D0412826

Paul Carr is the author of *Bringing Nothing to the Party*. He has founded numerous businesses with varying degrees of abysmal failure. He currently has no fixed abode.

www.paulcarr.com

THE
Upgrade

*A Cautionary Tale of
a Life without Reservations*

PAUL CARR

PHOENIX

A PHOENIX PAPERBACK

First published in Great Britain in 2011
by Weidenfeld & Nicolson
This paperback edition published in 2012
by Phoenix,
an imprint of Orion Books Ltd,
Orion House, 5 Upper St Martin's Lane,
London WC2H 9EA
An Hachette UK company

1 3 5 7 9 10 8 6 4 2

Copyright © Paul Carr 2011

A CIP catalogue record for this book
is available from the British Library.

ISBN 978-0-7538-2867-0

Typeset by Input Data Services Ltd, Bridgwater, Somerset

Printed and bound by CPI Group (UK) Ltd, Croydon, CR0 4YY

The Orion Publishing Group's policy is to use papers that
are natural, renewable and recyclable products and
made from wood grown in sustainable forests. The logging
and manufacturing processes are expected to conform to
the environmental regulations of the country of origin.

For Robert and Sarah –

I'm still alive, and it's all your fault.

'What you probably don't yet realise about Paul Carr is that he is a pathological fantasist with full-blown Narcissistic Personality Disorder. He is extremely charming, smart, disarming, but he is also a chronic liar who has carved a swathe of misery and confusion through a small corner of the UK New Media world.'

Email received by the publisher,
prior to publication of the author's previous book

The following is a true story.

Prologue

I don't notice the man in the grey suit taking my bag.

I mean, I do notice him – but in his smart grey Savile Row suit and his patent leather shoes, he looks just like any other hotel guest. I'm dimly aware of him gliding past me as I'm signing the guest register but, by the time I turn around, he's gone. And, with him, my bag.

A professional.

I smile.

The receptionist hands me back my debit card, having pre-authorised it for any incidentals I might incur during my stay. In other hotels they take as much as two or three hundred pounds. But the Lanesborough – the most expensive hotel in London – has just swiped a grand from my current account, just in case.

Given the cost of a room at the hotel, the pre-authorisation wasn't too outrageous. The standard – or 'rack' – rate for my suite is a little over £800 a night. I do the mental maths. £6000 a week. £312,000 a year. Plus tax and gratuities, of course. No wonder the Lanesborough is one of the few hotels in the world where they don't charge you extra for the in-room pornography.

Another thing they don't charge for is your butler. Mine is called Marcus and he's entirely at my disposal during my stay. If I need a copy of *The Times* or a pot of tea, Marcus will fetch it. If I should suddenly desire a Dalmatian puppy, painted green, Marcus will paint it. Marcus will do anything I ask him to do, providing it's legal. He'll also do lots of things that I haven't asked him to; hence my disappearing bag.

Room 237. I slide my key into the electronic lock, and once the hotel's elaborate security system is satisfied that I'm me – tick, tick, beep – the door swings open. I smile again. In the few minutes it took for the receptionist to electronically cut me a spare room key – it's cheesy as hell, but girls love being given their own key – Marcus has been hard at work.

My clothes are hanging in the walk-in wardrobe, except for a creased shirt that he's taken to be pressed, ahead of tonight's party. My razor and toothbrush have been removed from my overnight bag and placed on a little folded towel next to the sink. The book that was stuffed into the back pocket of my laptop bag is now on the table next to the gigantic bed with a bookmark placed where I'd folded down the corner of the page. My laptop is on the desk in the living room.

The living room. On the table sits an ice bucket and two half-bottles of champagne, compliments of the manager. Perfect. There's an unexpected touch, too: a dark chocolate cake with a message piped in thick white icing.

'Happy 30th Birthday.'

Aww. Sweet.

I sit down in one of the two leather armchairs and tear open the envelope that had been waiting for me at reception, but, before I can remove the card inside, there's a knock at the door.

I know it isn't Marcus – I'd been careful to flip the Do Not Disturb switch as I walked through the door. After ten hours on a plane I need to get some sleep. In a few hours I'm heading to Adam Street – my club, just off the Strand – for my birthday party. It's going to be a long night; especially if the girl I've invited to fly in from Italy shows up. She better had, given all the trouble Marcus is taking to press my shirt. That's going to cost me a twenty-quid tip.

Another knock.

'What?' I shout through the door.

'Open the fucking door, you twat.'

I do – and before it's even fully open I'm grabbed by two enormous arms and pulled into a crushing bear hug.

'Happy birthday, darling!'

'Robert! Thank you so much,' I gasp. 'Broken ribs. Really, you shouldn't have.' I force myself out of his grip. 'How did you know which room I was in?'

'Your butler sent me up – but I wrote down your room number wrong. I just nearly barged in on some Arab guy and what looked suspiciously like a hooker.' He paused. 'More importantly – you have a fucking butler.' Another pause. 'Congratulations. Your life is officially ridiculous.'

Robert Loch knows all about ridiculous. This is, after all, the man who the *Financial Times* – of all papers – once called 'the Hugh Hefner of London' after he rented a penthouse in Leicester Square and spent a whole year sitting in his rooftop hot tub, seducing Brazilian models and Russian ballerinas while building his latest online business.

And yet, right now, as he looks around my room, at the antique furniture and the fully stocked bar and the television – full of free porn – rising from the top of the bureau at the touch of a button, there is no mistaking the look in Robert's eyes.

Envy.

Envy for me – a loser who, less than two years earlier, had lost everything: my business, the love of my life and my home. Me, who has been fired from every job I've ever had, including two where I was technically my own boss. Me, whose only marketable skill is an ability to humiliate myself in ever more creative and entertaining ways.

And now here I am. My weekly outgoings aren't any more than they were two years ago – probably less, adjusted for inflation – and yet now I have my pick of fully-staffed accommodation in every major city on earth, a fleet of luxury cars at my disposal night and day and year-round access to a villa in the Spanish mountains, with more of the same across most of Europe.

I arrived at the Lanesborough in a limousine from Heathrow, after flying in from San Francisco. The previous evening I'd been out on a date with a pretty blonde journalist called Charlotte who wanted to profile me for some magazine or other. After dinner and drinks, we'd ended up back at my hotel with a girl we'd met in the bar. My real birthday celebration, though, is tonight at Adam Street, surrounded by nearly a hundred of my closest friends.

Then, tomorrow morning, while those same friends drag themselves bleary-eyed back to their desks and the forty-hour week that allows them to afford their exorbitant London rents, I'll hop on the Eurostar to Paris where I plan to complete my entire week's work in less than two hours, sitting in a café on the Champs-Elysées, eating foie gras and watching pretty French girls go by.

For me, this isn't a break from the pressures of my normal, everyday life – a nice birthday treat before returning to the rat race. This is my normal, everyday life. And it's all because of my membership of a very unusual club. A club with no joining fees and where anyone is welcome – even losers like me. All I had to do was to make one simple, life-changing decision.

What follows is the story of how I made that decision. It's a story of fast cars and Hollywood actresses; of Icelandic rock stars and six-thousand-mile booty calls. It's a story of eight hundred female hairdressers dressed only in bedsheets. It's a story of nights spent in prison cells; of jumping out of cars being driven by Spanish drug dealers and of trying to have sex with a girl knowing there's a dead woman in my wardrobe. And, more than anything else, it's a story of booze.

Lots and lots and lots of delicious booze.

Chapter 100

Walk Softly and Carry the US Pacific Fleet

'Eight fucking quid for a rum and Coke.'

A little less than two years earlier and my life was not going exactly according to plan.

It was a few days into 2008 and Robert and I were sitting in a dark corner of Jewel, a bar just off Piccadilly Circus. Robert was listening, somewhat patiently, as I railed against the cost of killing myself with booze in London. I'd just turned twenty-eight.

Following a spectacularly unsuccessful attempt to start a dot com business with my ex-girlfriend – so unsuccessful that I'd ended up writing a Schadenfreude-packed book called *Bringing Nothing to the Party** about how I'd lost them both forever – I had been forced back into freelance writing to pay the rent on my tiny London flat. Fortunately the latest instalment of the advance from the book just about covered the cost of drinking myself into a coma every night of the week to numb the pain of failure. Just about.

'I wouldn't mind but it's not even good rum.'

Jewel is that most vexing of things: an overpriced dive bar. A place where you go if you're a visitor in town and you think you're too good for the *Cheers* theme bar across the street. It's also something of a magnet for American girls, which was the sole reason I had insisted we move on there after spending most of the evening in a pub in Soho. My most recent ex-girlfriend was American (as was the previous one) and there was still something about the accent that made me fall instantly – and temporarily – in love whenever I heard it.

---

* If I didn't, at this point, urge you to read that book for that whole sorry saga then I wouldn't really be doing my job as a whore.

'Seriously, Robert, everything – absolutely everything – in my life is shit.'

'If you say so. What happened to life being great now that you've decided what you really want?'

Robert might as well have put the words 'great' and 'really' in airquotes. Like all of my friends, he was bored of hearing me complain. Even though my book wouldn't be published for almost six months, he'd read a preview of the Epilogue in which I bragged about finally realising that all I wanted to do was be a writer rather than some rich and famous entrepreneur. He knew I'd been paid a decent amount of money to write a book about being a loser. He knew that thanks to the book my freelance earnings were up as commissioning editors asked me to write stories about genuine dot com millionaires. And he knew that I was slowly but surely getting over my ex-girlfriend,* even if I was doing it by picking up a succession of almost identical American girls in dives like Jewel.

'Yeah, it's great – objectively,' I explained, draining my glass as the Eastern European waitress approached with another overpriced round. God, even I was tired of listening to myself. 'But I'm just bored. This time last year, all these ridiculous things were happening – I was writing a book, crazy American girls were setting up websites about my being shit in bed,† I was being fired from yet another company, I was being thrown in jail!'

'But you were miserable.'

'I know. But at least I wasn't bored. In less than two years I'll be thirty. That's the age when you're supposed to put away ridiculous things and start being responsible. But I'm twenty-eight – I've fallen into my rut two years early. Nothing ridiculous happens to me any more.'

And with that – exactly as would happen in a film, if there were a film shit enough to be filmed in the Jewel bar – something ridiculous happened.

---

* As demonstrated by the fact that this is the second time I've mentioned her.
† Google it. I'll wait.

101

Had the man who had just walked in been dressed normally, the first thing Robert and I would have noticed was his size. He was fucking enormous. But he wasn't dressed normally; he was wearing full US Navy dress uniform complete with a chest full of medals and a white hat pinned under his arm. He swaggered – that's really the only word for it – up to the bar, laid down his hat and ordered a drink. Turns out if you want to get served straight away in a crowded London bar, you should arrive wearing full US Navy dress uniform.

'Jesus. Look at that cunt,' I half slurred, pointing my rum and Coke towards the sailor. There was no doubt in my mind, of course, that he was a cunt. Only a cunt would walk into the Jewel bar wearing full naval dress uniform. Hell, only a cunt would walk into the Jewel bar. Robert and I were cunts, but at least we weren't in fancy dress.

He was also clearly not a real sailor. American naval officers tend not to hang around in Piccadilly Circus dive bars on their own, especially not wearing medals and with gleaming white hats under their arm. No, I'd read about his type: pick-up artists who prowl bars dressed in attention-seeking costumes, picking up vulnerable divorcees or drunk girls from the provinces who would buy their 'sailor-on-shore-leave' crap, despite the fact that they were 120 miles from the nearest US naval base. I had to give this guy style points, though – most fraudsters just slip on a dog tag from Camden Market and knock up a fake ID – they don't bother renting the full costume, complete with medals. Kudos, fraudster. Kudos.

Ah well, at least it would be good for ten minutes of fun. I knocked back my drink and marched over to the bar. Robert, reluctantly, followed close behind – all the better to drag me away for my own safety once the fists inevitably started to fly. He'd spent enough time around me drunk to know how this would end. I just couldn't help myself.

'I'm Paul,' I said, extending my hand to the costumed giant, 'who are you?'

'I'm Mark,' replied the man, taking my outstretched hand in a vice-grip and shaking it just once. His accent was unmistakably American and, oddly, he didn't seem fazed by the fact that he was shaking hands with an angry looking drunk stranger.

'Mark what?' I demanded, refusing to let go of his hand. With his free hand he reached into the pocket of his trousers and pulled out a business card. It looked like it had been produced on one of those vending machines you get in motorway service stations. Minus one style point.

'Mark Kenny.'

That proved it. Never trust a man with two first names.

'Oh please,' I said.

'What's the problem, sir?' he asked, his face a picture of innocence. The cocky bastard.

'Oh come on.' I said. 'Look at you, dressed like that in the fucking Jewel bar. We both know you're not really –' I squinted to read the job title on his card as the last rum took its grip. 'The US Navy Commander for the Center for Submarine Counter-Terrorism. Ha! Does that job even exist?'

'I hope so, otherwise I've wasted a lot of training,' he lied.

'He's good,' I said, turning to Robert, 'I'll give him that.' Robert was tapping away on his phone, presumably looking up the name 'Mark Kenny' on Google – or Wikipedia, or something – to prove that the guy was lying. Without looking up from the screen, he asked the question that would clearly prove to be the undoing of this 'Mark Kenny'.

'What do you think about Rudy Giuliani?'

Bit of a left-field question to open with, I thought. To the best of my knowledge the former mayor of New York wasn't a naval man. And I couldn't see what this guy's opinion about American politics was going to prove either way. Still, I had every confidence that Robert knew what he was doing.

'He's a good man,' replied 'Mark'. 'I've spent a little time with him.'

'Interesting,' replied Robert, his eyes still fixed on his phone.

'Oh, come on, Robert, you're not really buying this shit? I mean – just look at this business card and what the hell are these medals supposed to be?' I turned back to 'Mark' and yanked at one of the half-dozen or so fancy-dress shop props pasted to his chest. It was pretty well fastened. Plus one style point.

'What did you say your job was?' Robert butted in again, making eye contact with 'Mark' for the first time.

'I didn't,' he replied, 'but your friend has it on my card. I'm with the Center for Submarine CT Operations.'

'Yeah, um, Paul . . .' But I didn't let Robert finish his sentence. There was no need. This had gone far enough. It was one thing this charlatan lying to gullible women, but now he was lying to me. And I was very drunk.

'OK, seriously . . . you expect us to believe you're in charge of submarine counter-terrorism for the US Navy and yet rather than being – I don't know – on your ship . . .'

'Boat . . .'

'What?'

'Boat,' he repeated, 'a submarine is a boat.'

'Fine – rather than being on your fucking boat, you're in the Jewel bar in Piccadilly fucking Circus. Let me guess, al-Qaeda are planning to smuggle suicide swans into St James's fucking Park to break the Queen's neck with their fucking wings.'

'Um, Paul . . .'

'Wait a minute, Robert. I mean, you're honestly saying that the US Navy gives out business cards like this and that its captains wander around foreign countries in dress uniform . . .'

'Actually, I'm not a captain I'm . . .'

'No, I know you're not a fucking captain, you're . . .'

'PAUL.'

There was something about Robert's tone – perhaps the fact that he was shouting it right into my ear, with his hand pressing firmly down on my shoulder – that made me pause.

'WHAT?'

'He's right. He's not a fucking captain, he's a fucking rear admiral.'

'Rear Admiral Mark Kenny,' said Rear Admiral Mark Kenny, Commander of the Center for Submarine Counter-Terrorism Operations, former commanding officer of the USS *Birmingham* and close personal friend of Rudolph Giuliani, extending his hand again. 'You know, you could have just asked to see my passport.'

He reached into his trouser pocket and pulled out his diplomatic passport.

Oh.

Shit.

Plus one thousand style points, Admiral.

I sobered up immediately, and started to – kind of – whimper.

'Um . . . I'm really sorry about the medals, man.' I assumed an American would like being called 'man'. 'Err . . . you could probably have me killed, right?'

'Probably,' he said, with a shrug. 'Or I could just throw you to the suicide swans.'

Robert's hands were on both my shoulders now, steering me towards the door. 'Shall we go, mate?' he asked, through his tears of laughter.

Yeah. I think that's probably a good idea.

102

'HA!'

I woke up the next morning with a laugh. Had I really accused a rear admiral of being a conman last night? Yes and – Jesus Christ – I'd even tried to tear off one of his medals. He could have snapped my neck, and then just walked away, claiming diplomatic immunity. I've seen *Lethal Weapon 2*; I know what goes on.

But, still, what a rush, eh? The first ridiculous – ridiculously stupid – thing I'd done in months. It was just like old times. Perhaps things weren't so bad after all.

I grabbed a slice of cold pizza from the night before,* and scooped up the mail from my doormat. A whole load of bills, of course – council tax, phone bill, broadband – but also a big brown envelope from my landlord. The lease on my flat was up in February and this would, presumably, be the contract to renew for another year. Another year in overpriced, dirty London. Memories of ex-girlfriends on every corner, and cold pizza for breakfast. The idea hardly filled me with joy.

But, no, it wasn't a contract, it was a letter. Due to the looming 'credit crunch' my landlord had decided that the 'generous' £900 a month rent I was paying for my tiny one-bedroom flat in East Dulwich wasn't enough. I had a choice: either accept a 20 per cent hike, effective immediately, or I'd have thirty days to find somewhere else to live.

A piece of cold pineapple stuck in my throat. First the girl, then the business, and now my flat – it was like watching a Slinky spring fall from grace.

Thlink . . .

    . . . thlink . . .

        . . . thlink.†

I threw the envelope on to the sofa and took the two steps across the room to my desk. There was no way I was going to be bullied into paying nearly £1100 a month rent for such a tiny flat – and not least because I couldn't afford it. I was earning less than £2000 a month – before tax – from freelance gigs and, on top of my £900 rent, I was paying about £75 a month in council tax, £30 for phone and internet, a tenner for a TV licence, £80 for a cleaner, almost £100 for a Travelcard just to get into the centre of town – nearly £1200 a month before I even left the house. Given the cost of living

---

* Takeaway pizza: expensive as one meal – a bargain as two.
† . . . thlink.

in London, paying £1100 in rent alone was out of the question, unless I wanted my next address to be a debtors' prison.

I opened up my laptop and fired up Google. There really is nothing more useful than Google at times like this. No matter what major life decision you need to make, you can rely on it to deliver site after site of utterly irrelevant trivia to distract you from it.

On this occasion, the major life decision I needed to be distracted from was which cheaper, scummier part of London I should move to at the end of the month – and Google didn't disappoint.

'London is too expensive.' I typed the words into the search box and hit the submit button. I wasn't really expecting an answer to the problem; I just wanted to vent my frustration.

On the first pages of results there was a site showing the real cost of living in every major city in the world. From that I was able to see – in stark bar-chart form – that, after Moscow and Tokyo, London was the third most expensive place to live on planet earth; 30 per cent more costly, on average, than New York City. Alarming stuff, but, given that I'd paid £8 for a rum and Coke the previous night, hardly surprising.

Click.

More cost of living trivia, this time from a site that was trying to encourage me to buy a flat in Europe. Did I know that moving to Frankfurt or Madrid would save me a staggering 80 per cent in rent and 40 per cent in general cost of living? No, I did not, Google, thanks very much for rubbing that in.

Anyway, Madrid might be fine for a weekend break – or at most a few weeks over the summer – but I wouldn't want to live there. I only speak about two words of Spanish, for a start; also I have no beef with bulls.

But then again, maybe a holiday wouldn't be such a bad idea. I didn't have to make the housing decision straight away, after all. If the cost of living was really so much less elsewhere, I could afford to put my furniture in storage and take a month out. Visit another city, check into a hotel for a month and decide on my options. Perhaps not Madrid, but maybe New York – I had lots of friends there, and I knew from experience that at this time of year I could negotiate a decent room in Manhattan for $100 a night if I stayed more than a week. At the current exchange rate – almost exactly two dollars to the pound – that was £50 a night. £1,400 for the whole of February.

The amount was a nice coincidence, actually. £1400 was exactly the same as I'd be paying in total if I agreed on the rent hike in London, when council tax, phone line rental and all that stuff were factored in. Stuff that I wouldn't have to worry about in a hotel. And, of course, by being out of London for a month, my cost of living would be hugely reduced – so I might actually have a better quality of life, for less money.

The more I thought about it, the more it seemed like a good plan. But why stop at a month? Under the US Visa Waiver Program – which allows Brits* to enter the US without applying for a formal visa – I could stay in America for up to ninety days. Maybe I could see a bit of the country – outside Manhattan, hotels would probably be even cheaper.

And after that – well, what was the rush to find a new place? There were bound to be hotels in Europe, or even in parts of the UK, where I could stay for less than £50 a night. Really I could travel for as long as I liked: one of the perks of being a freelance writer is that I can pretty much work from anywhere there's a desk and a decent wifi connection.†

It was at that exact point, as I took another bite of cold pizza, that somewhere deep inside my brain a synapse fired. Tzzziz.

A whole minute passed, although it seemed longer. I just sat, staring at my laptop, paralysed by the idea. It seemed so obvious, but at the same time so . . . what was the word . . .? Ridiculous.

A ridiculous adventure.

That settled it.

---

* And people from thirty-four other countries.
† And an off-licence.

103

I've always loved hotels. I love drinking in their bars, I love eating in their restaurants and above all I love staying in their rooms. Which is lucky as, for much of my childhood, that's how I lived.

My parents have been hoteliers for their entire career — some eighty years, combined. The day after I was born, they carried me, in a little basket, back to their suite at the King Malcolm Hotel, where my dad was the manager. I spent my first Christmas in a hotel, I ate my first solid food in a hotel restaurant and I drank my first Diet Coke (not entirely legally, I suspect) in a hotel bar. Before speaking my first word, I dialled nine for an outside line.

When I was three, my dad's job took our family to Luton in Bedfordshire, where we lived for two years in the penthouse of the Strathmore Hotel. I did my first piece of homework on a hotel dining table and, while other kids' parents rented McDonald's restaurants for their birthday parties, my parties were held in the hotel's ballroom. In the absence of a back garden, I learned to ride my first bike on the hotel's flat roof, a mere ten storeys above street level.

Even during the few years when we actually lived in a proper house, my dad's long working hours meant that almost every significant occasion — Christmases, New Years, Easters, birthdays — found us celebrating in a hotel restaurant, surrounded by hundreds of paying guests. It's perhaps unsurprising, then, that I've always felt more comfortable in hotels than I do living in a house.

It's also perhaps unsurprising that, when I found myself nearing thirty, feeling stuck in a rut and craving one last burst of youthful irresponsibility, my first thought was to run back to the world of hotels.

Specifically, the idea I had — as I took that bite of cold pizza — was to give up my flat, pack a few possessions into a suitcase and embark on a year-long experiment. Rather than renewing my lease for another year, I'd spend that year on the road — exploring whether it was possible to live in nice hotels in other cities for the same cost as surviving on cold pizza in my shitty flat in London.

The idea isn't entirely without precedent. Lots of travelling salesmen live in hotels for extended periods: spending most of the year shuttling from Holiday Inn to Hilton, surviving on room service and takeaways and missing their (ex-)wife and kids. But they live that way out of necessity, rather than choice.

My theory was that, if you do it through choice, on your own terms, living in hotels – as a kind of high-class nomad – could actually be a practical, and luxurious, alternative to home. And history agrees with me . . .

America in the mid-1800s was growing rapidly, with hundreds of new towns and cities springing up every year. As each new town was founded, one of the first buildings to be erected was usually a hotel, to provide essential accommodation for new inhabitants. What started out as a temporary housing solution soon became established as a permanent way to live for many of those early city-dwellers. It made sense: even for the relatively well off, the cost of buying a family home and employing servants to run it was prohibitive. A good hotel provided all the comforts of a luxury home – complete with porters, cooks and maids – at a far more affordable cost. Why not make that hotel your home?

The idea took off, and, by 1844, a Chicago census found that one in six of the city's residents was living permanently in hotels. In New York the number was even higher – according to A. K. Sandoval-Strausz's book *Hotel: An American History*, in 1856 nearly three-quarters of the city's middle and upper classes gave a hotel as their primary address.

As hotel living became more popular, wealthier occupants began to demand more and more homey facilities – private kitchens so they could hire their own cooks, for example – while those less well off tried to cut costs by turning their backs on daily house-keeping and catered meals. These demands soon led canny developers to create a new hybrid living space: centrally located properties with many of the communal facilities offered by hotels, but with all of the comforts of a private house. And so the modern apartment building was born.

If history was on my side, then so was my own experience. Through seeing my parents at work, I know how hotels operate. A hotel bedroom is a highly perishable commodity – if it hasn't been sold by the end of the day, it's gone forever. I know the times of the year when rooms are hardest to sell and, as a result, when bargain rates are there for the taking. In most cities, the first couple of months of the year are slow so I knew I'd find some good deals on rooms in New York as long as I didn't stay much beyond the middle of March. After that I could head to second-tier cities, or even small towns, where cheaper rooms are available all year round.

I also know that the longer you stay in a hotel, the better the deals get. Hotels love long-staying guests: not only are those guests filling a room for a month or longer, but they're also very likely to use other hotel services like laundry and room service and the bar. For all these reasons, there isn't a hotel on the planet that won't give you a decent discount for a long stay. You don't even have to haggle: just ask. One little-known, but extraordinarily useful, fact is that in most cities you don't pay local tax (10–15 per cent in most US cities) on stays over thirty nights. In the UK, stays over twenty-eight nights are VAT-free.

Armed with just this basic information – and a willingness to learn more as I travelled – I was confident that living in hotels was a perfectly feasible way to spend a year. By the end of April I'd have to leave America so I didn't overstay the visa waiver, but then I could travel around Europe for a bit before heading back to the US once a decent amount of time had elapsed. Friends had told me that, as long as you leave a couple of months between visits, you can pretty much travel back and forth on the visa waiver indefinitely.

Then, by December, I'd head back to London for Christmas and start house hunting in time for January. That would still give me an entire year to figure out what I was going to do with my life before I turned thirty.

And if living in hotels didn't work out? Well, then I'd just come home early.

104

There's one more thing you need to know about living in hotels for a year.

It's fucking brilliant.

It is also 'living the fucking dream'. These are all things you learn when you start telling your male friends that you're thinking about doing it.

'That's a fucking brilliant idea,' said Robert when I told him my plan. 'Anyone can live in a hotel for a month. That's just a long holiday. But living in them for a whole year. That's living the fucking dream.'

I could see his point. It's hard to see a downside in spending twelve months in a place where a woman dressed as a maid comes to your room every morning, delivers fresh towels, recovers the remote control from behind the bed, replenishes the fridge with beer and tiny tubes of Pringles and leaves a mint on your pillow. A place with a bar and restaurant downstairs, and a uniformed man whose whole purpose is to get you things that you ask for, and to call you 'sir'. Oh, and an entire television channel dedicated to porn.

The fact that you can have all of these things at home, if you pay enough money, that no one has left a mint on a hotel room pillow since 1972 and that the Internet has all but destroyed the hotel room porn industry does little to alter the perception, for most of my male friends, that living in a hotel is as good as it gets.

For most of my female friends: not so much.

'A year? That sounds like an unmitigated living hell,' enthused my friend Kate when I explained my plan.

Girls, explained Kate as their spokesperson, like to live in their own places, surrounded by familiar things. They like having their own shelves and cupboards and wardrobes to house those things.

They like having their own kitchens to cook their own food. Girls like owning cushions. To live in a hotel, they would have to leave their cushions behind: bringing your own cushions to a hotel is like bringing your own salt to a restaurant.

To make things even more interesting, and probably partly to send Kate further into meltdown, I'd decided that my cushions wouldn't be the only thing I was leaving behind in London.

My original plan had been to pack as much of my life as possible into a suitcase, and then to put all of my other possessions into storage for a year. I may not have been as attached to my stuff as Kate was to hers, but I still wasn't entirely certain I wanted to get rid of it for ever. Keeping at least my furniture in storage meant I could pick up my life from where I left off when I got back.

Another hour of Internet research, though, showed me that even the cheapest storage company in London wanted £100 a month in rental fees – $200 straight off my hotel budget, to rent a tiny little metal flat for all of my possessions to live in while I was away.*

It was at that point I determined that, if a ridiculous adventure is worth doing, it's worth doing properly.

Heading back to the Internet – honestly, what did we do without it?† – I fired up the East Dulwich Forum, a site where people in London SE22 can sell their unwanted possessions. With my laptop balanced on one arm, I walked around my flat listing everything in sight: my bed, my DVD collection, my sofa, my plates, even the contents of my kitchen drawers. 'Spatula – hardly used – quick sale essential – no reasonable offer refused.'

On hearing this, as I'd hoped, Kate lost her mind. 'You can't sell all of your stuff!' she screeched. 'What about all of your books? And you've got those lovely brown suede cushions. You can't sell them!'

'I'm going to give the books to a charity shop,' I replied. 'You can have the cushions if you like.'

---

* Somehow that defeated the object. Although it did lead to me wonder if I could get away with putting myself in storage for a year.
† We watched hotel room porn.

'Really? OK!'

Girls really like owning cushions.

In the days that followed, half of East Dulwich came to my flat. They came in cars, and camper vans and even bicycles. My sofa went to a man called Peter who had been kicked out by his wife and was starting again from scratch. 'I'll be needing a sturdy sofa for all the women I'm going to be bringing back,' he said, in no way creepily.

My DVD collection – about a hundred discs that I never watched – went to a woman from some kind of local youth group who was hoping they'd 'keep the kids out of trouble', in the way that only *A Clockwork Orange* and *If . . . .* really can.

It doesn't matter how unattached you are to 'stuff', watching strangers coming and going, each visit leaving your flat slightly more bare than before, is a freaky experience. Like being burgled in slow motion, in exchange for money.

Less than a week after posting my first ad, all I had left was a sleeping bag, a couple of pillows, my clothes, a small pile of personal bits and pieces that I was planning on taking with me, a flatscreen television and my guitar.

The guitar and the television were the last – and the most heart-warming – things to go. During my first year at university I'd decided that I was going to learn to play the guitar in order to impress girls. I chose the most expensive guitar I could afford – a Fender Stratocaster – on the flawed justification that, having spent so much money on the damned thing, I'd have to learn to play it. Of course I never did. Instead, I carried it from house to house for almost a decade, never once so much as connecting it to the amplifier. It was the most expensive hatstand I've ever owned; not least because I don't own a single hat.*

And then, less than a week before I was due to move out, a fifteen-year-old kid called Stuart turned up at my flat. He'd brought

---

* There are two types of men in the world: men who look ridiculous in hats, and men who look great in hats. There is no middle ground. I am the former.

his mum with him because – it soon became clear – he couldn't understand why some guy would sell a Fender Stratocaster guitar and amp for fifty quid, and so assumed the advert was a trap.

Still, after listening to my ridiculous explanation of why I had to get rid of everything I owned by the end of the month, Stuart seemed satisfied that I wasn't planning to rape and murder him. He picked up the guitar, handling it like a doctor might pick up a donated kidney – confidently but respectfully. Five minutes of tweaking and plucking and tuning later, he cranked up the volume on the amp, paused for some dramatic effect … and then … blaaaaaaaaaang . . . the first chord that my hatstand had ever played. I don't know anything about music, but I know when I hear someone playing the shit out of a guitar. And Stuart played the shit out of the guitar. 'Wow,' I said when he was finished. 'I didn't know it could do that. Maybe I'll hold on to it after all.'

Stuart looked horrified. It *was* a trap!

'I'm kidding – I'm just glad someone is going to get some use out of it finally. Hey, you don't by any chance want a free flatscreen television do you?'

'What – for nothing?'

'Yeah. Help yourself, it's by the door.'

I'm not sure if Stuart learned anything that day about the value of money, but I certainly did. After waving him and his mum off with the last of my possessions, I went to the kitchen drawer where I'd been keeping the proceeds. I slid the drawer from its runners, tipped the contents – a small pile of notes and a few coins – on to the worktop and started counting.

Ten seconds later, I finished counting. My entire life was worth £540. I laughed. I laughed partly because it was such a tragically small amount of money for almost everything that I'd spent nearly three decades acquiring. But I also laughed because £540 was precisely the cost – including tax and booking fees – of my plane ticket to New York.

Fate had given my plan its stamp of approval. It was time to go.

Chapter 200

Naked Brunch

Wednesday 20 February 2008. Virgin Atlantic flight VS045 from Heathrow to JFK. I remember it vividly.

I arrived at the airport with less than an hour to spare, dropped off the suitcase containing my entire life, and headed towards security. I've never understood the 'arrive two hours before your flight' thing, especially if you've checked in online – but even so, given that my flight was due to take off at 2 p.m. and it was now half past one, I was cutting it a little fine.

Luckily there was only the merest hint of a line at security and, after the usual twatting around with shoes and belts and laptops, I was walking – maybe jogging slightly – down the jetway on to the plane.

'Paul!'

I almost never turn around when I hear my name shouted in public. The odds just aren't in favour of reacting; nine times out of ten, you end up waving, through reflex, to a total stranger. But then came a jab from behind; right in the spine. I reacted to that. It was my friend Zoe, out of breath, having clearly made it to the airport even later than I had.

'Hey! What are you doing here?' I asked idiotically, given that we were on a jetway, a few feet from the door of a plane, and Zoe was also dragging a suitcase. 'Well, obviously you're flying to New York. But why?'

'Oh, just some interviews, publisher meeting – they've arranged a reading, I think; usual bullshit. You?'

'Long story. Sort of an extended working holiday.'

'Really?' asked Zoe. 'You got the I or the O?'

For some reason, my friends love to talk about visas – partly, I think, because they can never quite believe any country has been stupid enough to give them one. Zoe was travelling under the I Visa – granting 'representatives of the foreign media' access to America for anything up to five years. For reasons that probably have nothing to do with freedom of the press, journalists are the only people not eligible to enter the US for professional reasons under the Visa Waiver Program. Many have tried, hoping they could just lie their way through immigration; most succeed but several have ended up in handcuffs, a holding cell and then back on the next plane home. If I was planning to do any reporting while in the US, I probably should have had an I Visa.

The O Visa, on the other hand, is for 'aliens of extraordinary ability'. Rock stars, actors, E.T. – people like that. I most definitely should not have had an O Visa.

'Nah, I'm just on the waiver. I'm not really going for work – more of a holiday. During which I might do some writing. For which I might get paid. But I'll just blag it at immigration; pretend I'm not really a journalist. Which won't be difficult, given that I'm not.'

Zoe isn't really a journalist either. But she's definitely a writer, and a successful one. A year or so earlier, her blog – a candid diary of her sex life – had been turned into a book: *Girl with a One Track Mind*. The UK edition had sold a zillion copies and now the US edition was doing well too. As befits Zoe's status as a hugely successful author, the words 'Premium Economy' were printed on her boarding card, while I'd be sitting in economy. The memoirist feudal system, as illustrated by airline seating. As we boarded the plane I glanced to the left, half expecting to see Dave Eggers enjoying a glass of champagne in Business Class.*

Realising that Zoe was on my flight gave me a momentary twinge. The same twinge that I suppose minor celebrities have when they find they're on the same plane as Bono or George Clooney. The realisation that when – inevitably – the plane plunges into the sea

* I'm not sure who that would put in the pilot seat: Maya Angelou? Anne Frank?

or plummets nose-first into a field in Pennsylvania, they'll just be a footnote in the coverage. Does it work the same way for writers, I wondered. If we skid off the runway on landing and burst into flames, would *The Bookseller* magazine mourn Zoe's death and forget about me?*

201

As it turned out, we didn't crash, giving me the full seven-hour flight to go over my plans, and to become increasingly excited about them. From the airport I'd take a cab to Manhattan, and the Pod Hotel on East 51st Street. I really like staying at the Pod: not only is it centrally located but it's inexpensive in the off-season and has flatscreen TVs, iPod docks, rainhead showers and free wifi. And for all of those reasons it's incredibly popular with young foreign travellers, making the place one giant pick-up joint.

With just a couple of emails to their reservations department, I'd managed to negotiate a double room for $89 a night – less than £45.

I'd decided to set my accommodation budget at £50–$100 – per night: about equal to the amount I'd be paying to stay in London if I'd accepted the increase in rent. I'd also agreed with myself that savings could be carried over, day to day, month to month, so each night I stayed at the Pod I was saving £5 that I could use for wherever I went next.

After my month at the Pod, I planned to head south. Although I'd visited America a dozen times or more, I'd only ever been to the coastal states – New York, California, Florida: the usual. Like an overgrown back-packer, I wanted to see the 'real America' so, like that same back-packer, I'd bought a book at the airport bookshop called *USA by Rail* with the intention of plotting a journey that would take me to all of the places I'd seen in films but never visited. Places like Utah, which I've always imagined is like a safari park filled with Mormons.

* Yes.

Flipping through *USA by Rail*, I was sucked straight into the dream. In the UK, travelling by train has lost all its romance – no one will write a love song about taking the 6.15p.m. from Nottingham to London St Pancras but in America the love affair lives on: the book listed routes with names like *Texas Eagle*, *California Zephyr* and *Empire Builder*.

My plan was to take the two-day *Crescent* service from New York Penn Station down to New Orleans, arriving in time for Mardi Gras at the beginning of March. I feel horrible admitting this, but at the back of my mind I figured that after Hurricane Katrina the city's hotel prices had probably gone down a bit.

After New Orleans, I'd hop on the *Sunset Limited* service and head west to Los Angeles. March was off-season on the railways too, so I'd booked a one-month rail pass for $470 which would allow me unlimited travel throughout the whole of the US, and some of Canada, for thirty days. I'd only have to spend five nights on the train rather than in a hotel before the pass paid for itself.

In fact, I'd become so intoxicated by the idea of seeing America by rail that, by the time I landed in New York, I'd planned a journey that lasted for the whole month of March. A huge circular route that would take me from Los Angeles to San Francisco to Salt Lake City (Mormons!) to Denver to Chicago to Pittsburgh to Washington, DC, and back to New York. Almost half that time would be spent on the train: a travelling hotel for less than $30 a night.

As we began our descent into JFK, passing low over Long Island and the tightly packed houses with backyard swimming pools that seem to cluster on the approach to every airport in America, I remember feeling happy, and strangely organised. Like a school-boy beginning a fresh exercise book, I had neatly copied my two-month travel and accommodation plan on to the first page of a brand new Moleskine notebook. As the year progressed, I was planning to use the book to plan each successive stage and to track how well I was keeping to my £50-a-day accommodation budget for the year.

The numbers looked good: assuming I didn't stray too far from my plan, February and March were going to come in well under budget, giving me plenty of flexibility for accommodation costs in April, May and into the peak season. Which was good, as I was past the point of no return: the last thing I'd done before going through to departures was to drop the key to my flat in the post to my (former) landlady along with a letter, politely but firmly telling her where to stick her rent hike. Now I had no ties, no fixed abode, and no responsibilities beyond a nightly hotel budget and the travel plan scribbled in my little black notebook.

The final plan I'd made, in the cab to the hotel, was to cut down on drinking for a while. London had given my liver a thrashing. I'd read online that one of the signs of liver failure was a yellowing of the eyeballs and horizontal white lines across the fingernails. The fact that I'd looked up those symptoms in the first place, let alone that I was now checking for them every morning, suggested a month on the wagon might not be a bad thing. Instead of boozing, I'd drink orange juice and eat salads and go for long walks around the city. I'd get healthy again.

Oh yes, I remember that all very clearly. The airport, the flight, the planning, the cab, the plan to stop drinking.

I remember checking into the hotel and putting my bag in my room. I remember having a shower and changing my shirt. I remember deciding to head out for a walk to orientate myself – to get a feel for where the local dry-cleaners and restaurants and bars could be found. I remember – ah, here we go, yes – I remember finding an Irish pub that looked friendly, Something O'Something's – there was a plastic leprechaun, I definitely remember that – and I remember noticing the pretty brunette with the ponytail, wearing a CUNY sweatshirt and sitting on her own. She was reading *Down and Out in Paris and London* which I remember I'd used as my opening line. 'I've always found the Rough Guides to be more reliable than Orwell . . .'

I shook my head, hoping it would hasten the return, if not of my memory then at least of the rest of my vision. I had a dim recollection of a bottle of wine and a conversation about how she was studying Contemporary World Literature. I'm sure I found a way – after we'd drunk, I think, shots of sambuca – to mention that I was a soon-to-be-published author, but at the same time to shrug it off like it was no big deal. I'm pretty sure we left the Irish bar and went to another place down the street where her friends were celebrating – what? – something. There was a bottle of champagne. But after that – nothing. I can't remember how I got back to the Pod. And I have absolutely no idea what possible set of circumstances led to my being slumped on the floor, head leaning against the closed door of my room.

I shook my head again and slowly I started to focus on how long my hotel room was. And narrow. Weird.

And that's when I realised the first of my two problems. I *was* slumped against my hotel room – I had that right – but, rather than being inside the room, I was outside, in the corridor. The second of my problems – and certainly the most pressing – was that I was stark bollock naked.

202

Think, think, think ... how the hell had I got there? Were my clothes inside my room? And, if so, had I made it into the room, undressed, and for some reason walked outside again? And if not – oh God – had I walked naked through the hotel?

My brain simply wasn't capable of processing all of these questions. All I knew is that I had to get back into my room before anyone saw me.

I tried the door. Locked, obviously. I gave it a half-hearted shove with my shoulder and immediately fell back down to the floor, still drunk. 'Hmm,' I thought, 'maybe that explains the slumping.'

I had no other option: I'd have to go down to the lobby and ask someone to let me in. I looked up and down the corridor. When this happens in movies, there's always some appropriately-comedic piece of bric-a-brac that can be pressed into service as a covering: a moose's head, a vase, something like that. Not in real life. The corridors in the Pod don't have windows; there weren't even any curtains.

No windows also meant I had no way of figuring out what time it was. What if I'd been slumped there for hours? What if it was 10 a.m. and a nice family with young children was checking in and the first thing they saw was a naked Brit emerging drunkenly from the elevator into the lobby, not-so-proudly cupping his genitals in his hands? That's no way to start a holiday. It is, however, a great way to start a lawsuit.

My only lucky break was that I'd been given a room right opposite the elevators. I pressed the call button and the door opened straight away, which was good – it meant less time in the corridor – but also potentially bad as it meant someone had arrived at my floor not long before. I prayed that person had been me.

As the car made its way downwards I caught a glimpse of my pathetic reflection in the elevator's mirrored walls. 'Dear God, Paul, you're a mess' I thought out loud.

Finally, the doors opened and I peered out into the lobby, trying my best to keep the rest of my body out of sight. All was calm and still, thank God; the clock behind the reception desk said 4.25 a.m. The only witness to my humiliation would be a solitary night porter sitting behind the reception desk, reading a magazine.

'¡*Ay Dios mío!*'

And a tiny Hispanic cleaner, mopping the floor right next to the elevator. I hadn't noticed her.

'*Lo siento,*' I said. My two words of Spanish.

'Don't worry, Maria, I'll go.' said the night porter, looking up boredly from his magazine. It was an interesting choice of words, 'I'll go', as if this kind of thing – naked men walking out of the elevators at four in the morning – happened at the Pod every night. He picked up a master key from behind the desk and ambled towards the elevator.

Even though I was still shit-faced drunk, the next thirty

seconds – which took the form of about three and a half years – were the most embarrassing of my life. I stood at one side of the elevator, still naked, arse pressed against the wall, genitals still cupped in my hands, while the tall night porter – I think he was Russian – stood as far on the other side as possible.

'Sorry about this,' I said.

He didn't say a word.

203

A few hours later – 11a.m. – I woke up in my hotel bed and, for a few blissful minutes, I completely forgot about my naked elevator adventure. I don't normally get headaches with hangovers, but this morning was different. My skull felt like it was full of burning sand – burning sand that was leaking down my throat. Stupid sambuca. I stood up and walked to the bathroom. Must drink water. Lots of water.

I turned on the tap above the sink and put my face in the bowl, letting the stream of water run over the back of my head and down the sides of my face. Then I tilted my head upwards and started lapping from the tap. Forget Evian or Perrier: there is no more delicious water than hangover water. After gulping down about half my body weight of the stuff, I shut off the tap and stood back up, gripping the sides of the sink for support, water dripping from my hair down the rest of my body. That's when I caught a glimpse of my naked self in the mirror.

And that's when the first flashback came.

'Oh fuuuuuccccccckkkkkk.'

There was no other mature course of action; I had to get out of there. There was simply no way I could face another thirty nights in the same hotel, with the same Russian night manager and the same small Hispanic cleaner. I was still drunk and I already felt sick with embarrassment. God knows how I'd feel when I sobered up.

204

A significant advantage of hotel stays over apartment rental contracts is that they're easy to renegotiate or cancel. Most hotels insist that you give twenty-four – or occasionally forty-eight – hours' notice if you decide to leave early. If you can't give notice – say, because you hadn't planned on waking up naked in a corridor – then you're still free to leave early but they'll usually charge you for the notice period. But that's all they'll make you pay. Some will try to insist on a small 'early check-out' penalty but the trick to getting rid of those is to be extremely apologetic, and to make it clear that you're looking forward to coming back to the hotel in future.

The only way you can find yourself trapped – financially at least – is if you've paid for the room up front – which some online booking sites force you to do to get their best rates. Paying up front can actually be a great idea if you're only staying for a couple of days and you're paying with a debit card. When a hotel pre-authorises your debit card for incidentals at check-in, the amount is immediately taken (or 'held') from your current account. For short stays, the hold might be more than the total cost of the room, and it can take as long as a week for it to be released and your money returned. By paying for the room in advance you can legitimately refuse to hand over your card for pre-authorisation at check-in as long as you're not planning to raid the minibar. The worst they can do is ask for a cash deposit, which they'll hand you back on departure.

In most other cases, though, paying up front is a terrible idea. You just never know when you'll need to escape.

I finally found my jeans thrown on a shelf – *interesting* – along with one of my shoes. The second shoe, it turned out, was hiding in the shower, along with my shirt and coat. I took some comfort from this as, firstly, it meant I'd obviously arrived back at the hotel fully clothed, and, secondly, because I was only travelling with one pair of shoes.

I quickly pulled on the jeans and shoes – my socks were apparently lost for ever – and swapped the shirt for a clean one from my suitcase. I hadn't even unpacked.

There was also no way I was going to go to reception to check out: the night porter would certainly have told the morning shift about the naked man from room 625. Instead, I grabbed my suitcase, took the elevator to the lobby – another juddering flashback – and, just before the doors opened, began talking into my mobile phone as if I was in the middle of a very important call. No one stops you when you're on the phone.

I walked straight through the lobby, past the reception desk and out on to the street, inhaling the exhaust fumes and food smells of freedom.

I didn't stop walking until I was three blocks from the hotel, where I found another Irish pub, this one with a wooden board outside boasting free wifi Internet access. I stood in the doorway for a moment and looked around – trying to remember if it was the same bar I'd been in the night before. No plastic leprechaun – good. I ordered half a beer – hair of the dog, that's all – and found a table in the corner. Opening my laptop I started to write an email ...

From: Paul Carr
To: The Pod Hotel (Reservations)

Dear Sir,

I am currently checked into room 625 for a one-month stay.
Unfortunately I have had to leave early on urgent business and so will no longer need the room. Please debit my card for the cost of my stay to date. I understand you have a 24-hour cancellation policy, so please feel free to charge me for one additional night.

Please accept my sincere apologies for any inconvenience, and I look forward to returning to the Pod soon.

Paul Carr

That last part was a lie, obviously – I could never set foot in the place again – but by acting like a potential future guest I knew there was less chance they'd try to charge me for the cancelled nights. Sure enough, when I checked my online bank statement a few weeks later, I found they hadn't even charged me for the extra twenty-four hours.

205

The email having been sent, all I had to do was find a new hotel, something that the Internet has made ridiculously easy, but also annoyingly absorbing. It's far too easy to spend hours comparing features and reviews and rates, when in fact the only questions that need to be answered are:

Are the rooms nice?

Is it near to where I need to be?

Does it have decent Internet access, not just in the public areas but in the actual rooms?

Are the online reviews from other guests favourable, particularly when it comes to the service?

Some people like a gym too.*

I took another drag from my beer to steady my hand for the task ahead. I could feel my hangover catching up with me – the last of the previous night's alcohol was leaving my system and I knew I'd either have to order a second beer or surrender to the worsening sickness.

Just one more.

I fired up Trip Advisor[†] – my go-to hotel review site, and ran a quick search for the highest rated hotels in Manhattan. I never look at the mid-range chain hotels – the four-star Marriotts, the Hiltons, the Sheratons – they're usually very nice, but they're also exactly

* I have no time for those people.
† http://www.tripadvisor.com

the same in every city on earth. Since my parents moved from managing chain hotels to owning an independent one, my loyalties have moved the same way. I've got as tired of cookie-cutter experiences as they have.*

Unless I already have a favorite hotel in a city, or a personal recommendation from someone I trust, Trip Advisor is indispensable. The site lists about half a million hotels, with more than thirty million reviews written by actual guests. Hotel sites generally use their own arbitrary ratings systems rather than anything official or internationally recognised, but anything with an average rating of less than four out of five on Trip Advisor is likely to be a dump in any language.

After the first batch of results came up, it was time to filter them based on price. Trip Advisor doesn't sell rooms itself; it just links to the major price-comparison sites. Some people swear by sites like Priceline which promise deep discounts on upscale hotels, as long as you don't mind them picking the hotel for you. It's only after you've confirmed the room – and agreed to pay for it – that you actually find out where you're staying. That idea has never appealed to me: not only are there too many unknowns but you have to pay up front.

I clicked on a few links.

With my budget of $100 a night, I ignored anywhere that was advertising a rate less than $75. With this hangover, I deserved better than a budget hotel in a shitty part of town. Had I been staying less than a couple of weeks I would also have ignored anywhere over $150 a night – but I still had twenty-seven days left in New York so I at least had a shot at some deep discounting. I eventually settled on a shortlist of three likely places – a process that would normally take me about ten minutes, but with my monstrous hangover took me the best part of forty-five. And one and a half beers.

---

* On a practical note, the mid-range chains also tend to be the hardest to charm for discounts unless you're part of their loyalty programme.

Then it was time to make some calls.

When my friends ask me for advice on scoring cheap hotel rooms, I always tell them that, once they have their shortlist, the first thing to do is call the hotel's reservations department. I coach them to explain that a friend has recommended the hotel as the best place in town but that they're travelling on a budget and were wondering if anything can be done with the rate advertised online? Hotel booking sites act much like travel agents – with hotels paying anything up to 15 per cent commission on any booking you make through them. If they can get you to book directly then they can afford to knock almost all of that commission off the price of the room and still come out ahead. The phone operators in big chain hotels don't usually have the leeway to make those decisions, but most independent places do. And they gladly will; people who book direct rather than through agencies are much more likely to become repeat guests.

The trick is to emphasise that you don't mind a bad room. Every hotel has rooms that are tough to sell: rooms that are smaller than the others, rooms with just a shower and no bath, rooms right at the top of the building, only accessible by stairs. These are the ones that usually end up on the anonymous hotel sites like Priceline, and these are the rooms that – particularly in independent hotels – are easiest to get discounts on.

Another bonus is that, in almost every case, the person taking your booking is not going to be the person you see at check-in. If the hotel is nice and the price is right, it makes sense to take whatever room you're offered and then, on check-in, if you're not happy with the room just stroll down to reception and complain. Politely. Pick something that you couldn't have known when you booked. The room looks out over the road and you're a light sleeper. It only has a shower and you're sure that on their website a bath was mentioned.* If one of the fixtures in the room – the shower,

---

* No one knows what it says on their own website.

the sink, the bed – is broken, you're golden. 'Is there any chance of getting a different room? Sorry to be difficult . . .' Nine times out of ten they'll upgrade you on the spot, or at least give you a nicer room in the same class. It's something every receptionist is empowered to do, no one has ever got fired for, and is far less hassle for them than arguing with you. And if you're still not happy, you can always check out the next morning and go somewhere else.

That's the advice I give to my friends, but this is as good a time as any to admit that it isn't the approach I always take. Sometimes I have my heart set on a particular hotel but the reservations department won't budge on price; maybe there's a big conference in town and everywhere else is full; maybe I'm just unlucky. It happens. In those cases, I have an absolutely foolproof plan B. And by foolproof, I mean it has never, ever, failed.

I play the press card.

Most upscale hotels employ a person whose sole job is to encourage journalists to say nice things about them. In large hotel chains, this person probably works in-house and is called Director of Marketing. For smaller chains and independents, the job is usually outsourced to a PR agency. As an occasionally published writer, and one who feels no shame in exploiting the fact for fun and profit, it usually just takes a quick email to the press office to get results . . .

From: Paul Carr
To: Any press office, anywhere

Hi, my name is Paul Carr. I write for [name of British newspaper – they never check] and I'm going to be in town for [x] days, starting from [date]. I've heard great things about [name of hotel] and I wondered what your media rate is for those dates? I'm happy to take whatever class of room you have . . .

'Media rate': those are the key words. Every hotel has one and, depending on how prestigious your publication or how convincing your email, the discount can range anywhere from 10 per cent off the rack rate up to 100 per cent. Even hotels that claim they don't discount for media, do. The Lanesborough says it doesn't have a media rate – why would it? It's the most prestigious hotel in London – and yet it certainly does. In December 2009 it was £350 for a £1000 room.*

The important thing is you're not asking for a discount, and you're not asking for a freebie – you're just enquiring as to what the rate for journalists is for those dates. Asking for a free room is always a bad idea as a) it marks you out as a blagger, and b) hotels tend to expect something in return. Although that can work, too: Zoe was once offered a free room in Manhattan in exchange for doing a book reading for hotel staff.

As far as I know, no hotel has ever actually checked my credentials with a newspaper. At most they might Google my name, find details of the various things I'd written and assume that all was on the level. It helped that I usually *was* on the level – but I've often thought that there's no reason why non-journalists couldn't pull off the same blag, if they did it with enough confidence. Of course, I never told my friends that. No sense in killing the golden goose.†

206

The hangover was raging with full force now, my second beer was finished and my laptop was warning me that it had less than 10 per cent power left. It was time to make a final decision. My best bet looked to be the Hotel QT, near Times Square: a boutique hotel, recently refurbished and a couple of steps up the ladder from the Pod. The Trip Advisor reviews were great

---

* More on how I know that – and why I didn't pay it – later.
† That sound you just heard was the death rattle of the golden goose.

and they were offering rooms for $139 a night. Oh, and they had a swimming pool in the lobby. Perfect; that's who I'd call first. I scribbled down the hotel's reservations number in my notepad: I reckoned the laptop probably only had about five minutes of life left and I wanted to quickly check my email before it died.

The UK is five hours ahead of New York so my inbox already contained a day's worth of mail from back home.* I scanned quickly down the list – ignoring the usual crap from Amazon and the spammers offering to make me a fortune – and opened the only two that were from people I actually knew. The first was from Robert who wanted to know how New York was treating me. I'd reply to that one later, when I got to the hotel – the naked elevator story demanded more than 8 per cent battery. The second was from my friend Michael and bore the subject line 'Vegas baby!' I clicked it open.

From: Michael Smith
To: Paul Carr

Hey mate!

A little bird tells me you're in New York. I'm at a conference in San Francisco today and I have to be in LA next week for a meeting but I've got a couple of days free. According to Facebook, Michelle is heading to Vegas tomorrow for her 30th birthday – was thinking of joining her. You in? Should be fun.

M.

Fun is the right word. Michael is one of my favourite people to party with. The founder of a string of multi-million-dollar businesses, he's hugely successful by any metric you care to

* I would continue to refer to London as 'back home' for about another three months.

use. But he's also the living embodiment of the phrase 'work hard and play hard'. A constant fixture on London's lists of 'most eligible bachelors', he also has a way with the ladies that makes him the ideal wingman for adventures with the opposite sex.*

Michelle too is always good for adventures – she's been friends with Michael and me for years and, as we'd both already had brief – very brief – romantic encounters with her, any odd sexual tension was long consigned to the past, allowing her to become an honorary guy for the purposes of wingmanship. Girls, we discovered, are less likely to be wary of men who are out with female friends.

Still, tempting as it was to join the two of them in Vegas, there was still no way I was 'in'. The whole point of my grand experiment in nomadic living was not to spend any more money than I would in London, both in terms of accommodation and also general cost of living. Assuming I managed to stick to that budget, I'd easily be able to pay my way with regular freelance gigs. I really couldn't justify any additional expenditure – including a flight to Vegas – this early in the trip, unless I could find some way of offsetting it against a saving somewhere else.

Three per cent battery.

I closed Michael's email. He'd have to have fun without me.

And that's when I noticed a third email. A one-line message, sent via Facebook, from Michelle.

'*Hey – come to Vegas – I've got a room. We'll share. – Michelle xoxoxo*'

Two per cent battery.

A free room for two nights: that would certainly go some way to offsetting the cost of the flight. But there were other considerations too, surely. I mean, I couldn't just abandon my meticulously

---

* When I told Michael I was writing this book, he insisted that I change his name to protect his reputation. Please, therefore, assume throughout that I'm referring to a different Michael Smith.

detailed travel plans on a whim and fly off to party in Vegas. That would be . . .

One per cent.

. . . what's the word?

Chapter 300

Beer and Togas in Las Vegas

Ridiculous.

'Fifty-seven men are in court today in Saudi Arabia, arrested on charges of "public flirting" in shopping centers around Mecca.'

The Fox News anchor tried to sound fair and balanced as he read the report, bless him. But it was a ridiculous story, and one that illustrated the gaping chasm – the gulf, even – between Western attitudes and those in the Middle East.

The arrest of fifty-seven people wasn't funny – not really – but hearing about it on an enormous flatscreen television in Michelle's room at the Excalibur Hotel, Las Vegas, I couldn't help but laugh out loud.

All of the oil money in Saudi Arabia couldn't afford to build enough prisons to house all of the flirters – and drinkers, and gamblers – in this place. A mecca of decadence and depravity, where even the check-in desks have gambling terminals built into them and drunken women on bachelorette weekends line every corridor, clutching two-foot tall plastic cups of alcoholic slush. Any one of the tiara-wearing, screeching, near-topless harpies I'd run into between reception and the fourth floor of the hotel would have eaten a Saudi flirter for breakfast.

The hotel itself was shaped like a piece of knock-off Disney merchandise. It was supposed to conjure up images of Camelot castle – all red and blue turrets and plastic knights holding injection-moulded swords – and yet, for all the millions they'd obviously spent on branding the place as 'the Excalibur', they apparently hadn't thought to spend $20 on a book about King Arthur's legend. The hotel's main restaurant was called 'the

Sherwood Forest' and the gift shop sold Robin Hood hats.

I should make clear at this point, that, even after receiving Michelle's message back in New York, I was still planning to phone the Hotel QT and check in for the rest of the month. Really I was. Then I'd decided to have just one more beer – for the road – and, while the bartender was pouring, I'd used the web browser on my BlackBerry to check the cost of flights to Vegas.

Jet Blue Airways was offering a special last-minute deal: a return flight for $120. That meant if I shared Michelle's hotel room I could fly to Vegas, stay for two days and then fly back to New York and still be under budget. If anything, it was fiscally irresponsible not to go. Four-beer logic.

301

My flight landed at a little after 1 a.m. Pacific Time – 4 a.m. New York time – and I took a cab straight to the Excalibur, where Michelle was waiting. She'd already been in town for six hours, having flown in from London, via Minneapolis – and yet, despite her jetlag and my hangover, we couldn't help checking out the hotel casino before sleep.

By 3.30 a.m., after dinner, a nightcap and a failed attempt to beat the slots, we finally made it to the room, where I'd flipped on the TV and started to unpack for the first time since leaving London. All I wanted to do was sleep, but the rest of the hotel was still wide awake, as if it were still the middle of the evening. Children still roamed the corridors, row upon row of bored-looking fat women pumped money into slots and the hen-night girls – those loud, loud girls – seemed like they were just getting started. Sure enough, at 7 a.m. we'd be awoken by them returning to their rooms – happy, drunk and singing Britney Spears' 'Toxic' at the top of their formidable lungs.

Michelle came out of the bathroom, dressed in a long t-shirt and what appeared to be bed socks, and climbed into one of the two double beds. I rescued the last shirt from the bottom of my bag –

its creases now permanent – and laid it inside the wardrobe, on the one shelf that Michelle had left for me.

'So, how's the sweepstake going?' she asked.

'What sweepstake?'

'Robert's sweepstake ... the one about you being ...' She stopped. 'He hasn't told you?'

'No, he hasn't,' I said. 'What sweepstake?'

'How long you'll be able to stay in America before you either get arrested, married or seriously injured. Everybody we know in London is playing.'

'You're kidding me. Even you?'

'It's just for fun.'

'I'm sure it is. How long did you give me?'

'Oh, I said it would probably happen this weekend. I mean, seriously, you, in Las Vegas? Ha!'

Click

She reached over and turned out the bedside lamp. 'Goodnight, honey.'

The cheek of it. OK, so I'd only been in the country for a day before ending up drunk and naked in a hotel corridor, but that – well – that was just a glitch. Getting it out of my system. And, anyway, compared to the animals I'd seen in the hotel lobby, I was a saint: a paragon of virtue, celibacy and self-preservation.

And yet, Sin City or no, after last night's madness I was definitely going to calm down for a few days.

302

The next morning I felt much better – human, almost. Michelle and I had breakfast at the House of Blues bar and restaurant – pulled pork sandwiches, with orange juice with just a touch of champagne. Hell, it was almost lunchtime anyway.

Michael's flight was due to arrive at noon, and it was now pushing 1p.m. so we headed down the Strip to his hotel. He'd texted to say he was staying at the Mandalay Bay Hotel, so that's where we sat, in the lobby, waiting. A stunning waitress – all legs and breasts and hair, she could easily have been a model, or I suppose an off-duty stripper – came to take our obligatory drinks order. One of the things you soon realise about Vegas is that there is no free seating; you sit, you drink, you pay. I ordered a Diet Coke. I really meant it this time: no drinking.

Twenty minutes passed. Half an hour. Where the hell was Michael?

After forty-five minutes, I texted him. 'Where the hell are you?'

The reply came in a few seconds: 'THEhotel/Mandalay Bay/Lobby, where you?'

'That's where we are.'

'No, you're not.'

I called the waitress over. 'Another round, sir? Something stronger?'

'No, thank you. I was just wondering – we were supposed to meet our friend in the hotel lobby – is this the only one? '

'Yes and no,' she said, 'this is the only lobby in this hotel. But it's not the only hotel in this building.'

'Um . . .'

'Is your friend staying at the Mandalay Bay Hotel, or the hotel at Mandalay Bay?'

I showed her Michael's text, and she smiled – this happened all the time. She pointed us the way from the lobby of the Mandalay Bay Hotel and through to the totally separate lobby of THEhotel at Mandalay Bay where, sure enough, Michael was waiting.

'I hope there's rum in that Coke, Mr Carr. There's a sweepstake, you know.'

Michael's voice echoed around the lobby. He was sitting with his feet up on a leather stool, and he was dressed for Vegas. A bright blue shirt – three buttons undone and with a picture of a tiger sewn on the front – blue jeans, and shiny purple cowboy boots, complete with rhinestones. He also had a stack of brightly coloured gaming chips in his hand. Had he brought them with him? Is that even allowed?

Hugs all around.

'So what's the plan?' asked Michael, dropping the chips into his pocket and clapping his hands for some imaginary camera, like croupiers do in films.

'Nikki's getting in at seven' said Michelle. 'She's schmoozing some client in town so she's going to buy us all dinner at Nobu and expense it.'

'Perfect,' said Michael. 'Then there's a club at the Palms that my cab driver was talking about. Let's see if we can blag our way into VIP there.'

'Perfect,' I said. I didn't even think to ask who Nikki was until much later. All that mattered was she was one of Michelle's friends who was buying us dinner on her corporate Amex. Another budget saving. 'And sorry to mess up your precious sweepstake, but I'm not drinking tonight.'

They both laughed. As well they might.

303

Thirty-three hours later.

I defy anyone to spend two days in Las Vegas and not come out broken – emotionally and physically. My liver felt like it had grown to at least four times its original size and I was pretty sure I'd put on about twelve stone in weight. I couldn't feel my legs properly.

The previous night we'd partied like rock stars, courtesy of our generous corporate sponsor: Nikki's Amex card. Dinner at Nobu first, then a table at Body English at the Hard Rock replete with bottles of Jack Daniel's and Premium Vodka. The drinking was interrupted only by a live performance by someone called 'Fat Man Scoop' whose spirited performance consisted mainly of entreaties to 'make some motherfucking noise', which is surely the worst kind of noise. Michael and I had decided to leave the girls to their vodka and head out to another bar.

And another. And another, before eventually arriving at the Palms, as recommended by Michael's cab driver. Curiously, we didn't see many people there who looked like cab drivers – but we did meet a group of girls who were in town to promote shoe insoles at a conference. 'That's a coincidence,' said Michael to the second prettiest of the girls,* 'my mother is a chiropodist.' For once, he was telling the truth.

'I don't know what that means,' said the girl. Apparently chiropodists are called something else in America.

Our next encounter was with a bachelorette party from – I think – Atlanta. We joined them at their table and were soon helping them work through a second bottle of vodka – which is about the time things started to come apart a bit at the seams. Fortunately I had my digital camera with me ensuring that I was later able to piece together more of the night's events. It seems at one point I got to wear the bride-to-be's veil. Always the bridesmaid.

The next morning's hangover was painful; the kind that makes one crave a full English breakfast. The Americans try, bless them, but they just can't get bacon right. They have a thing they *call* bacon, but really it's just thick strips of fat with a faint pink outline that may or may not have once been part of a pig. I settled instead for a pile of pancakes and a Bloody Mary.

'What time did we get back last night?' I asked, hoping Michael wouldn't remember either. Some knowns are better left unknown.

'About four, I think, whatever time Eye Candy closed.'

'Eye Candy?'

'Some hotel bar or other; I found the receipt in my wallet. Do you remember the strip club?'

'No, Michael, I do not remember the strip club. When did we decide to go to a strip club?'

'*We* didn't. You told the cab driver to take us somewhere fun. I wanted to play blackjack back at the Hard Rock – win some of my money back – but you insisted he take us somewhere where there'd be hot girls.'

---

* Michael is all about strategy.

'So he took us to a strip club?'

'You really don't remember? Jesus, that was only about two, I think. We got in and they said they couldn't serve alcohol as it was a fully nude club or something. So you ordered two Red Bulls for $20 each and then we had to run away after they tried to force us into a $400 private show'

'Interesting,' I said, 'all I know is that this morning I had a text message on my phone from a 404 area code – which is Atlanta, apparently. See what you make of it . . .'

I handed Michael my phone, and he read the message out loud: ''@ airport flight in half hour u coming . . .' do they not have punctuation in Atlanta? Wait – was this girl – I assume it was a girl – waiting for you at Atlanta airport or here?'

'I have no idea.'

'Ha!' said Michael, '404. Memory of last night not found.'

I didn't have the energy to laugh at Michael's geek joke.* Nor could I muster much enthusiasm when he started talking about his amazing room at THEhotel with its spa bath, home cinema TV and near-panoramic view over the city.

'You lucky bastard. Are you expensing it?'

'Wouldn't dream of it,' Michael replied, looking almost offended. 'Anyway, it's only a hundred bucks a night. Booked it online. Vegas rooms are stupid-cheap during the week at this time of year.'

A hundred dollars. Exactly on my accommodation budget – another sign, surely – and I could really, really use a spa bath right now. I'd just have to figure out some other way to offset the cost of the flights. By the time Michael had finished drinking his coffee and flirting with the waitress, I'd booked the room using my BlackBerry.

304

After breakfast, I checked into my new room, tested out the spa bath and then slept for the rest of the day while Michael – who

* http://en.wikipedia.org/wiki/HTTP–404

obviously hadn't been nearly us drunk as me the previous night – headed off to play in, and eventually win, a poker tournament in the hotel's casino. The prize money wasn't much – $500 or so – but it was enough that he'd promised to buy dinner, seeing as I'd bought the $20 strip-club Red Bulls.

We arranged to meet in the lobby of THEhotel at seven. Michael was still giddy after his win so we decided to walk about a bit to see what our food options were: Michael had heard there was a good Wolfgang Puck close by. In Vegas, you're never more than twenty feet from a Wolfgang Puck.

As we walked, Michael started to pitch an idea he'd had between poker games. Rather than him flying to his meeting in LA, me heading back to New York and Michelle going back to London, how did I feel about the idea of the three of us renting a car and driving across the desert from Vegas to Los Angeles? He had a meeting in LA, but apart from that we could just hang out – see some sights, meet some nice local girls before finally driving down the coast to San Diego for ETech, the annual West Coast technology conference which was happening the following week.

I had to admit, it was a good plan. A bit too good in fact – I suspected Michael might have been working on it since before we'd arrived in town. But no, I'd had my fun; I had to get back to my planned travel.

'It sounds great, mate, it really does, but I really do have to head back to New York. I've had enough craziness these past few days.'

Michael wasn't letting it go, though. 'Who said anything about craziness? I have serious work to do when I get to LA. I've just always wanted to drive through the desert in a convertible. It'll be like *Fear and Loathing in Las Vegas*. You know, with the bats.'

'First of all, Michael, don't think for a second that I don't realise you're trying to play into my Hunter S. Thompson fantasies. Second of all, Raoul Duke and Dr Gonzo were on their way *to* Vegas when they saw the bats. And third, as you well know, there weren't any actual bats: they were on a shit-ton of drugs. Is that part of the road trip, too? Because I have to tell you, the last twenty-four hours in

Vegas have nearly killed me, without any narcotics.'

'No, of course not, I just meant it'll be fun. You know I'm right. I'll even let you drive.'

He was right, of course, especially as I could probably parlay the trip into some work – convince an editor back home to pay me to write about ETech or some technology companies in LA – and cover all of my costs at a stroke.

The problem was, the way I was going I might also end up having an actual stroke. I could feel myself getting hooked on the buzz of having no responsibilities. Whatever Michael said, a trip to LA – especially with Michelle coming too – would surely mean more drinking and partying and madness. It would also trash my already shaky-looking budget. I already had flights to recoup.

'I just want to stay on the right side of ridiculous – that's all,' I said. 'You're good at knowing when to stop but I'm really not. I just don't want to make the sweepstake too easy.'

'Dude, look . . .'

'I know what you're going to say, Michael, but . . .'

'No,' said Michael, 'Dude. Look.'

'Holy shit.'

Walking towards us were the three most beautiful women either of us had ever seen. Dressed head to toe in black – knee-length black skirts, black shirts, black jackets – they looked like spies. Sexy female spies, with the most perfect hair you can possibly imagine.

Men aren't really supposed to notice hair – boobs, yes, bums, yes, but not hair. And yet there was something about these girls that just screamed it: LOOK AT MY HAIR.

And so we did. We looked at their perfect hair, and then we looked their perfect faces and their perfect, young – maybe twenty-two-, twenty-three-year-old – bodies, all dressed in black, as they walked towards and then past us, chattering excitedly about whatever it is that girls like that talk about.*

---

* Hair care, probably.

'I can't believe we didn't say anything to them,' I said.

But Michael couldn't speak either. 'I know, but, I . . . I mean . . . did you . . . the hair . . .'

'I know.'

We carried on walking, Michael still pitching our working road trip and me still demurring on the grounds of sanity, and us both still thinking about the girls with the hair. And then, as we rounded the next corner – still no sign of the Wolfgang Puck – there they were again. Except they weren't the same girls. They were dressed the same – head to toe in black – and their hair was just as perfect, but this time one of them was a redhead and the other was Asian.

And they kept coming. More and more of these girls, in little groups of two, or five or six. All the same; all with the perfect hair.

We finally found our courage, and our voices, just as two blonde girls – they could easily have been twins, had one not been a foot taller than the other – came into view.

'Excuse me, ladies,' said Michael, being sure to exaggerate his accent. Strategy.

They giggled. 'Ohmigod, are you English?!' asked the taller girl.

'Good ear,' I said. 'I'm Paul and this is Michael. We couldn't help but notice that there were so many beautiful women in the hotel tonight. We just wondered whether you were here for some kind of convention? Do they have beautiful women conventions here?'

'Yes!' shrieked the shorter one. They both talked in exclamation marks. 'Not beautiful women conventions, I don't mean!' – giggle – 'We're here with the Paul Mitchell Hair and Beauty School. It's our annual conference!'

'Goodness,' said Michael, 'so you're all hairdressers?'

'Stylists!' said the taller girl. 'Yes, all of us from all the schools across America. There are, like, two thousand of us!'

Holy. Fucking. Shit.

'No way!' said Michael. 'What an amazing coincidence. I'm Michael, and my friend Paul and I are hair stylists, too.'

He caught himself. Two male hair stylists? Idiot. We might as well have been holding hands. Also, we do not have the hair of hair stylists.

'Well,' I jumped in, 'actually our friend Robert in London is the stylist, we're just his investors. He's opening a new salon in Soho.'

'No way! That's awesome – what's it called . . .?'

'British Hairways.'

305

Looking back now, I wonder how different my life would be if we'd arranged to meet for dinner slightly earlier. Or if I hadn't moved hotels and we'd met instead at the Excalibur. Mainly, though, I wonder how my life would have been different if Michael hadn't been so good at puns.

Had Michael not been so good at puns there's a very good chance I'd have flown back to New York the next day as planned, picked up my train ticket and continued my travels. I'd probably have stuck studiously to my budget and, after twelve months of moving around the world from hotel to hotel, I'd have got back to London and maybe written a book: 'How I spent a year living in hotels', or some-such. One of those crazy middle-class adventure books with a very clearly defined goal that you know the 'hero' is going to achieve from page one. Maybe, had Michael not been so good at puns, when I moved into my new flat on 1 January 2009, I'd have a girl on my arm. A fellow traveller – an American, obviously – who I'd met in a Holiday Inn in Salt Lake City and fallen in love with and decided to bring back to London to start a new life with a dog and plans to procreate. Maybe had Michael not been so good at puns then I'd have actually met a fucking Mormon.

Michael, though, *is* good at puns. So if you picked up this book hoping for Mormons, we're both in trouble.

306

'British Hairways.'

The girls stopped for a second, processing Michael's words. And then they dissolved into fits of giggles.

'No way! That's sooooo funny!' said the tall girl, turning to her friend. 'Ohmigod! They have to come meet Janet – that's our tutor – and tell her that. She'd love it.' She stopped bouncing up and down and remembered that she still hadn't introduced herself properly.

'I'm Sandi!'

'And I'm Mandy!' said the shorter girl.

I swear that's what they said.

'No fucking way,' I said.

'What do you mean?!' said Sandi, offended.

'He means we'd love to meet your tutor,' said Michael. 'What are you ladies doing later?'

307

'A toga party.' Michael put down his steak knife and shook his head.

'I know. Thousands of those girls, dressed in bedsheets. I have to say, mate, British Hairways was inspired.'

'I know. I have no idea where it came from.'

We carried on eating our dinner. We hadn't found the Wolfgang Puck, but the steak joint we had found was fine, and anyway we had far more important things on our mind than food. We'd briefly discussed whether to scavenge some bedsheets from the hotel to make togas, but had instead settled on fashioning some of the fake plastic ivy from the lobby of the Excalibur into makeshift laurel wreaths to wear on our heads. That way if, as was highly likely, we didn't make it into the toga party, we wouldn't be stuck looking like twats for the rest of the night.

'AUSSIE, AUSSIE, AUSSIE!'

Apparently not everyone was concerned about looking like a twat. The guy standing at the bar had been shouting those same three words – over and over again – the whole time we'd been eating. He was doing shots of some kind of clear spirit, each one punctuated with the same irritating war cry. An Australian, obviously. We might have told him to shut up had he not been so gigantic – well over six feet tall with enormous arms and a huge barrel chest, squeezed into a skin-tight t-shirt.

He was still going strong when Michael and I decided to leave and head to meet the hairdressers. Unfortunately there was no way to get out of the restaurant without walking past the bar.

'Hey, fellas,' shouted the Australian as we tried to creep by. We ignored him and carried on walking.

'Hey, fellas!' louder this time. Sigh. We stopped and turned around.

'You guys wanna do tequila suicides?'

I sighed – *Australians* – and started walking again, putting my laurel wreath on my head as I went. We had a toga party to get to. But Michael couldn't help himself.

'What are tequila suicides?' he asked, genuinely curious. I admit I was wondering the same thing but had decided it was unwise to ask.

'That's the spirit, mate! Barman! Three tequilas, and slice up some more lemons! What's your name, mate?' He grabbed Michael's hand, crushing it on purpose. Michael smiled through the pain and introduced himself.

'Nice to meet you, Mikey, I'm Jonesy – and a tequila suicide is like this . . .' The Australian grabbed a slice of lemon from the bar, tilted his head back and opened his eyes wide.

'First, you squirt the lemon in your eye.' He did so, without even wincing. I winced for him.

'Then,' – he picked up a drinking straw and a salt shaker, pouring a line of salt on to the bar – 'you snort the salt . . .'

Snnniiiiiiifffff . . .

Jesus Christ.

'And then . . . you drink the tequila.'

'AUSSIE, AUSSIE, AUSSIE!'

Slam.

'Now, come on, Michael – your turn. Might help you grow some balls.'

Michael smiled again. 'Maybe later.'

308

Two hours later and the toga party was in full thrust. As antici-pated, we'd almost been turned away at the door by the two burly security guards hired to keep the likes of us well away from these poor, impressionable girls. But Sandi and Mandy had spotted us and dragged us inside. 'Come on! Janet is dying* to meet you.'

We followed Mandy and Sandi to the buffet table and free bar where Janet – an older women wearing what was clearly a pro-fessionally made toga, rented for the occasion – was standing with a group of other tutors. They looked like serious people; we'd have to bring our A-game, as Americans might say.

And how the lies flowed.

No, we didn't know much about hair ourselves – our friend Robert took care of that side of things – we were more the business people; the brains who kept everything on track. 'He cuts hair, we cut costs,' I joked and we all laughed. Seriously, where was this shit coming from? And it got worse.

'Paul and I would love to visit your school,' I heard Michael saying.

And then I was nodding: 'A guest lecture? We could definitely do that, couldn't we, Michael?'

'Oh, definitely.'

'This coming April? Perfect.'

Sandi and Mandy were standing a couple of feet away, lapping it up. We finished talking to Janet and got her business card –

---

* Once you've heard one hairdressing pun, you start to hear them everywhere.

which I've carried in my wallet ever since, just to prove to myself and anyone else that it really happened – and promised to call to arrange the lecture. Then, after promising Mandy and Sandi that we wouldn't leave without them – as if – we'd grabbed a couple of ridiculous Hawaiian cocktail things and headed towards the dance floor.

'So,' said Michael, 'what do you think about the road trip idea now? This could be us every night in LA and San Diego. Blagging our way into parties at night and working hard all day.'

Frankly, at this stage of the evening I couldn't have given less of a shit about work. I'd figure that out later. All I could think about were the possibilities this party had shown me; how ridiculous life could be with a little bit of effort. Thanks to our ability to lie convincingly, but basically harmlessly, Michael and I were drinking free booze in Las Vegas, surrounded by hundreds of beautiful girls dressed only in bedsheets. We were the only straight men in the room. There was a very real chance I'd be taking either Mandy or Sandi back to my spa bath tonight: in the room that was costing me the exact same as my flat in London. Why the hell would I ever want to go back to that life?

If it wasn't for the fact that the Hawaiian punch was my first drink of the day – I'd been too hungover until then – I'd think it was the booze talking. But it wasn't. This was a totally sober epiphany.

What if I didn't ever go back? What if I stopped thinking of this as a one-year experiment with a neatly defined goal at the end and just made it my life? Living in hotels, blagging my way into adventures and supporting myself with freelance gigs? If tonight was anything to go by, I'd hardly be short of things to write about: surely at least one editor would be interested in the story of me, Michael and a few hundred girls in togas?

I'd been telling myself that I had to cut down on drinking and figure out my life before I was thirty – but why? I remembered Michael's earlier allusion to Hunter S. Thompson. Like most young ego-driven writers, I'm a ridiculous gonzo fanboy, but the fact remained that Thompson – and writers like him – had shown the world that it was entirely possible to spend your whole life drinking and partying and having ridiculous adventures and yet still somehow survive. Hell, when Thompson shot himself he was nearly seventy.

What was it he always said? 'Buy the ticket, take the ride'?

Michael was still waiting for me to answer his question. 'So? LA? Shall we go?'

'What a ridiculous question,' I said. 'Of course we shall.'

309

We bumped fists – the ironic post-Obama handshake – necked our ridiculous drinks and trod carefully across the dance floor towards the door, all too aware that one misplaced step could trigger a wardrobe malfunction of epic proportions.

We could quite happily have stayed in that room all night – all week, even – but Mandy and Sandi were ready to leave and we didn't want to let them out of our sights. All being well, we'd see the rest of these amazing girls in April when we visited the Paul Mitchell school in San Diego to deliver our acclaimed lecture (with Power Points) on the Business of Hair. The fact that our lecture didn't exist and that neither Michael nor I knew the first thing about opening a hair salon was a trivial detail.

'I mean,' I said, as we walked past the bouncer, who was busy explaining to a giant Australian drunk that he wasn't his 'mate', 'it's only hair. How much can there be to know about hair?'

'Well, exactly – that's what Wikipedia's for, right?'

310

'Good morning, gentlemen.'

Ten a.m., and the parking valet outside the Mandalay Bay Hotel was grinning, as well he might. The jet-black Mustang convertible that Michael had rented earlier that morning, using my credit card, was a beast of a car – with gleaming chrome wheels and a V8 engine. None of that power would be much use in Los Angeles traffic, of course, but that problem was six hours and an entire desert away. Right now, all I cared about was that I was about to get behind the wheel of a car that made me drool.

With a satisfying clunk of the release mechanism and a whir of hydraulics, the roof of the Mustang slid back. Michael threw his duffel bag into the back, tipped the valet the last of his poker winnings and leapt, *Dukes of Hazzard*-style, into the passenger seat beside me. I tried to do the same thing, but hadn't bargained for the steering wheel.

Now we just had to locate Michelle. She was supposed to meet us outside the hotel at 9.30, but was already half an hour late. We called her mobile, and her room at the Excalibur, but there was no answer at either. We were just starting to get worried, when finally she emerged, blinking at the sunshine, hair pulled under a baseball cap that we'd never seen before, pulling her suitcase along behind her. She was clearly wearing last night's clothes. And a huge grin.

'Good night, dear?' I asked as she scrambled over Michael's bag into the car's tiny back seat, wedging her suitcase in beside her.

'Oh my GOD yes!'

'You didn't seem to be in your room when we called earlier,' Michael said, with a smile.

Michelle's grin broadened. 'I met someone last night. He was amazing!'

'We probably don't need to hear the details,' said Michael, trying to figure out how to get some music out of the satellite radio.

But Michelle couldn't help herself. 'Oh my God, babes, I'm not kidding, he was so hot. And he had these amazing arms. He just picked me up and threw me around the bed like a rag doll. It was the best sex I've ever had. I think he was Australian – Nikki and I met him in the hotel bar. You won't believe what he was drinking . . . He put this line of salt on the bar and . . . what?'

With a screech of expensive tyres, I gunned the Mustang out on to the Strip, Michael gripping the armrest with both hands.

'You have driven on the right before, haven't you?' he yelled, with only a hint of panic.

'The right? Oh, yeah – shit – thanks.' Even when lurching across four lanes of traffic to avoid a head-on collision with a stretched Humvee, the Mustang V8 handles like a dream.

After only a couple of wrong turnings and a misunderstanding involving a stop light and some more oncoming traffic, we were soon heading towards Interstate 15, on the correct side of the road. In a few hours we'd be in Los Angeles. The City of Angels – where every day a dozen dreams are realised and a thousand are shattered; where every cab driver has a screenplay on the passenger seat and all the waiters are just 'resting'; where even the dorky girls are ten feet tall and where they sell casting couches in Ikea.

And where I'd decided to open up the throttle on my new life as a permanent, hotel-dwelling nomad. A man bouncing from adventure to adventure, supporting himself through a combination of writing gigs and bullshit. A man with no responsibilities, just a determination never to get stuck in a rut again.

A man without a plan.

Ticket bought, let the ride begin.

Chapter 400

What the Hell Was I Doing, Drinking in LA?

FADE IN . . .

                        VO
        'We were somewhere outside Barstow, on the edge of
        the desert, when I pulled over to update my Facebook
        status. I remember Michael saying something like "you
        really are a dork, you know that? I'm going into the gas
        station shop to buy some root beer and a pack of Junior
        Mints."'

OPENING CREDITS – A MONTAGE OF SCENES FROM A
ROAD TRIP

A rented black convertible Mustang tears along a desert road.
PAUL is driving, MICHAEL is in the passenger seat while
MICHELLE sleeps on the back seat, a ridiculous grin on her face.
For some reason.

   They arrive in LA, three hours late, after sitting in ten miles of
traffic outside the city. MICHAEL leaves the car and walks into
his luxury hotel in downtown LA, paid for by the company he's
meeting in town. The hotel has no more vacancies.

   PAUL and MICHELLE drive around for another hour before,
battered by tiredness, PAUL insists they check into the next hotel
they see: the Super 8 Motel. The Hollywood sign can be seen in
the distance.

INT. HOTEL ROOM – NIGHT

PAUL and MICHELLE sit in their hotel room. It's like the inside of every motel room you've ever seen: two double beds with faded topsheets, a small bathroom with a bare light bulb. The wifi is broken. Paul is hunched over, trying to check his email on his phone while Michelle eats the yoghurt that she insisted PAUL stop to buy even though she knew he was fucking exhausted and just wanted a beer.

> PAUL
>
> The good news is the *Guardian* replied to my pitch. They're interested in a piece about the tech industry in LA if I can find a good angle. I was thinking I might write it in the style of a screenplay.

> MICHELLE
>
> Why, babe?

> PAUL
>
> Because we're in Hollywood. It'll be funny.

> MICHELLE
>
> Or just annoying. People will think you're trying to be clever, like Douglas Coupland or someone like that. 'Ooh, look how I play with the format and break through the fourth wall. Look at my pop-culture references that maybe three people will get . . .'

> PAUL
>
> Douglas Coupland? Fuck off. I'm nothing like Douglas Coupland.

> MICHELLE
>
> I'm sorry, babe, you're right. You're nothing like Douglas

Coupland. People have heard of Douglas Coupland.
Douglas Coupland has sold millions of books. Doug . . .

> PAUL

Fuck offfff.

> MICHELLE

So in this screenplay of yours, will you be mentioning
the ridiculous stripe of sunburn across your forehead?
I think that would add . . . what's the word you use?
Colour.

PAUL looks up from his phone and we see he has a thick stripe of
sunburn running, like an angry red sweatband, across the top of
his forehead. He does look ridiculous.

> PAUL

It's not funny. How was I supposed to know the sun was
burning me over the top of the windscreen?

> MICHELLE

The car has no roof, babe. And we were driving through
the desert. At noon. What did you think was going to
happen? You should have asked to borrow my baseball
cap.

> PAUL

Technically, it's still Jonesy's baseball cap. Anyway,
I need a beer. You coming?

PAUL picks up the baseball cap, pulls it over his burnt forehead
and heads for the door.

> MICHELLE

No thanks, babe – early night for me.

PAUL

Suit yourself. The less time I spend in this shithole the
better. Still, at least it only cost us sixty dollars a night.
Fifteen quid each. I'm back on budget.

SLAM. PAUL closes the door behind him.

MICHELLE
(Shouting through the door):
Nice exposition, babe.

PAUL (OS)
Fuck off.

FADE OUT.

401

I called Michael. It went straight to voicemail; either his meeting
had run very late, or he had decided to crash early too. Light-
weights, both of them. Ah well, I'd just find a bar, text him the
address and see if he turned up. I walked the length of the street –
something unheard of in LA – but could only find one place that
looked like a bar; literally a hole in the wall with an old Mexican
man selling beer to patrons sitting on plastic stools. I decided
instead to rely on the old taxi driver recommendation trick. I hailed
the next cab that passed and hopped in the back. The clock on the
dashboard said 11p.m.

'Hi, I'm looking for somewhere to get a drink – something not
too touristy. Where do people go around here?'

The cab driver looked at me through the rear-view mirror. 'What
you like? You like girls?'

'Not if I have to pay for them. I just want a bar that stays open
late.'

'Everywhere shuts at two a.m. – California licensing laws. But I know a good place.'

We drove for ten minutes, although I couldn't say in what direction. I was too busy looking at Trip Advisor on my phone, hoping to find a better hotel for the next night. At one point we turned on to the freeway, which worried me slightly – either that I was being kidnapped or that his 'good place' was in a different state – but before long we were back on a residential street, pulling up outside what seemed to be a closed bar. Just a black door and a window containing a broken neon light spelling out the word Coors.

'Here?'

'Here!'

I paid the driver – $20 including the tip – and pushed open the black door. The bar was empty – just me, a super-cute blonde girl cleaning glasses and one other guy, wearing a faded blue t-shirt and a beanie hat, sitting at the far end of the bar. I sat at the other end – near the door – and ordered a rum and Diet Coke. I'd just have one drink then I'd text Michael.

The cute bartender came back with my drink. 'Six dollars.' I gave her a ten and slid my change back across the bar as a tip. She picked it up and dropped it in a tip jar, at which point the guy at the other end of the bar drummed his hands, hard, against the bar. A sort of mini-drum roll – like he was celebrating my having left a four-dollar tip. Weird.

I finished my first drink inadvisably fast. I was thirsty, and tired. I ordered another, and then another. Every time I ordered, and left the obligatory tip, the guy in the beanie did his little celebratory drum roll. It wasn't so much annoying as incongruous. Why the drumming? Why only when I tipped? And why wasn't the girl behind the bar telling him to stop being so fucking annoying? Judging by the attention he was paying her, the guy in the beanie hat would do anything the cute blonde girl told him to do. I ordered another one-drink round – I still hadn't texted Michael – and headed down the bar.

'Hey, man,' said the drummer as I sat down beside him.

'Hi,' I said. 'I'm Paul.'

'Matt.' He raised his glass.

'Hi, Matt. Sorry to bother you but I have a theory I wanted to run past you.'

'Shoot.'

'Well, I was sitting down there listening to you drumming on the bar every time I leave tip and I thought – 'Hmmm; that guy is being really fucking annoying. And . . .'

Matt leaned in closer.

'And?'

He had looked smaller from the other end of the bar. And less likely to punch me in the face. But I was six drinks in, so I pressed on.

'. . . And . . . well . . . I thought to myself, the only way anyone could get away with being that annoying without being asked to stop is if either a) he owns the bar, or b) he's sleeping with the bartender.'

Matt didn't say a word. He just stared at me, and then looked over at the blonde girl who had stopped cleaning the glasses. She looked horrified. Had I really said that? Matt leaned in even closer, and then put his arm around my shoulder. With his free hand he picked up my empty glass. Uh-oh.

'Where you from, Paul?'

'London,' I said. I figured he didn't want to hear my whole hotel living story. Not before he glassed me in the face.

'Well, Paul from London . . .

. . . as it happens you're right on both counts. This is my bar and that,' – he pointed my glass towards the blonde girl who had turned a bright shade of red – 'is my bartender. Didn't mean to annoy you, man; just messing around; let me get you another drink.'

We drank another round – rum for me, whisky for him – and then moved on to shots of tequila, as only seemed proper. I told Matt that I was a writer and that I was planning to live life on the road, moving from hotel to hotel, blagging my way into parties and generally living like a king for the same as I was spending languishing in London. Then I explained to Matt what 'blagging' means.

'Blagging. I like that. Well, Paul, I might be able to help you out there.'

He walked behind the bar like – well, like he owned the place – and grabbed a handful of bills from the register and a bunch of car keys lying next to it. Then he kissed his girlfriend goodbye – for just long enough to make me feel uncomfortable – and headed to the door.

'Follow me.'

Follow him? Some guy I'd just met in a bar in LA who had picked up his car keys despite drinking more than me? Sure. OK.

There were only two cars in the parking lot: a busted-up gold Toyota and a grey Aston Martin DB7. The alarm on the DB7 blipped, the lights flashed and the doors unlocked. No way. The DB7 is one of my top three dream cars after the DB5 and the Vanquish. All Aston Martins, obviously. Never trust a man whose top three cars aren't all Aston Martins. I explained my Aston Martin theory to Matt. I was drunk, and apparently starting to ramble.

'You wanna drive it?''

'Oh *please*.'

'I'm serious. If you're really a writer, I want to make sure I make it into your next book.'

For a moment I really considered taking the keys. But two decades of British drink-driving adverts had had their desired effect and I realised that driving on the wrong side of the road, in a foreign country, while borderline plastered would probably be a bad idea. There was also the matter of the sweepstake.

'No, thanks, I'm happy in the passenger seat.'

As Matt drove, down some boulevard or other, past restaurants and bars and clubs and palm trees and beautiful people going about their late-night business, I sobered up just enough to realise how well my new plan was going. I'd been in town less than a day and I'd already scored a liver full of drink, a ride in a DB7 and a new LA friend. Life was good, the fact that I was probably going to end the night drugged, raped and buried in a shallow ditch notwithstanding.

We pulled up outside our destination: a much cooler bar this time – no Coors sign in the window – with huge oak doors guarded by two overinflated male models in matching Gucci suits. Matt got out of the car and handed his keys to one of them, who greeted his boss like an old friend: a beaming smile and a powerful man-hug. 'Hey, Paul' said Matt, 'come meet my best employee, Tobias.'

'Nice to meet you, Tobias,' I said.

Matt put his arm around my shoulder again. 'Paul is my new friend from England. He's a writer and I'm trying to make sure I'm in his next book. Remember his face – for as long as he's in town, Paul and his friends never pay for a drink, OK?'

'Sure thing, boss' said the bouncer, opening the door for us.

'So how many bars do you own?' I asked.

'Too many for one night.'

Inside was rammed. Wall-to-wall guys in tailored black suits with crisp white shirts and women dressed like they were heading to the Oscars. Wait – was it actually Oscar night? No, that was the previous week; I suppose these people didn't need an excuse to dress like movie stars. Matt was working the room – hugging men and kissing women on the cheek – so I headed to the bar.

'A rum and Diet Coke, please.'

'Coming up.' I took out my wallet. The bartender looked towards the door, where Tobias was standing. Tobias shook his head; the bartender nodded in reply.

'That's fine, sir. On the house.'

Shit, I guess Matt wasn't kidding about drinking for free. And not just me: 'Paul and his friends never pay for a drink' – just wait till I told Michael and Michelle; they'll shit themselves. This is the blagger's holy grail.

The rum was strong and the Diet Coke was weak, and before long I was seriously hammered. So much so that I'd been talking to the girl for about ten minutes before I focused on what we were actually saying. Where had she come from, anyway? I seemed to remember that she'd come over and sat down on the stool next to mine – or possibly I'd met her on my way back from the toilet and convinced her to join me at a table. I really couldn't remember for certain, what with the room spinning the way it was. But however it had happened, I suddenly wasn't at the bar any more but was sitting in a booth in the corner, still talking to her: this brown-haired supermodel in a bright green dress. There was a bottle of champagne in a bucket next to us and two glasses on the table. I wasn't sure if I'd ordered it or not. I'm pretty certain I hadn't paid for it.

Across the bar, the bouncer was shouting for closing time.

'Shit,' I said, 'I guess it's time to go.'

'Don't worry about it,' said the girl. 'Matt says we're cool.'

And so we were. After the last of the paying customers had been ushered into the night, the doors were closed and the lock-in began. There were maybe a dozen of us – Matt's friends, old and new – and the drinks kept coming.

More time passed, more drinks and suddenly I'm in a different room. It's a disabled toilet, I think – there are handles on the wall and a long red pull-cord hanging from the roof. And the brunette in the green dress. Except now she's only in the bottom half of the green dress and she's pressing me against the tile wall, and we're kissing.

And . . .

402

I wake up with absolutely no idea where I am. At least this time I'm in bed rather than in a hotel room corridor. And I'm not naked; in fact, I'm still wearing all of my clothes. There's someone else in the room; a television is on. I blink and the world starts to come into focus – the faded topsheet, the clatter of the ancient air conditioning. I'm back at the motel. How the hell did I get home?

'Good morning, drunkard.'

Michelle.

'Jesus Christ. What the hell time did I get in last night?'

'This morning, actually, about six. You insisted I wake up so you could tell me about some girl called Chloe.'

'Chloe?' I thought for a moment. 'Did I mention a green dress?'

'Yes, you wouldn't shut up about her bloody green dress – and some nonsense in a disabled toilet. Honestly, you can't just go around fucking girls in disabled toilets.'

'Actually, I can. I think. Did I tell you about the drinks?'

'What about them?'

I sat up in bed. It was all coming back. 'That's why I was out till six,' I explained excitedly. 'I met the owner of a bar and we had this ridiculous lock-in. But before we did, he told the bouncer that me and you and Michael can drink for free while we're in town.' I acted out the whole scene with bouncer and the hug and the 'this is my friend Paul'.

When I'd finished, Michelle just stared at me. 'You're shitting me.'

'I am emphatically shitting you not.'

'That's amazing. Where is this bar?'

Uh.

'I have absolutely no idea.'

'What do you mean you have no idea? We have free drinks in not one but two bars in LA and you can't remember where they are? How drunk were you?'

'I think I had sex with a girl in a disabled toilet. How drunk do you have to be for that to happen? I think pretty drunk.'

But it was fine; this wasn't my first time having to retrace my steps after a night out – and I had a foolproof plan. My jacket was still lying on the floor, where I'd apparently thrown it when I came in. I jumped out of bed and started rifling through the pockets, looking for a telltale slip of white paper. My usual trick when I can't remember what I did the night before: check my receipts – a time-stamped paper trail of shame.

But then I stopped. The realisation kicked in at the exact same time as the hangover. I didn't have any receipts. Of course I bloody didn't. In the first bar I'd used cash – and after that I hadn't paid for a single drink all night; that was the whole point. Somewhere in Los Angeles there was an open bar and a girl with a green dress, both with my name on them. And I had no way of finding either of them again.

'Ha! Brilliant,' I said. 'Just perfectly brilliant.'

I turned over and slept until dinnertime.

403

'So what happened to you last night?'

When we met for dinner at the Geisha House on Hollywood Boulevard, Michael had some explaining to do. If he had answered his phone, he'd have been with me at the bar the previous night and could have helped me retrace my steps today.

'Sorry, mate, I had a date.'

'With who?'

'Just a girl I met before I flew to meet you guys in Vegas. Veronica – she's a video game designer. And, anyway, from what Michelle told me this morning, you didn't need any help from me, you stud. Tell me, though, what was it like having sex with someone in a wheelchair?'

'We've been through this, Michael. The girl wasn't disabled. The toilet was disabled. She was . . .'

'Able?' said Michael. 'Sounds like it.'

'Ho ho. So what's the plan tomorrow? Drive down to San Diego in the morning? I need to call the car rental people and renew the car.'

'Actually,' said Michael, 'can you just return it? I've made other plans.'

Michael's 'other plans', as he explained, had come while he was preparing for his hot date the previous night. He'd switched on the TV in his hotel room and had caught part of *Vanishing Point*, the 1971 movie in which Barry Newman is hired to deliver a car from Colorado to San Francisco. It's a great movie: filled with car chases and cops and a naked woman on a motorcycle. It's also a movie in which the car – a 1970 Dodge Challenger – is indisputably the star.

'You're not seriously telling me you rented us a 1970 Challenger?'

'Of course not,' said Michael. 'I asked at the rental place but apparently Tarantino bought most of them to trash in *Grindhouse*. They're pretty rare now.'

I was disappointed, of course. Even after the DB7 the night before, a 1970 Challenger would be amazing. Especially if I'd actually been sober enough to drive this time.

'Yeah, sorry to disappoint,' said Michael, removing his iPhone from his pocket and flipping to the photo album application. Pausing for dramatic effect, he slid the phone across the table just in time for the in-built accelerometer to flip the picture from portrait to landscape. 'This is the best I could do.'

Holy shit.

'You're. Kidding. Me. Where did you find that?'

'Beverly Hills Luxury Car Rental,' he said. 'Called them this morning. They didn't have a 1970 Challenger, just a 1971 – would that do?'

404

Michelle and I drove to the airport the next morning to return the Mustang. As we headed to meet Michael at his hotel, I was literally bouncing on the back seat of the cab with excitement: not only were we renting the Challenger, but Michael had agreed to pay all of the hire fees, on the basis that I'd paid for the Mustang and he was the one obsessed with *Vanishing Point*. I'd happily agreed, especially given that Beverly Hills Luxury Car Rental was charging us a grand a day for two days, plus an additional full day's rental for them to come to San Diego and collect it – *plus* a five grand deposit in case we trashed it.

'I get why Michael feels obliged to pay,' I said to Michelle as we neared the hotel, 'I just can't understand why he's letting me drive. Who pays all that money and then lets someone else drive?'

It was only as we pulled up at the hotel and saw the beautiful hunk of purple steel, roof down and classic American rock pouring out of the retro-fitted CD player that everything fell into place. There, sitting in the back seat next to a gigantic suitcase, was a pretty girl who couldn't have been a day over twenty-one.

'Aha!' I said, 'you must be Veronica.'

405

The fact that Michael hadn't told us he had invited Veronica along on the next leg of the road trip didn't bother me in the slightest. I was behind the wheel of a nearly-forty-year-old classic car, with an engine that purred like a grizzly bear receiving a hot stone massage. Veronica seemed like a nice girl – smart for her frighteningly young age, and really pretty – and as long as she and Michael were happy squashed in the back seat with all the luggage, then the more the merrier. I glanced back as we pulled on to the I-5. They seemed happy enough.

One thing that did bother me, though, was that Veronica kept talking about things we were going to do 'when we get back to LA'. I'd ignored it the first couple of times, assuming Michael and she had made plans, but when she referred to 'the drive being even quicker on the way back', my suspicion was confirmed. Michael had convinced this poor girl to drive down the coast with us – hundreds of miles from her home – without telling her it was a one-way trip. How the hell was she going to get home? Christ, she probably still lived with her parents.

I looked over at Michelle in the passenger seat. She looked back. We were obviously both thinking the same thing. Ah well, those logistics were Michael's problem not ours.

A guy passing in his truck sounded his horn. He was pointing at the car, giving it – and us – a thumbs-up, 'Nice,' he mouthed through the window. 'Thanks,' I mouthed in return.

Michelle turned up Huey Lewis and the News and we carried on south.

406

We decided to break the journey with a stopover in Laguna Beach, for no other reason than we'd all watched the reality show of the same name and it looked dreadful. All beach bunny bimbos and fake breasts and guys wearing backwards baseball caps and shell necklaces. 'Douche central,' Veronica had called it.

Keen to avoid another Super 8 Motel fiasco, I'd actually taken the opportunity of a lunch stop to look up hotels in the area. There was a nice-sounding one on the main drag, according to Trip Advisor. I hadn't had time to call and negotiate over the phone, so we'd have to try our luck at the desk.

We rolled into town about four, and soon found the hotel, right by the sea, as advertised. It certainly looked nice – easy access to the beach, a restaurant and bar, wifi. I left Michelle to park the car while I went in to sort the rooms.

The board behind the reception desk advertised a rack rate of $125 per room. That wasn't going to break the bank but still I decided to pull a variation of the upgrade trick, just for fun.

'I'm looking for three double rooms,' I said, sliding my passport across the desk. 'Is $125 the best rate you can do?'

'I'm afraid so, sir,' replied the guy at reception. He looked even younger than Veronica. 'We're pretty slammed tonight.' He took my passport and, despite the fact that I hadn't actually confirmed that I wanted the rooms, he walked into the back office to photocopy it, while the registration cards began to print.

'I'm just going to need a credit card,' he said when he came back.

'Actually,' I said, 'is there any chance I can see the rooms first?'

'You don't want them?' said the receptionist, irritated by all the effort he'd put into the photocopying.

'Oh, no, I'm pretty sure we want them, I just want to look at them first.'

The receptionist sighed; he was the only one on duty. He handed me the three keys and I promised to be right back once I'd checked out the rooms. They were absolutely fine – not huge, but decently sized and beautifully decorated, with views over the beach. And for $125 a night. A bargain, really. I went back to reception and explained that, unfortunately, I'd have to leave them.

'But I've already printed the registration cards.'

'I know,' I said, 'and I'm sorry to mess you around – it's just that I'm a journalist and I'm writing a story about my road trip for my paper back in London. *The Times*,' I lied four times in quick succession.

The receptionist seemed to perk up at this. '*The London Times*? Serious?'

'For my sins,' I lied again.

'OK – I shouldn't do this, but if you pay the $125 I could upgrade one of the rooms to our honeymoon suite. It has a Jacuzzi and a deck that leads to the beach. How would that be? Apart from that, I don't think we have any other rooms.'

I made a big show of thinking about it. 'That's good enough for me.'

He gave me a huge smile as he traded one of the double-room keys for the honeymoon suite. 'Enjoy your stay, and if you need anything at all during your stay, I'm Malcolm.'

'Thank you, Malcolm – I'll remember that when I write my article.'

I considered for a second taking the honeymoon suite for myself, but after Michael had dropped three grand on the car, I figured he'd earned his night of passion with Veronica. And not least because, presumably, he was going to dump her the next day when we got to San Diego.

407

Our night in Laguna Beach passed without incident. Except for the part where a ghost invited us to her wake.

We got to know a bit more about Veronica – as much as there is to know about a twenty-one-year-old – and we drank cocktails in a bar just a little way down the beach. At about midnight, Michael and his date headed off to bed, leaving Michelle and me to one last nightcap before we hit the sack ourselves.

We still had a two-hour drive in the morning, and then a full day's conference to attend. The *Guardian* were still keen on the idea of me writing something for them, a fact I'd used to blag a $1000 conference pass for free, plus a hefty discount on a hotel room.

All I had to do was finish my drink, say goodnight to Michelle and walk the – I dunno – two hundred yards from the hotel bar to my room.

408

Michelle and I woke up at ten the next morning. I know this because she was lying beside me. We were both fully clothed – which was a good sign – but we were also both in the same room, which was less good. On the dressing table were two gigantic – and I mean *gigantic* – bottles, one half full of Captain Morgan rum and the other maybe a quarter full of Smirnoff.

The memory came back in chunks, but mostly in the right order. We'd been about to leave the bar – Michelle had gone to the toilet and I was paying our tab – when I looked up to find a skinny girl with a pointy face and terrifying bulging eyes staring right at me.

'You!' said the girl.

'Me?' I sought to clarify.

'You!' she confirmed, 'I know who sent you.'

'Actually, I'm not from around here. I think you probably have me confused with . . .'

'Yes!' she said, 'of course you're English. She would have sent someone from England.'

'I'm sorry, I really don't understand what you're talking about.'

She put her face even closer to mine. I don't think even the girl in the green dress had got this close. Things had got very weird, very quickly.

'Kos sent you to party with us.'

Michelle got back from the bathroom and picked up her coat from the chair behind me. 'Don't let me interrupt,' she said, somewhat misreading the situation. But the girl with the skinny face turned to Michelle.

'You!'

Here we go.

'You what, babe?'

'She sent you too . . .'

'Kos . . .' I explained to Michelle. A mistake: skinny-face girl took this as a confirmation and, grabbing Michelle in one arm and me in the other, began pulling us across the bar to where her friends had been standing watching. Happily, her friends were slightly less mental and they were able to explain that they were in town for the funeral of their friend Kos who had died a few weeks earlier of a drug overdose. 'They drugged her. They put something in her coke,' explained one of the boys in the way that crazy people explain 9/11.

'They spiked her drink?' I said. 'That's sick. Did they catch who did it?'

'No,' said the boy, as if I were the one who was stoned, 'not her Coke, her coke. And we don't know who. She had enemies, dude.' The others in the group nodded their agreement. They were all totally fucked. And now Michelle and I had been dragged into a weird drink-and-drug-fuelled wake, apparently on the basis that one of the girls – Mel, the others called her – had received 'like a total psychic feeling' that Kos had sent Michelle and me to get drunk with them.

Still, who were we to argue with a dead girl? We'd seen the end of *Carrie*; we knew what happened to people who did that.

We spent the rest of the night back at the kids' hotel room – a vast suite, paid for by someone's dad apparently, with five or six bedrooms and a kitchen full of catering size bottles of booze. One of the boys had a guitar on which he could only play covers of Semisonic songs and every so often one of the group would excuse herself to vomit over the balcony, onto the cars parked below. I prayed Michelle had closed the roof of the Challenger.

Still, the drink was free, the company was certainly entertaining and I knew that one day it would all make excellent fodder for an article. Michelle and I had eventually left at about 5 a.m., but not before grabbing a bottle each for the road.

And now we were waking up to a monstrous hangover and the guilt of having crashed some poor girl's wake and stolen her friends' booze.

'I can't believe we did that,' said Michelle.

'It's what Kos would have wanted,' I replied.

'That's true,' said Michelle. 'She must have known the risks when she invited us.'

409

The drive down to San Diego was exactly as painful as we deserved, and Michelle and I had to take turns with the driving while the other slept. Michael and Veronica sat in the back again, but even through our hangovers we couldn't help notice that their dynamic had changed overnight. Veronica was far more huggy and kissy than she had been the previous day while Michael was the precise opposite – polite, but distant. He spent the trip on his laptop, catching up with some work.

'Do you think they've had a fight,' I whispered to Michelle as we neared San Diego.

'No, babe,' she replied, like I was some kind of idiot, 'I think they had sex.'

410

As agreed with the hire company, we left the Challenger in the parking lot of the conference hotel: the Marriott in San Diego. The

Marriott is a chain hotel with a rack rate of $250 a night, but I'd been able to swing a discount by sweet-talking Maureen, the conference PR coordinator, with promises of extensive coverage in some newspaper or other.

At the end of her email confirming the discount, and my free conference pass, she added a PS . . .

'Hope you enjoy the conference – can't promise any girls in togas though.'

In response to Rob's constant emails demanding news, I'd started writing a blog about my travels, one of the first posts on which had included a photo of some of the hairdressers we'd met in Vegas, really only to make Rob sickeningly jealous. Clearly Maureen had been reading too.

Michelle and I headed off to check into the hotel and collect our conference badges. 'I'll catch up with you guys,' said Michael. He pointed at the Amtrak station that was directly across the street from the hotel, 'I'm just going to walk Veronica to get a train.'

Wow. Had they talked about this last night, or were Michelle and I witnessing the world's most casual and insensitive dumping? 'You don't mind going back on your own, do you? It's just that I'm going to be busy with this conference for a couple of days.'

Veronica just stared, first at Michael, then at Michelle and me. 'Uh, no . . . that's fine.'

'Do you think he knew the station was opposite the hotel before we got here?' Michelle asked as we walked on ahead.

'I have absolutely no idea,' I said, 'but that was so horrible to watch it was almost brilliant.'

Michelle punched me on the arm, hard. 'God, I hate boys.'

411

For the duration of the two-day conference, I worked really hard, making careful notes during seminars with names like 'How Technology Almost Lost the War in Iraq' and 'Sexual Identity Online'. It was actually nice to have a couple of days off from hardcore boozing. As we sat at the back of one panel, Michael introduced me to a new social networking site called Twitter which he'd apparently become addicted to. I didn't get it: it seemed to be a bit like updating your Facebook status, but for the whole world rather than just your friends. I told him I'd give it a try.

Between sessions we lounged by the pool and I read a book called *The 4-Hour Workweek*, which I'd borrowed from Michael. It was well enough written, but the author – a guy called Timothy Ferriss – seemed to be arguing that the secret to a happy life was never replying to emails, selling herbal supplements on the Internet and then buggering off to Argentina to learn to dance. Fuck that, I thought; the secret to a happy life is getting drunk, going to the occasional conference and then writing about it for whoever pays the most.

Chapter 500

The Freaking Rolling Stones or Something

After ETech, my original travel plans now a little more than a distant memory, I decided that I would fly to Austin, Texas, for the South by Southwest Festival.

Held every March, the festival brings together tens of thousands of independent filmmakers, musicians and – in recent years – Internet people to meet their peers, listen to panels and talks and, in the evenings, to get blind drunk at a succession of sponsored parties. The Internet portion of the festival is often described as 'spring break for geeks'.

My decision to attend was all Zoe's fault: her readings in New York had gone well, and her publisher had secured her two gigs at South by Southwest: a reading and also a spot on a panel about online privacy.

She had found a place to stay in Austin – an 'amazing' two-bedroom condo right across the street from the conference centre, and emailed to ask if I wanted to share it with her. Despite my not really knowing what a 'condo' was, I agreed. The price was $100 a night and I had nothing better planned after San Diego.

The whole idea of the festival being a party for geeks fascinated me and on the flight from San Diego International Airport to Austin I wrote a pitch to an editor I knew at the *Financial Times*, likening the event to Woodstock in 1969 . . .

Mark Zuckerberg from Facebook is headlining and then there are a thousand other acts booked to speak on pretty much all aspects of interactive media. It seems that almost everyone in the UK and US dot com industry is heading there – and not just for the legendary parties. Oh, the parties!

And yet behind the scenes, it's a really critical time for the industry where increased consolidation and lots of 'cool' businesses coming to the end of their first funding round means that young entrepreneurs are under pressure to find a 'liquidity event', preferably through acquisition. To grow up, in other words. Like Woodstock in 1969, this year's SXSWi could well mark the end of an era – and I'd very much like to get under the skin of it.

I titled the pitch 'Fear and Coding in Austin, Texas' and felt very pleased with myself for the rest of the flight.

501

On the second night of the conference I stumbled through the door of the condo at about 3 a.m. Right behind me was a girl called Eris, an interactive designer from San Francisco who I'd met a few hours earlier at a roof-top party. The circumstances of our meeting at the party had been slightly odd.

Zoe had just introduced me to some famous website editor on whom she had a crush and, as required, I was making polite small talk about what a nice – and, unbelievably, available – girl Zoe was. My friendly duties complete, I was just about to leave them to their flirting when a small brown-haired girl ran the full length of the roof deck and jumped on to my back. 'Heeeyyyy!' she shouted, swinging from my neck like one of those stuffed monkeys you sometimes get, 'how are yoooooooouuu?'

'Heyyyyy!' I replied, 'uh . . . whoooooo are yoooouuuu?'

The girl let go and landed in front of me. She stared in my face, confused but still beaming: 'I'm sure I know you,' she said. I swear to God, I had a horrible feeling that her next words would be 'Kos sent you'.

But, actually, the crazy brown-haired monkey girl probably did know me. I have a terrible memory for faces at the best of times, but I also meet a lot of people when I'm drunk and then have to deal with the embarrassment of having absolutely no recollection when I see them again. 'Oh, yes,' I said, desperately looking for clues 'where was it I last saw you?'

'I think it was in San Francisco,' said the girl.

'Ah,' I said, 'then we definitely haven't met. I've never been to San Francisco.'

'Oh, well,' said the girl, 'let's meet now. I'm Eris.' She kissed me full on the mouth. 'And by the end of tonight I'll have convinced you to come to San Francisco.'

I liked Eris immediately.

502

As Eris and I spilled through the door of the condo, drunkenly kissing and grabbing at each other's clothes, I realised that I should probably have phoned ahead.

Zoe's bra was in our fruit bowl and a line of her clothes, plus those of a mystery stranger, formed a path from the leather sofa to her bedroom. A pair of thick-rimmed glasses was lying on the countertop.

I led Eris into my room and closed the door, wondering for a split second who the lucky guy Zoe had brought home was. Ah well, I'll find out when she blogs about it tomorrow morning.

It's amazing what some people consider 'work'.

Tomorrow morning duly arrived and Eris left early, heading for an early panel about interaction, or design, or something before catching her flight home. 'You really should come to San Francisco,' she said. 'I think you'd love it.'

I promised her I'd think about it, showed her to the door and then went back to bed to await the inevitable hangover. And, sure enough, by the time I was woken up half an hour later, it was raging with full force. So I really could have done without the shouting from the kitchen . . .

'Fuck. Fuck, fuck, fuckfuckFUCK.'

Zoe's morning was apparently not shaping up as well as her previous evening had.

'FUCKKKKIING HELLL.'

I stumbled out of bed, pulled on my jeans and opened the door.

'What's wrong?' I groaned. 'You can't possibly tell me you're suffering from post-coital guilt. Doesn't seem your style somehow.'

In fact Zoe had a much more serious – and hilarious – reason to be upset. An hour earlier she had woken up – cheeks still flushed from her adventure on our rented upholstery – and switched on her laptop to catch up on the day's news and gossip. And that's when she had discovered the horrible truth – a commenter on a geek gossip site had seen her leaving the party with a guy and had decided to write about it. The blogger had become the blogged.

Stifling a grin – with limited success – I poured her a cup of coffee and listened as she explained what had happened. The problem was not that she'd been spotted leaving the party with a guy – that was hardly news for someone who blogged about one-night stands – but, rather, the identity of that guy. Not only was he Internet-famous too, but he was even more well known than Zoe.

'You mean, the guy last night was _____?' I said, barely able to contain my laughter.

'Yes.'

'Holy shit. He's like a fucking member of the geek A-list'

'Yes, I know,' she said.

'Oh dear.'

503

But if Zoe thought her fifteen minutes of unwanted fame was traumatic, it was nothing compared to what would happen, a few hours later, and less than a mile from our rented apartment – to a business reporter called Sarah Lacy.

Lacy had first come to prominence when she wrote a cover story for *BusinessWeek* magazine about Silicon Valley's new breed of young Internet entrepreneurs, the twenty-somethings responsible for popular sites like Facebook and MySpace and Digg. The article had been so well received that she'd been commissioned by publishers Gotham to write an entire book on the subject, with the title *Once You're Lucky, Twice You're Good*.

The book was due to be published the following month, and, while researching and writing it, Sarah had won the trust of many of her subjects, including Facebook founder Mark Zuckerberg, whose net worth had recently been valued at one and a half billion dollars. Very much the man of the moment, Zuckerberg had reluctantly agreed to be interviewed on stage at South by Southwest – but only if Sarah conducted the interview.

The event was the conference's hot ticket – so much so that two auditoria had been set aside for it: one for the interview itself and a second where the whole thing would be broadcast on a huge screen for those who couldn't fit into the main room.

'You going to the Zuckerberg interview?' Zoe asked as we left the condo, heading for a late brunch.

I hadn't planned on it. 'One point five billion reasons why I'm going to say nothing interesting and you're still going to lap it up?' I said. 'Yeah – sounds fascinating.'

'Not jealous at all then?'

'Of Mark Zuckerberg? Please.'

'Suit yourself. I hear this Sarah Lacy girl is cute.'

'Really?' I said. 'Well, I might poke my head round the door. See if there's anything in it for the *FT* article.'

'Thought you might. See you there.'

504

Sarah Lacy was indeed cute, especially for a business reporter. Wearing knee-length designer shorts and with her dark curly hair held back in a hairband, she was certainly in marked contrast to Zuckerberg who prides himself on his geek chic look – a black fleece and Adidas flip-flops.

'When online dating goes horribly wrong,' I whispered to Zoe as we sat at the back, waiting for the interview to get started.

The room was chock-full o' nerds and their excitement at seeing their hero was beyond embarrassing. As Zuckerberg walked on to the stage, accompanied by thumping techno music, a group of men in the first two rows stood up and started dancing.

'I'm not sure I can cope with this,' I said to Zoe. 'Pretty reporter or not, I may have to get out of here.'

'Yeah,' she said, 'and I assume you've noticed that the pretty reporter is wearing a wedding ring.'

'Jesus, Zoe, how can you see a wedding ring from here?'

'Comes with the job, darling.'

The interview got underway and it soon became apparent that the organisers had made a terrible mistake. The computer programmers and web designers that comprised the majority of the audience couldn't care less that Facebook was a multi-billion-dollar company: all they were interested in were the technical details of how the site ran, how it was coded and what features were coming next.

Lacy, though, is a business reporter, and so wanted to press the world's youngest billionaire on how he saw his role changing over the coming months. It was a classic case of right content, wrong audience. Another problem that soon became apparent was that Zuckerberg is a really, really difficult interview subject: much more comfortable in front of a computer than an audience. From the start, he answered Lacy's questions with defensive one-word answers and awkward jokes. Lacy, for her part, tried to put him at ease by playing on their friendship to the point where she was almost flirting with the world's most unflirtwithable man. It was painful to watch.

I was curious what the rest of the audience thought, so I called up Twitter on my phone. I'd used the service a few times since Michael had introduced me to it, but not to the point where I was convinced of its purpose. But looking at the 'tweets' relating to the Zuckerberg interview, I suddenly understood it. 'This Lacy chick is the worst interviewer ever,' wrote one Twitterer. 'This interview sucks ass,' said another. Twitter was the perfect tool for hecklers who are too cowardly to actually shout something out. I could learn to like it.

By this point, I actually felt sorry for both Lacy and Zuckerberg – the former was asking good questions and was doing her best to coax answers from her subject; the latter was clearly uncomfortable on stage and just wanted to get back to his nice safe office. It was a terrible interview, but it was hard to decide whose fault that was. The audience, though, was suffering from no such uncertainty – here was some *woman* interviewing the great Mark Zuckerberg and not even asking any technical questions.

'Ask a proper question!' One of them found some courage and started to heckle.

I couldn't take it any more. I walked out of the auditorium and headed to the bar. For the amusement of my friends back home – and maybe Maureen – I decided to kill some time writing a post for my blog: a fake transcript of the speech, with Zuckerberg parodied as a monosyllabic idiot savant and Lacy as an overfriendly bimbo . . .

Austin Convention Center Ballroom A – 2p.m.: BusinessWeek *journalist Sarah Lacy enters, followed by Mark Zuckerberg. The audience applauds wildly.*

Sarah Lacy (SL): 'Thank you – thank you all so much. Now let's hear it for this guy – Mark Zuckerberg everyone! So, I wanna start by asking – as I did in my book – why do you think Facebook . . . which I use, like, all the time – is so great?'

Mark Zuckerberg (MZ): 'Well . . .'

SL: 'What I mean is – what is it about Facebook that has attracted not just me but millions of other people like me to sign up?'

MZ: 'Er . . .'

SL: 'I totally agree. Can you say more?'

MZ: 'Sure . . .'

SL: 'Can you believe this guy? Wow – I mean his answers are so

short – seriously, I think he's the biggest loser I've ever interviewed. Hey, Mark, can I tell the story about the first time you
allowed me to interview you?'

MZ: 'Uh . . . I guess.'

SL: 'OK, so, like, I'm interviewing Mark – and we've been talking
for like twenty hours and Mark was, like, 'I need to pee' and I was,
like, 'that's so interesting and sexy', tell me more and he's, like, 'no
I really need to pee' and I'm like talking about my book and, like,
the next thing I know he's peed all over the floor and it's like so
cute and hilarious.'

MZ: 'Thanks for sharing that.'

*Audience breaks into spontaneous standing ovation, in awe at Zuck-
erberg's razor-sharp retort. Fat guy at the front screams and faints.
Twitter crashes.*

It was cruel, really, and not very funny. But then again it was only
really intended to be read by my friends and the maybe two
hundred other people who were by now reading my blog regularly.

What I definitely hadn't expected was that the *Guardian*'s technology reporter, Jemima Kiss, would quote me in her coverage of
the event. Thanks to that link and the couple of dozen other
bloggers who then re-posted the link on their own blogs, by the
end of the day my parody of the Lacy/Zuckerberg interview had
been read by almost 100,000 people.

505

Later that evening I began to have serious second thoughts about
the blog post. On Twitter and other social networks, the reviews
of the interview had got worse as the day had gone on – most of
them apparently written by people who hadn't actually been in
the room, but had heard about the train wreck online, from blogs
like mine. Bashing Lacy and Zuckerberg had become the game of
the day, with Lacy getting the bulk of the abuse, as so often happens

with women in the male-dominated world of technology.

But what started out as criticisms of Lacy's professional abilities had quickly become highly abusive, personal attacks. The final straw came when I noticed one commenter on a popular blog had written that he wanted to rape her. This over an interview at a geek conference. Suddenly the jokes weren't funny any more.

I'd like to say that at this point I took the post down. Zoe was right: the truth is that much of what I wrote stemmed from jealousy – Zuckerberg was younger than me and worth more than a billion dollars; Lacy was a successful *BusinessWeek* journalist – attractive, wealthy and considerably better known that I was. And after today's performance, she was only going to be more famous. Damn her.

But, then again, both Zuckerberg and Lacy were celebrities, of a sort. The rape threats were pretty extreme, but they must be used to this kind of stuff: people making jokes and silly threats online – it's just the price of fame.

Meanwhile, my inbox was full of messages from people congratulating me on my hilarious parody. People were stopping me in the corridors of the convention centre to tell me they thought I was 'freakin' awesome'. They'd asked about my upcoming book, having read about it on my site, and said they were looking forward to reading more of my stuff. If I took down the blog post all of that attention would go away. Wasn't I entitled to some fame too?

In the end I decided on a compromise: I left the post up, but attached a note emphasising that I thought Lacy was a great reporter who'd just had a bad gig and attacking those who were posting abusive comments about her:

A quick update: the following post was written straight (literally) after I walked out of the Zuckerberg keynote. I hadn't seen any Twitters or other blog comments – it was just my own (hopefully mildly amusing) take on the performance of participants.

Since I posted it, the coverage of the event on certain blogs has got really personal – mostly directed at Sarah Lacy. There's a huge difference between mocking someone for a bad gig and abusing them personally and pronouncing their career over. My intent in this case was very much the former – and I stand by it; Lacy had a duff gig and Zuckerberg was the most boring interviewee imaginable.

What I can't abide, though, are the jealous little fucks hurling shit at a journalist just because they would give their right arm to be in her position. It's a cliché to ask this but I do wonder whether people would be being quite so personally vile to her if she were male. And – hell – you have to give her kudos for making a thousand or so people feel sorry for a twenty-something billionaire.

I still felt like a coward and a hypocrite; wasn't I one of those jealous little fucks? But any further soul-searching would have to wait. Michael had just texted: he'd decided to fly into Austin from his meetings in San Francisco and was ready to party. Tonight would be one last hurrah after the roadtrip before he flew back to London and I continued on my travels.

506

By the time Michael and I arrived at Pure Volume – a huge white tent erected on wasteland opposite the convention centre – it was nearly 2 a.m. The tent had an all-night licence, with a free sponsored bar, and so every night, when all of the other bars in the city closed, all of the conference attendees headed there to keep drinking. The queue snaked around the block, and it didn't seem to be moving. 'Fuck this,' I said to Michael and headed to the front of the line, press credentials in hand.

The venue looked half empty, but the bouncer waved away my press pass. 'We're full,' he said.

'But it's dead in there,' I pointed out, not unreasonably.

'Sorry, guys – we need to leave room for the VIPs,' he replied. 'We just had to turn away the DJ's girlfriend.' Presumably the DJ booth was full as well.

But whether there really was a capacity problem or if, as seemed more likely, the sponsors wanted to keep the number of peasants inside low to save on the cost of free booze, we knew there was almost no chance of us getting in before daylight. It was time to figure out a plan B.

We thanked the bouncer for his time and ever-so-casually sauntered away, waiting until we were out of sight before ducking down the alleyway behind the tent.

Our way was barred by another bouncer, standing guard over the flap of canvas leading to the VIP area at the back of the makeshift venue. He too claimed that he couldn't let anyone else in.

'But the whole place is empty,' I argued. 'Last night it was ten times more full and we still got in.' A harmless lie.

'I have to say I agree with you guys,' said the bouncer, 'but I want to keep my job.' At least he was acknowledging the ridiculousness of the situation – but the simple fact remained that Michael and I weren't famous enough to get into the VIP area. Clearly the bouncer hadn't been one of the 100,000 people who had read my blog. I mean, that was a type of fame, wasn't it?

Our fruitless negotiations were interrupted by the arrival of what appeared to be a Green Day tribute band – five or six nice middle-class boys with torn clothes and punk hair – led down the alleyway by a besuited promoter. He marched up to the bouncer as his teenage charges stood sullenly and patiently behind him like schoolchildren queuing to get into a museum.

'Hey, dude,' said the promoter to the bouncer, 'these guys are with me – you've got to let them in; they're like the freaking Rolling Stones or something.'

Michael and I looked the band up and down. Here's a quick list of ways they were like the Rolling Stones . . .

1) They had feet.

And yet the promoter's confidence – likening a group of children to the Rolling Stones as if the similarity were a statement of fact – had paid off; the band was whisked inside. The bouncer didn't want to risk getting fired for refusing to let the 'freaking Rolling Stones or something' in.

Well, if that's how this has to work, I thought, so be it. The promoter was still outside the tent, making a call on his mobile. Presumably he needed to warn the band's mums that their sons would be home late. Michael and I waited until he'd finished and made our approach.

'Excuse me,' I said, 'who were those guys?'

'They're called 'October'.'

We stared back blankly.

'You might not have heard of them – but they're, like, huge – like the Goo Goo Dolls or something.'

'The Goo Goo Dolls? Cool! Actually, maybe you can help us – we're journalists from the *Financial Times* in London, and we're in town covering the best new bands at South by Southwest. Actually, this our last night in town,' I lied, three times – the bit about it being our last night was true.

Michael picked up the lie. It was like being back in Vegas – I secretly hoped there'd be call for a pun. 'If you can help us to get in and meet October, then I'm sure we could find a way to mention them in our article. I've heard they're pretty good.'

'Like the freaking Rolling Stones or something,' I added, helpfully.

'Journalists?' His eyes widened. 'Hey!' he shouted to the bouncer 'these guys are from *The London Times* – they're with me too.'

The VIP area was weird. An uneasy mix of music, film and interactive celebrities. You could tell the Internet-famous straight away; the Internet, as a medium, hadn't been around long enough for any of its celebrities to figure out how to act cool. The web kids looked like first-generation immigrants to planet fame.

You could spot the old-media-famous easily enough too, because they actually had recognisable faces. I saw Moby standing at the bar talking to Mark Cuban – the billionaire owner of the Dallas Mavericks who had made his fortune founding technology companies. On the other side of the room, a guy who looked suspiciously like Will Ferrell was talking to a girl who I'm pretty sure was Kate Hudson. And tucked away far in the corner, the boys from October were playing Guitar Hero – and losing, badly.

We'd been in the room three whole minutes, so of course Michael was already chatting up a girl. I couldn't place her at first, but then I realised she was Justine Ezarik – or 'iJustine' – an Internet-famous spokesmodel who produced web-based promotional videos for companies that wanted to play up their geek cred. Justine was clutching an old-fashioned lunch pail with the Junior Mints logo across the front, which was all the 'in' Michael needed. He reached into his pocket and pulled out the half-empty pack of Junior Mints he'd been carrying since Barstow and offered her one.

Michael's latest business is an online puzzle company called Mind Candy. The name is a play on the phrase 'eye candy' and has nothing – I can't emphasise this enough – to do with actual confectionery of any sort. And yet as I walked past, I overheard a snippet of their conversation . . .

'So what do you, like, do?' asked Justine.

'I run a company called Mind Candy.'

'OhMyGod I *love* candy!'

'Well,' – offering a Junior Mint –'that's what we make.'

Nice work, Michael – but he could have iJustine; I was far more interested in the girl I'd spotted standing by the bar, drinking from a very large plastic cup of what I would later confirm was neat vodka.

507

'Hannah!'

Hannah is Canadian, but she lives in London where she works as design director for a very successful website. We'd only met properly once before, and it would be fair to say that we hadn't really got off on the right foot. Much of this had to do with my being very, very drunk and deciding that it would be hilarious to accuse her of being an American. Repeatedly. For about an hour.

After sixty minutes of my drunken bullshit, Hannah had responded in the only appropriate manner: by physically propelling me across the room into a table of drinks.

I'd liked Hannah immediately. In fact, I'd had a ridiculous crush on her from the moment she pushed me into that table. Who wouldn't fall for *that* girl? The fact that she was astonishingly sexy, with bright red hair and lipstick to match, also helped. What didn't help was the fact that she had a long-term boyfriend – and that she thought I was a drunken asshole.

And yet, tonight she didn't seem particularly un-pleased to see me. In fact, she greeted me as if I were her best friend in the world. 'Paul! I was looking for you! I read your blog post about Sarah Lacy and Mark Zuckerberg. I had no idea you were so funny. Wow – that Lacy chick sounds like a *cunt*.'

'Actually, I feel terrible about that post. I'm sure Sarah Lacy is a lovely person and a damn fine journalist; I was just being jealous and stupid.'

That's what I should have said.

But Hannah – lovely, sexy Hannah – thought I was funny. In fact, I got the distinct feeling she was flirting with me. Holy shit – Hannah thinks I'm funny? Because of that horrible blog post?

'Yeah, total cunt.' I said. 'So, how have you been?'

Chapter 600

French Toast in a Bowl

I left Austin the following morning on Amtrak's *Texas Eagle* service, having finally arranged to pick up my rail pass from the local ticket office. The pass was actually supposed to have expired a few days earlier, but when I explained that I was a journalist from London, researching a book about great American train journeys, the ticket agent had kindly agreed to postdate the ticket so that I could use it for the full thirty days.

Only two trains a day stop in Austin — one heading north towards Chicago and one heading back in the opposite direction. Miss your train and it's a twenty-four-hour wait in a station that's essentially a concrete shed next to a railway line. So infrequent are the services — and so slow are the trains — that they haven't even bothered to build a proper platform: passengers just mill around next to — and sometimes on — the tracks. It's more than a little freaky to watch a group of children picking out coins and other conductive debris from between what would, in the UK, be live rails.

The real difference between the railways in the UK and the US, though, is with the trains themselves. My *USA by Rail* book had prepared me for them to be impressive, but when the *Texas Eagle* finally rumbled into view it was like the bit in *Jurassic Park* when Jeff Goldblum and Laura Dern first see a dinosaur.

The carriages are huge double-decker beasts filled with what must surely be the largest train seats in the world. Even when occupied by Texans they still look big. Sleeper cars are available but, given how much leg room there is, there's really no need to spend the extra money; just bring a blanket and a pillow.

One other feature of the seats, though, that I hadn't expected:

they're almost all empty. And there's a good reason – train journeys in America are long. Really, insanely, long.

I had decided finally to make my way back to New York, first travelling up the middle of the country to Chicago, before changing trains to head east back to Penn Station in Manhattan. The Austin–Chicago leg alone would take twenty-nine hours, and the man in the ticket office had warned me to add another three or four on to that for delays. 'Your problem' he explained, 'is that outside of the major metropolitan areas, there are no routes designed specifically for passengers.' Instead, Amtrak's services run on freight lines, which means that freight services take priority. If a train loaded with coal or Mustangs needs to pass, the Amtrak service pulls into a siding and waits, even if that means having to reverse back along the tracks for a few miles first.

If I were trying to get somewhere in a hurry, Amtrak would be an enormously frustrating way to travel. But I wasn't in a hurry. I still had almost two months left in the country under the visa waiver and no particular place to be, just a couple of freelance articles to write about ETech and South by Southwest, and maybe some adventures to have on the way to New York. With those goals, the train would be perfect: a moving office where the view from the window changes every second and I could get on and off at any time if the opportunity for adventure presented itself.

Like, say, if as I was boarding I overheard two girls talking about how they were leaving the train in Dallas – just six hours north – to celebrate St Patrick's Day.

601

Dallas. You have to love a town where the banks display signs politely reminding you that you're not allowed to bring concealed weapons inside. I hadn't needed to negotiate on the hotel room, having found a family-owned place a couple of miles from the centre of town with a rack rate of $60 including breakfast. There was no wifi – which, had I been staying more than one night, would have been a huge problem. But for one night – meh; I'd survive. It was already getting late and I was ready to head out and experience St Paddy's Day, Dallas-style.

With no idea of the geography of the town, I fell back on the cab driver recommendation trick and was soon in a place called Lower Greenville, which the driver had assured me was 'exactly what you're looking for'.

Apparently 'exactly what I was looking for' was a shit-load of students: Lower Greenville was swarming with them. Every bar was boasting drink specials – 'beer for a buck' screamed one sign – and, in a subtle nod to the day, they were all plastered in gaudy shamrocks, inflatable pints of Guinness and crocks of plastic gold. The students had got into the spirit of things too: the guys were all wearing comedy leprechaun hats while the girls were wearing bright green t-shirts with slogans like 'Kiss Me I'm Irish' and – confusingly – 'There's Whiskey in My Jar'. I actually wrote that second one down in the hope of translating it later.* Both genders wore strings of colourful beads, made of metallic plastic, around their necks; I asked one chap what they signified and he explained: 'you ask a girl to flash her tits, bro, and if she does, you give her the beads.' It seemed like an excellent system.

After stopping for a quick bite of sushi – which, I accept, was an odd thing to choose in Dallas– I found the only bar that wasn't totally packed with children and ordered a beer. On a small stage at the far end of the room, a band called Sold for Gold was playing a protest song, of sorts:

> *The damage is done*
> *it's about the government.*
> *About the United States*
> *They fucked up the government, man.*

I took out my notepad again and began making notes. After the

---

* My best guess is that by 'jar' she means vagina and by 'whiskey' she probably does actually mean 'whiskey'.

Lacy/Zuckerberg transcript, the popularity of my blog had spread far beyond Robert, Maureen and my friends back in London. Total strangers had started to email me in response to my mini-travelogues and I wanted to keep them interested. Surely a night in Dallas – on St Patrick's Day – would provide some good copy.

I'd only written a few lines when a tall blonde girl, wearing a baseball cap but, disappointingly, no beads, came and sat on the stool beside me.

'What ya writing?'

'Oh, just taking some notes,' I looked up and realised how amazingly beautiful she was. 'I'm a journalist.'

'No way! A music journalist?'

Why not? 'Sure,' I replied, 'I'm writing about bands in Texas who decided not to go to South by Southwest.'

'That's so cool! Hey, my friends and I are just heading down the street to another bar – our friend's band is playing. You wanna come with?'

Obviously I do, yes.

602

The problem with the first night in a new hotel is that, even when you wake up sober and in your own room, it's still disorientating. But the next morning I had neither of those comforts. The blonde girl's friend's band – I'd forgotten to write down their name; some music journalist I turned out to be – had been excellent, especially after the half a dozen beers the blonde girl and I drank while we waited for them to come on.

After the gig, we'd ditched the rest of the group and headed to a club for a nightcap. Unfortunately we'd just missed last orders so, really, there was no alternative but to head back to her apartment. 'My room-mate is in Austin for South by Southwest. We can drink her vodka – I'll just fill it with water.' Students.

Now waking up in that same apartment, I realised I had less than two hours to get back to my hotel, shower, grab my luggage and make my train to Chicago. Not for the first time I was glad I hadn't had a chance to unpack before heading out to get pissed.

603

The *Texas Eagle* service to Chicago takes twenty-six hours and the range of books available at Dallas's Union Station made the average airport newsagents look like the Smithsonian. Instead I bought *Esquire*, *GQ*, *Vanity Fair*, *The New Yorker* and every other magazine I could find that wasn't porn and didn't promise 'five hundred tips to drive your man wild'. Even having applied the porn filter, the woman behind the counter – who couldn't have been older than thirty-five – looked at the cover of *GQ*, with its photo of model Adriana Lima, and raised both eyebrows. 'You want a bag for this one?'

No, I felt like saying, I'm just going to finish off here.

As the train rolled out of Dallas, I wandered down to the viewing car and sat in one of the swivel chairs that line both sides. Sooner or later during the journey, everyone on the train would have to pass through where I was sitting: the viewing area was above the bar and next to the dining car. What better place to people-watch and hope for adventures?

Riding on the *Texas Eagle* the previous day I'd assumed that the idea of the observation car – what with the floor-to-ceiling windows and all – was just to allow passengers to look outwards – to see the Capitol building in Little Rock (a replica of the US Capitol in Washington, DC) or to take a photograph of the station at Texarkana where the train pauses briefly with half in Texas and half in Arkansas, or to marvel at the views of the mighty Mississippi, as we passed over it ...

But if that were the intention then the service wouldn't pass all of those places in the dead of night. In fact, as I began my second *Texas Eagle* journey I became convinced that the huge windows and the pitch darkness outside and the bright lights inside had exactly the opposite purpose – to turn the entire observation car into a giant inward-facing mirror. A custom-built environment for people-watching. Certainly, in contrast to the barren wastes and sleepy towns passing by outside, a huge variety of human life could be found in the observation car; marines returning home from Iraq, young teachers grading piles of paper while their pupils slept in the adjacent coach, students on their way to spring break, the old, the young, the black, the white, the rich, the poor. And, with nothing to see but each other, they couldn't help but talk.

I met a teacher – she couldn't have been a day over twenty-three – who was taking a carriage-load of kids on a school trip to somewhere or other, on her own. The respect she commanded from her charges was astonishing, and we talked for a while about the differences between education in the UK and the US. She couldn't grasp why I was concerned about her ability to handle such a large group. 'But they're children,' she kept saying, 'and I'm an adult.'

Over dinner, I made the acquaintance of three frat boys (I forgot to write down their names – but I know at least two of them rhymed*) who were on their way back from what sounded like a memorable spring break in the south. We got talking after I overheard them discussing one particularly successful romantic encounter from the trip . . .

'Dude, I'm serious – she said I made her come like three times. She said I was the fuckin' best she'd ever had . . .'

'Dude! You gonna tell Beth?'

'Fuck no. But – yunno – fuck Beth. Beth's fuckin' frigid, man . . .'

'Yeah, but she had some sweeeet tits.'

'True, man. That's fuckin' true . . .'

I was sitting quietly, reading one of my half-dozen magazines, for at least ten minutes before they noticed that the waiter had seated me opposite them.

'Oh shit, sorry, man . . . that was pretty rude.'

'No problem,' I replied. 'I dated Beth for a while. I know what you mean.'

---

* So after Mandy and Sandi, you wouldn't have believed me anyway.

'Ha – you're all right man. You Australian?'

Sure.

604

Back to the observation car – having paid $21 for my three-course meal, including a New York strip steak – I decided to settle down for the night rather than heading back to my proper seat. A group of college kids, drinking half-bottles of house* wine, had produced an iPod and some speakers and it wasn't long before the carriage was rocking to the sounds of the Beach Boys' 'Wouldn't It Be Nice'.

For the rest of the night I listened to a succession of iPod play-lists – the Beach Boys turned to Soulja Boy turned to Cher turned to Snoop Dogg – and met even more people.

I met two cheerleaders on their way back to school in Detroit who hated Hillary Clinton with a passion I expect they'd normally reserve for pre-makeover geeks. 'If she becomes President then this country is screwed,' said one of them. 'You know who'd make a great President? Oprah.'

I met a marine who was travelling home with his wife and nine-month-old baby. He'd been in Iraq for a year and this was the first time he'd met his daughter. The three of them – the marine, his wife and the baby, slept across two seats on the train, cuddled up against the cold. They couldn't afford to fly, he explained. 'And, anyway, I don't trust planes.'

I met a guy called Mike who travels the country by railway, making his money from people who are about to have their homes foreclosed by the bank. He explained how his business works: 'I arrive in a new town and walk around the poor streets looking for foreclosure notices. Then I knock on the door and introduce myself. I offer to buy the house for fifty grand. It's a fraction of the real value, but by selling to me they don't get foreclosed which

* Train.

means their credit rating isn't affected. They can take the money I give them and start again.'

'What, start again in a tent?' I asked, amazed by the shitty deal he was giving these poor people.

'Sure, if they like. The point is, I'm giving them a better break than the bank would. These are people who took out mortgages they couldn't afford. What did they expect? The way I see it, they'll lose their home anyway. At least I give them money to start again and their credit is clean.'

'And then what do you do with their houses?' I ask.

'I call the bank. Offer them maybe 40 per cent of the true value of the place. They always take it. No one wants to be stuck with a house with a recession coming.'

'You think there's a recession coming, then?'

'No doubt about it. You know there's a recession coming when business is this good.'

At around 4 a.m., the train pulled to a halt, I assumed because a freight train needed to get past.

The party in the observation car had finally wound down, and Mike and I were the only two people still there, except for a couple of girls sleeping in the seats opposite. But then a curious thing happened. From the sleeping carriage two cars down, people began to emerge, wearing pyjamas or wrapped in sleeping bags, rubbing their sleepy eyes. From the main carriage, too, passengers who had clearly been asleep were waking up and padding down the train steps, out on to the platform. It was freezing cold outside and the station building looked deserted.

'What's going on?' I asked Mike. 'Where is everyone going?'

'We're at Poplar Bluff. It's a smoking stop – last one before morning.'

'They're waking up to smoke?' I said, taking another swig of my beer. The bar was closed but I thought I could see a bottle of whisky peeking out of the top of a bag belonging to one of the sleeping girls, so all was not lost.

'Yep,' said Mike, 'addiction is a hell of a thing.'

605

I slept for a couple of hours in total, but kept being woken up by people walking through the carriages.

Truth is, I didn't really want to sleep; I was enjoying watching the towns rolling by outside the window and thinking about how sorry I felt for all the people out there who owned houses. I thought about what Mike had said – 'no one wants to be stuck with a house in this economy' – and I thought about those people who would dearly love to be stuck with their houses, but who were forced to sell them to people like Mike. The girls opposite – more cheerleaders, as it turned out, heading back to school in Chicago – had given me the rest of their bottle of whisky in return for promising to mention them in my book about great American train journeys.* I took another swig and settled back for another nap.

Breakfast was served in the restaurant car and, to make sure I got a seat, I'd made a booking the previous night for 8 a.m. Spending the night in the observation car had been fun, but also freezing cold, so I was looking forward to a big American breakfast. I'd even be prepared to overlook their problem with bacon.

But as I arrived at the restaurant car, the waiter was taping a hastily handwritten sign on the restaurant car door. 'Sorry – continental breakfast only (bananas, Rice Krispies, oatmeal, yoghurt and coffee).'

'Bananas and Rice Krispies?' I said. 'What continent is that breakfast from?'

'Sorry – that's all there is. We were supposed to get a delivery of plates last night but they didn't show up. We won't have any until St Louis so we can't serve any hot food.'

I sat down at one of the communal tables, across from an oversized man in a red checked lumberjack shirt. He introduced himself as Doug, 'a steelworker until I finally came to my senses and retired'.

* You're welcome, cheerleaders.

We talked for a while, about Tony Blair – once he'd placed my accent – and how he wanted to thank us for our support of America and George W. Bush. He hoped we'd support President McCain just the same. I smiled and said all the right things until the waiter came over to take our order.

Doug had read the sign about the lack of breakfast choices, but he had a plan. 'I don't need a plate,' he said. 'I'll just get some French toast in a bowl.'

The waiter stopped scribbling on his pad. 'I'm really not sure we can do that, sir.'

'Why not?'

'Our French toast is served on plates.'

But Doug wasn't budging. 'Son, I've seen most things in my sixty-nine years – I think I can handle French toast in a bowl.'

I liked Doug.

The waiter explained that he'd have to check with the chef, and scurried off to do exactly that. As he left, the school teacher from the previous night came and sat down with us. I was also growing to like the communal seating on American trains as opposed to British trains where only the mentally disturbed would make so much as eye contact with a stranger.

'Good morning, gentlemen,' she said, 'and what's the news this morning?'

'Doug just ordered French toast in a bowl,' I explained.

'A bowl? What's wrong with a plate?'

'The plates are meeting us in St Louis,' said Doug. He didn't skip a beat. And neither did the teacher . . .

'Great. I could use some French toast in a bowl.'

The waiter came back just in time to hear the teacher also setting her heart on French toast in a bowl. The poor man looked like he was going to cry. 'I'm sorry, sir, ma'am, but the chef says if we give you French toast in a bowl, we'll have to give everyone French toast in a bowl.'

'So what?' asked Doug, raising his voice just loud enough; 'tell me, son, would society crumble if that happened? Would the terrorists win if every man, woman and child on this train were to be served French toast in a bowl? Because I'd say our freedom to enjoy French toast in a bowl is what makes us Americans. In fact, if the terrorists could see us now, I'd say they'd be taking some measure of joy from our inability to manage to take some French toast and put it in a bowl, wouldn't you say, son?'

'I'm sorry, sir, that's just what the chef says.'

'Well,' said Doug, his voice creeping even louder, 'you tell the *chef* that Doug Anderson of Hawley, Pennsylvania, has two things to say in reply. Now, you should write these down in your little notebook there so you get them right.'

The waiter kept his pad in his pocket.

'First off,' Doug continued, 'the customer is always right. And second, if all you do is prepare Rice Krispies on the railroad, you got no business callin' yourself a chef.'

His piece said, Doug ordered the oatmeal, which I couldn't help but think was unwise given that he'd just insulted the chef. I've seen *Fight Club*. I know what goes on.

I ordered a sealed pot of yoghurt.

606

Chicago.

'Oprah, Obama, Michael Jordan, Mr T. So what you're basically saying is that Chicago is home to all of white people's favourite black people?'

The girl sitting at the next table in Starbucks didn't laugh. 'That's inappropriate,' she said and returned to her book. Until then she'd been giving me an enthusiastic verbal tour of the city after over-hearing my accent as I ordered coffee.

I smirked to myself and opened my laptop to email Robert. He and I had a long-running competition – now entering its third or fourth year – to see which of us could elicit the words 'that's inappropriate' the most times from American girls. The concept of 'appropriateness' is much more real to Americans than it is to Brits, despite us being the ones who are supposed to be stuffy and formal. I'd noticed it a lot with swearing: while Brits of both genders will be quite happy, among friends, to use the word 'fuck' – as a verb, a noun and adjective or an adverb – a surprising number of young Americans blanch at the idea. Rather, they'd talk about 'dropping the F bomb', as if four letters were capable of levelling Nagasaki. Why actually use the word when the very threat of it was enough? Worse, of course, was 'the C bomb', which I took particular delight in dropping at every available opportunity. Perhaps it's the fact that my dad's family hail from Glasgow but, used outside of its gynaecological sense, it's always been one of my favourite words.

Actually, that was one of the many reasons I liked Hannah: being Canadian, she had all of the spark and energy and attractiveness – and accent – of an American, but with none of the silly coyness. We'd only met once before and yet she hadn't hesitated to call Sarah Lacy a cunt.

As if summoned across two continents by those thoughts, five minutes later an email arrived with Hannah's name in the 'from' line. I'd sent her a short note from the train, using my phone – nice to run into you again, we should catch up when I'm back in London, all that bullshit – but I hadn't really expected her to reply. And yet . . .

From: Hannah
To: Paul

Hey – sorry for the slow reply. I had to talk my way out of jail or deportation during a five-hour interrogation at Gatwick, break up with my boyfriend and drink a bottle of Bourbon. So it's been a busy week. I could hardly do justice to these stories over email. If you're coming back to London one day I suggest you buy me a gin martini or two in exchange for a story of terrorism and drama.

Hx

This was unbelievable. She's single again, and I'm in Chicago. 'Cunting fuck shit,' I cursed to myself. The girl at the next table let out a loud sigh. So inappropriate. I tapped out a reply, something casual.

From: Paul
To: Hannah

Hey!

Sorry to hear about the breakup.

No, wait, that's probably the most disingenuous thing I've written all week. No man is really all that sorry when he hears that a pretty girl is single. Let me rephrase: I'm sorry to hear you had to go through a breakup; they're never fun. I'm back in London towards the end of April. The gin martinis are on me.

Px

It took me about forty minutes to get the casual, spontaneous wording just right. After I clicked send and my email began its journey across two continents, I noticed another message had arrived – this one from Eris. You wait all year for a pretty designer and suddenly two come along at once.

Eris had been looking at my blog and had read a post I'd written on the train from Dallas about how it wasn't really a city that I could see myself spending a huge amount of time in. It was just too spread out, too nondescript. It just seemed to lack character. Of course, I'd decided all of this during a twelve-hour stay, much of which I'd been either drunk, asleep, in bed with a pretty blonde girl or all of the above.

From: Eris
To: Paul

Dallas. I never felt like I really belonged there, either (and I lived there for 10+ years). I found small places that felt like me, but navigating through the city as a whole made me feel very disconnected. I think I left as an act of self-preservation.

I got the call offering me a job in San Francisco. I told them I'd be there in two weeks, and I was. I packed up everything that was important to me at the time (computers, cats, books, some clothes), put it in my car and drove halfway across the country. I didn't look back, I didn't think how not-very-smart it was for a 24-year-old girl to drive by herself through the middle of nowhere. I just knew I had to leave.

I know many people with similar stories to this one. I have two friends from Chicago, for instance, who were overcome with the desire to leave that city. With all the cities you visit, there's someone who left them. Fled. These stories are fascinating, and somehow we've all found one another and found salvation in San Francisco.

With Dallas and Chicago and most of the rest of America, you're basically taking a tour, not of cities, but of disappointment. And when all that's done and you come to San Francisco, we'll be here.

Eris

I read the email twice. Her story about feeling like she didn't belong in Dallas and knowing she had to leave was very similar to my feelings about London. I mean, I absolutely loved the city, but I also knew I couldn't live there. All the drinking and the memories and the drudgery and the cost just ground me down. I could see how, as an interactive designer, San Francisco was the obvious place for Eris to go: it's the heart of the technology industry and a city packed with artists and creative people.

For me, the whole world was my San Francisco. I wanted to keep travelling and experiencing new things and knowing that, if I ended up in trouble, I could always hop on a plane or a train and head somewhere else.

I was suddenly aware of a figure standing over me. Tall, skinny, about eighteen years old and wearing a Starbucks apron. I looked up. Yes?

'Excuse me, sir,' he said, with a pomposity that belied his years. 'One of our customers has complained about your use of "language". I'm afraid I'm going to have to ask you to leave. There is a bar next door if you'd like to curse.'

'My use of language? Oh, for fuck's sake.' The girl at the next table was looking over, a self-satisfied smile playing around her lips.

It was time to head somewhere else.

Chapter 700

Diss me, Kate

I slept quite a lot of the way between Chicago and New York, taking care to put all of my valuables into my laptop bag before wrapping the strap around my feet and pushing it under the seat in front. The people on the train looked like a trustworthy bunch, but you can never be too careful. I'm quite a light sleeper, which made the subsequent theft of my iPod, my phone and my *USA by Rail* book somewhere between Charleston and Cincinnati all the more mysterious. The thief must have crawled under the seat. For some reason, though, he'd left behind my laptop and charger.

The loss of my phone was sort of a mixed blessing – God only knows how much of an international roaming bill I'd racked up in the past couple of months. I'd realised back in LA that I hadn't given my phone company in the UK a forwarding address – mainly because I didn't have one – so there was no way for them to bill me. I figured I'd just use the phone until they cut me off and try to fix things when I was next in London.

But still, as the *Cardinal* service pulled into Penn Station, the absence of wifi on board – score one for British inter-city trains – meant that I'd been out of touch with the outside world for twenty hours. I knew how those smokers back in Poplar Bluff felt.

When I finally found a bar with a decent Internet connection, there were no more messages from Eris, which was disappointing as I'd got used to her daily cajoling to get on a plane to San Francisco. There was, however, an email from my friend Caroline, a comedian from New York who also happens to be Joan Rivers' niece. She is precisely as much fun as you imagine that person to be.

From: Caroline
To: Paul

Hey, I see from your blog you're heading to New York. Are you going to be here on Saturday? If so, you're coming with me to the screening of 21 (new Kate Bosworth/Jim Sturgess flick), and then celeb-spotting at the after-party.

A quick check on the Internet Movie Database told me that *21* is the movie adaptation of *Bringing Down the House*, Ben Mezrich's book about a group of MIT students who applied their geek maths skills to count cards in Vegas. I'd read the book back in London and so was definitely keen to see the movie, even though I didn't have the first idea who Kate Bosworth or Jim Sturgess were.

The only thing stopping me was the fact it was already Saturday evening, I hadn't booked a hotel room and the screening had started an hour ago, halfway across town. Ah well, at least I could get to the after-party early and avoid the queues.

Rather than trying to check into my hotel before the party, I decided to leave my bags in storage at the station and collect them afterwards. Or at least that was the plan until I learned that Amtrak will only store bags for passengers who have an outward ticket. I showed the man at the baggage check my rail pass – still valid for three whole weeks – but he shook his head. I had to be actually booked on to another train. 'It's to stop terrorists leaving bombs here,' he said, with the look of a man who knew he was enforcing a ridiculous policy.

Exploiting what seemed to be a reasonably obvious loophole in Amtrak's plan to foil terrorism, I dragged my suitcase to the ticket office and used my rail pass to book myself a free ticket on to a train back to Chicago. They gladly accepted the bag. Now all I had to do was remember to collect it before 6.55 the next morning, otherwise all of my possessions would be on their way back west without me.

701

Sure enough, there wasn't a queue at the after-party. There was, however, an officious-looking woman with a clipboard.

'Hello,' I said, 'I'm here for the *21* party.' The clipboard woman looked me up and down – I looked like a man who had been on a train for twenty hours – and instantly made her judgement.

'Are you on the list?'

'I honestly don't know, I was supposed to be with someone. My name is Paul Carr. I'm with the *Guardian* in London.'

That, as it turns out, was precisely the wrong thing to say. She gestured to a gaggle of photographers standing next to a black SUV, waiting for the first of the celebrities to show up.

'Oh, no, I'm not here to cover the party. I'm a guest,' I said.

'You're not on my list,' she said. 'I'm sorry. It's a very strict guest list tonight. Fire regulations.'

I felt like an idiot. My 'I'm a journalist' card might work to get past a bouncer in Austin, but it certainly wasn't going to work with a professional celebrity PR in Manhattan. This woman probably spent half of her life keeping journalists out of things, citing fire regulations. I'd have had more luck if I'd claimed to be a fireman.

I shrugged and headed back down the street; I'd just have to wait an hour or so for Caroline to show up. But then, as I trudged forlornly away, one of the photographers who had been watching my unsuccessful blag shouted behind me: 'nice try!'

You know in *Back to the Future*, when someone calls Marty McFly a chicken, and his ego just can't stand it?

Yeah. That.

Fuck *you*, I thought. I knew I should keep walking; that I'd get into the party eventually if I just waited for Caroline. But now I wanted to make a point: show that photographer what a 'nice try' really looked like. I turned and twisted my face into my well-practised 'little boy lost' face. Combined with the English accent that one of my female American friends had described as 'kryptonite to American women', it had worked in most situations like this before. The question is, would it work with a hard-nosed New York PR? It had better do, otherwise I'd be laughed away from the party permanently.

'Yes?' said the PR.

'I'm sorry to bother you again – I know you're very busy,' I lied. Twice. 'I just wondered if you could give a message to Ben for me? Just tell him Paul said he was sorry he couldn't get in, but that I'll call him tomorrow.'

'Who is Ben?' said the PR.

'Oh, I'm sorry,' I said, feigning shock that there might be some other Ben at the party, 'Ben Mezrich. Assuming, of course, that *he* is on the list. We worked together at *The Times* a couple of years ago. He said to swing by if I was in town tonight.'

I was gambling on a number of things here. Firstly, that Ben Mezrich – who I've never met – was still trapped in the screening and so was uncontactable in person or by phone. Had the PR checked my story, I'd be completely screwed. Second, I was gambling that, by choosing the writer of the book that inspired the film as my friend rather than one of the stars, my story would be inherently more believable. I mean, who would claim to be friends with a writer? And thirdly, I was gambling that the PR knew so little about Mezrich, or journalism, or anything but Hollywood stars, that she wouldn't know that Ben Mezrich has never written for *The Times* – either the one in London, or the one in New York.

'Yeah, no problem,' said the PR. 'I'll give him the message.'

Shit. She was calling my bluff.

Then, a sigh. She looked again at the dishevelled figure standing in front of her, holding a laptop bag. I certainly looked like a journalist.

'Ben's not here yet,' she said, 'but you're welcome to wait for him inside if you want.'

'Oh, that's very kind of you,' I said, and walked inside, pausing only to give the finger to the photographer by the black SUV.

Nice try indeed.

702

An hour of so later – enough time for me to drink about half a bottle's worth of free champagne – the party had started to fill up with familiar faces. If the secret to meeting A-listers is to act like you don't even know that they're famous then my terrible ability to recognise faces puts me well ahead of the game. I have good friends who I'd met five or six times before I finally stopped introducing myself. Tom Cruise and Angelina Jolie could walk up to me in the street and I'd probably shoo them away, telling them that I had no spare change.

But even with my limited facial recognition powers, the *21* party quickly started to make me feel star-struck. Helena Christensen was the first A-lister I saw – and for the next five minutes I couldn't stop staring at her. She was about to turn forty and yet still looked as beautiful as the girl my friends and I had gawped at in *FHM* when we were at school ten years earlier. Next, from the other end of the A-list, and age range, came Katrina Bowden from *30 Rock* chatting to Meryl Streep's daughter, Mamie Gummer, and a stream of other starlets. There was an Olsen. I'm not sure which.

Even the waitresses were stunningly beautiful. One in particular stood out, a tall blonde girl holding a tray with two glasses of champagne. I wondered what she was thinking as she looked around the room: she was at least as pretty as the celebrities at the party and yet here she was, working as a waitress, serving them champagne, probably to pay her way through college or something. She was way – waay – out of my league but I figured everyone else would be hitting on the celebrities – trying to bag an Olsen – so for once I might have a shot. And, of course, the great thing about hitting on waitresses is that you don't need an excuse to approach them.

'Can I take one of those?' I asked, pointing at the glasses on her tray.

'Actually, they're for this table.'

'Oh,' I said, impressed at my own ability to be brushed off by beautiful waitresses just as aggressively as all other beautiful women, 'are you going to get any more?'

She looked at me as if I'd just insulted her mother. 'The bar is just over there. It's free, help yourself. Excuse me ...'

And then she walked away. Wow, a new low – great work, Paul; you really must look like a guy who slept on a train last night. Fortunately my embarrassment had witnesses – I looked over at the bar and saw Caroline had arrived and was laughing her arse off at my ineptitude. She beckoned me over with a drink.

'Hey!' I said, kissing her on both cheeks while simultaneously taking the drink.

'Hey! So what were you saying to Kate Bosworth?'

'What? I wasn't talking to ...'

Oh. Shit.

'... uh, you don't mean Kate Bosworth, the tall blonde girl over there with the champagne, do you?'

'Duh, yes. The Kate Bosworth that you'd have recognised had you made it to the damn screening. Tell me you didn't say anything bad to her.'

'I just asked her to get me a drink. I thought she was a waitress.'

Caroline screamed and then burst into even louder howls of laughter. When she finally regained her composure she put a pitying arm around me.

'Well, it's fair to say not many men will use that line on her tonight.'

Having insulted the guest of honour, my work at the party was done. It was time to get drunk. 'But just to be on the safe side, Caroline,' I asked, 'can you warn me who else is here just so I don't have a repeat performance?'

'OK,' she said, leaning in, 'well, Clive Owen is here – he's ...'

'I know who bloody Clive Owen is,' I said, probably slightly too loudly. 'He's British. The guy who was in those awful BMW web ads, and *Inside Man*. Jesus Christ, that was a shit movie. Don't worry, I watch a lot of shit movies, I'll definitely recognise Clive fucking Owen . . .'

Caroline was staring at me.

'Sorry,' I said, 'I'll stop ranting now.'

She was still staring.

Oooohh. I looked in the mirror behind the bar. There, right behind me, talking to Caroline's friend – was Clive fucking Owen. He'd heard every word.

For the remainder of the evening, I avoided insulting anyone, mainly because I was sure to treat everyone like they were a celebrity. Caroline introduced me to Jeff Ma – the maths wizard on whose life the book was based. He was standing next to Jim Sturgess, who played him in the movie. I'd love to have been in the meeting where someone said – 'OK, who can we get to play an Asian American math geek?' to which the reply came – 'Well, there's this white English guy who looks like he should be in the Arctic Monkeys.' I also met Kevin Spacey's partner – 'production partner' he kept saying as if for some reason people often thought differently – and took the opportunity to pitch him my brilliant idea for a John McCain biopic starring John Travolta. 'It's brilliant,' I said, 'Travolta can do all the flying himself – I mean, apart from the crashing part, of course.' He excused himself and went off to talk to someone famous. And less drunk.

Then, in the corner, I noticed a guy standing on his own. He looked just like Hayden Christensen, who was apparently in *Star Wars* but who I've only seen in *Shattered Glass*, the movie about the *New Republic* journalist who got caught faking his stories. It was a great movie, and his performance was hugely underrated. I decided to go and tell him this.

'Hi, I'm Paul,' I said, extending my hand.

'Hi, I'm Ben Mezrich' said Hayden.

Ah. I looked back over at Jim Sturgess and Jeff Ma, both surrounded by admirers who wanted to get close to the famous actor and the man whose life they'd read about or seen on screen. And yet the guy who actually did the research and wrote the story? Just standing on his own in a corner, alone and unloved. This is why I only ever write about myself, I thought, and headed off in search of an Olsen.

At some point I must have left the party. I remember there being an after-after-party downstairs where Jeff Ma told the story of the time when he and Caroline had spent a weekend in Vegas. David Copperfield had tried to pick up Caroline's friend Meredith, apparently, but with limited success. I also remember a vague feeling of panic at about 2 a.m. when I realised that I still hadn't arranged a hotel room, or collected my bags, but with my drunken confidence I was sure I'd fix the problem. Anyway, I'd been distracted by someone who I'm sure was Ben Mezrich walking past, towards the toilets, with a Victoria's Secret model on his arm. Maybe he wasn't such a dork after all.

703

'Housekeeping!'

I looked at the clock beside the bed. It was 11a.m. A maid was knocking on the door, loudly.

'No thank you,' I shouted. Obviously I'd forgotten to put the Do Not Disturb sign on the door. I looked around my room. Wait – was this even my room? My laptop bag was on the floor, as was my suitcase, still with its Amtrak label attached – but there was no sign of anyone else's belongings. I must somehow have found a hotel, checked in and climbed into bed. That was pretty impressive, given that I'd have had to hand over my passport, fill in a registration card and swipe my credit card. More impressive still was the fact that I'd somehow remembered to reclaim my suitcase. Ah well, at least I wouldn't have to worry about doing that hungover today.

I sobered up enough to realise that I needed water. I looked across the room to the bathroom door. It looked familiar. As did the flatscreen TV and the iPod dock alarm clock next to the bed. No wonder I'd been able to find this place and check in while drunk – I'd done it a dozen times before.

I was back at the Pod. And the guy who had checked me in must have been the night porter.

'Oh fuuccccccck.'

I had to get out of there.

Again.

Chapter 800

I Left My Heart, Liver in San Francisco

'You're really coming?' Eris was delighted.

'Yeah. I've decided I probably shouldn't stay in New York more than one night at a time.'

'Great! I'm going to take some time off work to give you the tour.'

'You don't have to do that.'

'Just get on a plane and leave everything to me.'

801

When Eris said she was going to take some time off work to show me San Francisco, I assumed she meant a morning, maybe even a whole day. In fact she took an entire week – unpaid – to act as my personal tour guide.

In the morning we'd go for breakfast in a different part of town: the Mission, Union Square, the Castro, SoMa, the Tenderloin, Nob Hill . . .

'Ha!'

'What's funny?'

'Nob Hill.' I explained why, with the same relish I'd felt the first time I explained to an elderly American woman in Florida why 'fanny pack' was so hilarious.

'Then you'll love what we call the area between the Tenderloin and Nob Hill.'

'Surely not . . .'

'Tendernob, yeah.'

. . . and then we'd spend the rest of the day exploring; drinking tea in Delores Park, riding cable cars and browsing books in City

Lights, the bookshop noted for its relationship with beat poets like Alan Ginsberg and where, in the fifties, owner Lawrence Ferlinghetti had famously been arrested for publishing and stocking Ginsberg's *Howl*. Eris is another Hunter S. Thompson fan and so much of the tour took us to places made famous in his writing, including – of course – the Mitchell Brothers' O'Farrell Theatre, the strip club where Thompson claimed to be night manager in the mid-eighties. Today the club still advertises itself using a quote from Thompson's *Kingdom of Fear* where he called the club 'the Carnegie Hall of public sex in America'.

Eris recommended that I stay at another piece of San Francisco history: the York Hotel, where in 1958 Hitchcock filmed the Empire Hotel scenes from *Vertigo*. The hotel was in the middle of being renovated and so, for guests who didn't mind some building noise, it was offering double rooms for $65 a night. I asked reception to cut an extra key for Eris and she moved in on the second night. I joked that she should expand her range of services to other cities: people would pay handsomely for a pretty tour guide during the day, especially if that same guide also stayed the night. We disagreed on how amusing the idea was.

802

I'd been in San Francisco two weeks before it occurred to me that I should probably do some work. The thought wasn't prompted, you understand, by any sense of guilt at having spent fourteen days laying in parks and getting drunk in dive bars – all in the name of sightseeing. Rather it was because an easy story landed in my inbox.

The subject line of the email read simply 'Webmission', and attached was a press release explaining that a group of British Internet entrepreneurs were flying into San Francisco to meet their American counterparts, sponsored in part by UK Trade & Investment. Would I like to sit in on their daytime meetings, and attend their after-parties?

Figuring that, at worst, I'd be able to get drunk on the British taxpayer's shilling at the after-parties, and at best I'd get to write about it afterwards for a newspaper back in the UK ('As a recent transplant to San Francisco . . .') I quickly agreed.

Webmission was an event that divided opinion among British web entrepreneurs. For those whose companies had been selected to attend, it was a hugely worthwhile initiative; an opportunity for Brits to build business relationships with US companies and for Americans to come to parties where everyone had an accent and the British government was picking up the booze tab. For those who hadn't been chosen to attend, it was just a piss-up at the taxpayers' expense. As far as I could tell, both sides were right.

Looking at the attendee list, I was pleased to see a few names I recognised: much as I was loving my time in San Francisco, I was starting to miss the British cynicism of my friends back in the UK. I was half hoping that Robert's name would be there, but his newest company – a site allowing people to recommend books, films and other things to their friends – was too young ('early stage' in business speak) to make the cut.

It was with no small measure of surprise then, that I opened the door of my hotel room on the morning Webmission began and found him standing there. He was wearing a set of plastic beads, plastic sunglasses and a bright pink baseball cap with the words 'San Francisco' emblazoned across the peak.

'Rob! What the fuck are you doing here?'

'I was missing you, mate. And I wanted to meet this Eris girl you keep blogging about. I convinced Scott that it would be a sensible use of company funds for us to fly over to take part in Webmission.'

Scott – Dr Scott Rutherford – was Robert's business partner, and basically the polar opposite of Rob. A former particle physicist-turned-web programmer who also had a sideline as a professional DJ, Scott wouldn't be seen dead in a set of plastic beads, or at least not since his Ibiza days. Scott was definitely the sensible one in the company. And yet somehow their partnership worked – Scott doing all of the technical work on building the site while Robert focused on what he called 'big thinking and networking'. Which in this case apparently meant flying halfway around the world to get drunk with me in San Francisco.

It was by total coincidence that Robert had booked himself into the York Hotel: it was only when he checked in that he realised it was the place I'd been writing about on my blog. Receptionists never give out a guest's room number, but Rob had switched on the accent and had quickly been able to get the information that had led him to my door. Kryptonite.

It'd only been a couple of months since I'd last seen Robert, but, given the adventures I'd had since leaving London, it felt like a year. I gave him a hug.

'Let's go and drink some wine in the sun,' I said. 'Eris finishes work in a couple of hours. I'll tell her to come and meet us.'

It really is amazing how much alcohol it's possible to drink in a little under three hours, if you set your mind to it. And we did. By the time Eris caught up with us, at a wine bar off Union Square, Robert and I had worked our way through the best part of four bottles of cheap pinot grigio, and a couple of beers. I'd told him all about Michael and me in Vegas with the toga girls; about the road trip, about South by Southwest and Dallas and New York. He was suitably jealous.

'I have to say, mate, this nomadic lifestyle sounds like it might be the perfect way to live. My lease is up soon on my place in Leicester Square – I think I might give it a go.'

'You absolutely should. In fact, everyone should.' I explained how much I was paying at the York – well under my $100 budget – and how the favourable pound-to-dollar exchange rate – still hovering around the 1:2 ratio – meant that my food and drink budget was far, far smaller than back in London. 'These bottles of wine are costing us less than six quid,' I said.

Robert looked at the small row of empties. 'The amount you're drinking, that's fortunate,' he said.

He was joking, but he had a point; I noticed that I was drinking twice as fast as him. I'd put it down to the fact that he'd just flown in from London and so was too tired to concentrate on hard drinking. But I had definitely been drunk more often lately; waking up not remembering the night before and, even with the exchange rate, discovering that I'd spent a fortune on booze. I realised that I'd been basically living in 'holiday mode'; the mode that Brits tend to go into when we leave the country for a fortnight in Spain. But this wasn't a holiday; it was my everyday life. Just because I could do my entire week's work – a couple of freelance columns and maybe a bit of time thinking about what my next book might be – in a day didn't mean I could spend the rest of the time paralytic. My liver was already a mess before I'd left London; God only knows what it must look like now. I glanced down at my nails – relieved to see there were still no little white lines – and, although it was hard to tell with the suntan, I'm pretty sure my skin hadn't turned yellow.

The clouds parted and the California sunshine hit us again, glinting off my empty glass and Robert's half-full one. I topped them both up, enjoying how the sun made the yellow liquid light up as if I was pouring out pure magic.

'So tell me about Eris,' said Rob.

'Oh, she's delightful,' I said, 'she's given me the grand tour and she's moved into the York with me.'

'So you like her then?'

'Well . . .'

Of course I liked her – she was great: cute, smart, funny – all the stuff that girls you like are supposed to be. But the more time we were spending together, the more I realised that it was only ever going to be a fling. For a start, she'd just split up from her long-term boyfriend and wasn't looking for anything serious, but more importantly she clearly wasn't that into me. A few nights earlier we'd had a huge fight after she disappeared with some guy at the end of a party and didn't turn up back at the York until the next morning. 'We're not boyfriend and girlfriend,' she'd pointed out, quite reasonably. But as well as denting my ego, it had also reinforced what this was: a bit of fun for both of us. Of course when

I explained all of this to Robert, I was careful to make it clear that, while Eris was hugely into me – possibly even entertaining thoughts of marriage– I wasn't going to be tied down by some girl.

'Well – yeah, she's fun and all, but I'm not sure I fancy her enough for it to be a serious thing. You know, she's cute – but there are some amazing women in California. Really amazing – you really have to see them . . .'

Robert wasn't responding. He was just looking at the girl who had sat down next to me while I was busy explaining all the flaws with Eris which meant that I wasn't interested in getting serious with her. I think I'd just got to the part about preferring girls with bigger breasts when I realised something was amiss.

'You must be Eris,' said Robert, finally breaking the silence.

'You must be Robert,' said Eris. 'And you,' she said, turning to me, 'must be drunk.'

I was absolutely plastered. The drunkenness hit me as if someone had emptied a cement mixer over me, starting from my head, and slowly trickling down over my entire body. I should have reined it back, told her I was only joking, apologised – anything. But I didn't. My brain was going into alcoholic shutdown and the only thing I could think of doing was pressing on.

'Let me finish,' I slurred, and then continued to explain, to both Eris and Robert now, why she was far from being my ideal woman. Looking back, it was ridiculous – I fancied the hell out of her and in a different set of circumstances – had she been looking for a relationship with anyone, let alone me, for example – I could prob- ably have started to fall in love with her. More than any of that, though, spending the previous week with her had made me fall in love with San Francisco. For that at least, she was one of the best things that had ever happened to me.

803

Waking up fully clothed in a bathtub wearing a pair of plastic sunglasses is better than waking up naked in a hotel corridor. That much we can all agree on. It is, however, still a far cry from waking up in a bed. Through the bathroom door I could just make out the time on the television clock. Eight a.m. Not bad, I thought, until I realised that my last memory was from seven o'clock the previous evening where I'd knocked over a whole bottle of wine during what I think was a very public argument with Eris.

I scrambled out of the bath and called Robert's room. He answered on the third or fourth ring.

'Hello, darling' he said, correctly reasoning that I was the only person who could possibly be calling his hotel landline at eight in the morning.

'So, meeting Eris last night was wonderful,' he said. 'Let's go for breakfast.'

We sat in a booth at the Pinecrest Diner down the street from the hotel – a place where, thanks to Eris's tour, I knew that in 1997 a cook had shot a waitress in a dispute over poached eggs. Sure enough, the menu now contains a prominent notice: 'we regret that we are unable to serve poached eggs'. Probably wise. Over scrambled eggs and crappy American bacon, Robert explained that my night had ended when – at about eight or nine o'clock – I'd finally finished lecturing Eris on why we could never be a couple, despite her making it clear that nothing could be further from her mind. Robert had at last convinced me to go back to my hotel, while he spent the rest of the night trying to do damage limitation.

'I think I convinced her that you weren't normally such an arsehole and that you were just very drunk.'

'I *was* very drunk.'

'I know, mate, but even by your standards you were impressive. Do you remember telling me – in front of her – that her breasts weren't up to your standards?'

'Oh God, really? Where the fuck did that come from. I like her breasts!'

The old man in the booth behind us tutted loudly. I lowered my voice.

'So do I,' said Robert, barely able to conceal a smile.

'Exactly, so . . . wait . . . what do you mean 'so do I'?'

'Well, after you left, she was really upset by what you said, so she asked for my opinion. Just took me to the corner of the bar and flashed me.'

I choked on my scrambled eggs and then couldn't stop laughing. Robert was right: Eris was brilliant.

'Now all I have to do is convince her ever to speak to me again.'

But making things up with Eris would have to wait. Robert had more news. The previous week back in London he'd been asked to arrange a networking event for a visiting American journalist who was in town meeting dot com entrepreneurs in her role as columnist for *BusinessWeek*. Robert had recognised her name, and a quick visit to my blog had confirmed where he'd heard it before. The journalist's name was Sarah Lacy.

'She's actually great fun,' said Robert. 'In fact I think you'd like her. You and she have similar senses of humour.'

'Uh, I don't think she'd agree with that if she saw what I wrote on my blog.'

'Oh, we talked about that,' said Rob. 'She doesn't read stuff people say about her online anymore, but I told her – more or less – what you'd written. She said you sounded like a dick, but I vouched for you and said you guys should meet when she was back in San Francisco. I emailed her yesterday; she's getting back to town tomorrow and is going to come to one of the Webmission events – a barbecue at some PR guy's house.'

Part of me knew that meeting Sarah Lacy was a bad idea. What if she'd decided to look up my blog after Robert had spoken to her? I'd already pissed off one woman in the past twenty-four hours. But, then again, after South by Southwest, I'd actually taken the time to read some of her *BusinessWeek* columns: they were insightful, funny and annoyingly well written, and from Robert's description she definitely sounded like someone I'd like to meet. I'd just have to suck it up, go to the barbecue and hope she didn't stab me with a steak knife.

804

'You Brits are actually far less offensive than people in the US.'

Saying that out loud was Sarah Lacy's first mistake, given that she was talking to me and Robert. She'd arrived at the barbecue a few minutes after us, and Robert had immediately dragged me over to say hello. I mumbled a few apologies about my South by Southwest post, which – to my relief, but also slight disappointment – she still hadn't read, but she dismissed my pathetic arse-kissing, saying that the abuse she gets from US commentators was far worse than anything I might have said. Having read some of that abuse, I agreed with her.

Still, though, Robert had taken her comments about our inability to offend as a challenge. I forget the joke he decided to tell but I know the punch line was 'it's lucky your party trick isn't a double-headed blowjob'. I know this because Robert insisted I video the exchange on my digital camera, but by the time I'd figured out the video setting I was only in time to record the punch line and Lacy's response. We were hoping for an on-camera 'that's inappropriate'. Instead all we got was loud laughter, and a concession that – OK – some Brits could be more offensive than Americans.

I liked Sarah Lacy. Her wedding ring – and constant references to her husband – had helped me to ignore the fact that, yes, she was astonishingly pretty and instead concentrate on how much we had in common when it came to work. She told me how 'everyone' in London had insisted that we meet, on the grounds that 'you're apparently the British version of me'. But she also admitted that, from the other reviews she'd heard from my 'friends', she had been expecting someone far drunker.

'You should have seen me yesterday,' I said.

'Well, how about later this week? Robert told me you have a book out about London entrepreneurs, and my book about their San Francisco counterparts is out next month. Let's get a drink one afternoon and compare notes.'

Back at my hotel – while I waited for Eris to come over so I could take her for the world's most grovelling apology dinner – I wrote an email to Hannah.

From: Paul
To: Hannah

I met Sarah Lacy today. She's not a cunt. In fact she's great. I feel like a traitor – I'm sorry.

The reply came back almost instantly.

From: Hannah
To: Paul

Oh, Paul, you haven't fallen for her have you?

'No!' I replied, 'I mean, only in so far as I fall for every American woman. But for once my crush is purely professional. She described me as the British version of herself, and I think she might have a point. I have a feeling we're going to be friends.'

'Dammit,' wrote Hannah, 'I nearly met her in London but everyone kept saying how nice she was and I couldn't bear it. Now you too. I suppose I'm going to have to start liking her too.'

805

I'd arranged to meet Sarah in Homestead, a bar in the Mission district that serves bowls of unshelled peanuts with the beer and encourages you to drop the shells on the floor. A huge dog wanders around picking up any stray nuts and every so often an old woman ambles in from the street, pushing a shopping cart, selling tamales with hot sauce.

I was twenty minutes late and, when I walked in, Sarah already had a beer in front of her, lined up next to a shot of Jägermeister. Yep, the American version of me, I thought.

'Hey!' I said, nodding at the full glasses in front of her. 'I assume you're OK for drinks?'

'Well, seeing as you're so late, you can get me a martini. Olives.'

The American version of me, who triple-fists drinks.

'So, I should probably start by telling you what I wrote in my blog post . . .' I put our drinks on the table, 'but if I do, I'd rather you didn't punch me on the nose.'

Knowing that she doesn't ever read stuff that's written about her, I could have kept my mouth shut. But for that same reason, I had to tell her – if only to apologise properly for it. By now I was feeling crushingly bad about the whole thing.

'Of course I won't punch you on the nose. I'm pretty unoffendable by now. But also I really don't want to know. I don't read stuff online because if I did it would upset me. What you wrote is a matter for you and all of the other people who have decided they hate me despite having never met me.'

Ouch.

It was a reasonable point, and it instantly made me feel even worse. I was just another chump on the web who tapped out hate from behind a screen. Just because I thought of myself as a professional writer didn't alter that fact. Lacy had a contract for *BusinessWeek*, her own weekly video show on Yahoo.com and had been invited to appear on stage at South by Southwest, while I sat in the audience talking shit on a blog.

'I'll probably take it down,' I said. What a coward. What a fucking hypocritical coward.

'You shouldn't,' she said, 'you should leave it up. You wrote whatever you wrote, and you should stand by it. To be honest, Geoff – my husband – cares more than I do. He actually does read this stuff and you can imagine how he felt sitting at home in San Francisco while people wrote on the Internet that they wanted to rape me.'

'Oh, you saw that guy then?'

'Geoff told me about it. There were several people saying stuff like that.'

Jesus. I thought about girls who I'd cared about – my most recent ex in particular – and wondered how I'd feel if someone had said that about her. Then I thought about how I'd feel if some dickhead blogger had written a transcript about her flirting with Mark Zuckerberg. None of it was funny any more.

We talked a bit more about the interview – even though she was understandably bored with the whole subject – and it was interesting to hear some context. How Zuckerberg had insisted on her being the one to conduct the interview and how, apart from a couple of guys who had heckled, they'd both actually come off stage thinking it had gone reasonably well. It was only afterwards when people told them about the Twitter backlash that they'd realised how controversial the whole episode had been.

The conversation finally moved on to less awkward subjects, especially as we had more drinks. After an hour or so, Eris came to join us – my apology dinner, but more so Robert's damage limitation, had worked, and she'd decided to give me another chance.

The three of us talked until closing time, comparing the difference between entrepreneurs in our respective countries, and with Sarah sharing her thoughts on friends of mine she'd met in London, including Robert, Michael and Michelle. We talked about writing and how, despite our similarities, neither of us could do the other's job. I was too much of an egotist to write about other people without putting myself at the centre of the story, and Sarah was too interested in business and billionaires to pad out her work with self-aggrandising bullshit.

At one point we ended up talking about unicorns and specifically whether eighties cartoon heroine She-Ra rode on a magical winged unicorn (as I insisted) or just a bog-standard magical winged horse (Sarah's recollection). Before we knew it, a wager was made: if I was right, Sarah would give me the advance copy of her book that she had in her bag, inscribed with a message of my choice. If she was right, I had to send her a copy of my book on publication, again with a custom message written in the front.

Robert was right: Sarah was fun.

As Eris and I headed back to my hotel for the last time, we held hands. It felt nice, but we both knew this was probably the last night we'd spend together. I only had a week left of my visa waiver and I'd been advised by friends who knew the system to understay slightly so that immigration didn't get suspicious on my next visit: people who stay for exactly three months look like they're abusing the system.

I'd bought myself a few extra hours by switching my return flight so I was flying directly from San Francisco rather than having to go back via New York, but still I was leaving in the morning. I felt sad at having to leave a city I'd fallen in love with, but such was the life of a nomad. The most important thing was that Eris and I were parting on good terms; a minor miracle after my ridiculous behaviour a few nights earlier.

I was also glad to have met Sarah. I looked down at the copy of *Once You're Lucky, Twice You're Good* sticking out of my bag. Of course I'd been right about the winged unicorn and, as agreed, Sarah had written an inscription in the front: a confession that, rather than me being the British version of her, *she* was the American version of *me*.

'*Dear Paul, I am the American version of you – and that's all I can ever aspire to be. Your friend and doppelgänger (I WISH!) – Sarah Lacy.*'

Your friend. That made me smile. After all the shit I'd written about her, I was ending my trip with a new friend. I promised to keep in touch by email and she promised (grudgingly) to look at my blog and keep track of my nomadic adventures.

'So where next?' asked Eris.

'Spain, apparently,' I replied.

It was Robert's idea. The more time he'd spent in San Francisco, hearing details of my travels that I'd conveniently left off the blog – Michelle and Jonesy, the lost night in LA, the hooker with the braces – the more jealous he'd become that he hadn't been along for the ride.

'I want to live like you,' he said.

'But you live in a penthouse in Leicester Square. With a hot tub on the roof.'

'Yeah, but you live in hotels and get drunk with hairdressers in bedsheets and fuck disabled girls in LA.'

'She wasn't disabled . . . wait, how did you . . .?'

'Michael told me.'

By the end of the week, Robert had made a decision: like me, he wasn't going to renew his lease. Like me, he was going to pack a few things into a suitcase and become a nomad. 'I've spoken to Scott and we've agreed that I can do everything I need to do on the road, as long as there's wifi. In fact, Scott's probably going to join us for a bit too.'

'Us?'

'Oh, yes,' he said. 'I knew there was something I meant to tell you – we're going to Spain.'

Chapter 900

Oh Deary Me

'If you're feeling kinda tedious
If life is seriously mediocre
Here's how to get that adrenaline flowing
Just step aboard a Boeing, going . . . high!'

Early May is still supposed to be the off-season in Spain, but high in the mountains of Andalucía the sun was so hot that I could feel its heat against my bare legs. And not just from above: it was hot enough to radiate off the patio, and up through the bottom of the hammock.

I adjusted my sunglasses and listened to the sounds of the mountain. We were an hour in any direction from the nearest town so really the only sound to hear was the goats. Every day a farmer led a couple of hundred goats, each wearing a small bell, down the steep path at the end of our driveway. We never saw or heard the goats returning at the end of the day, leading us to assume that they were being herded to some kind of goat pie factory. Poor old jangly goats.

And that's all I could hear: just the soothing sound of two hundred goats ambling to their deaths, the ringing of bells, the occasional sound of the farmer shouting something in Spanish.

And then, suddenly, one other sound.

Louder than the goats.

The unmistakable sound of Robert having a blazing row with an award-winning Hollywood actor about the price of an ornamental goose lamp.

901

Almost a month had passed since Robert had made the decision to give up his London lease and join me in living the life of a high-class nomad. We'd joked that with just me travelling it was an adventure, but with two of us we had the beginnings of a club. The 'Kings of the Road Club' we'd called it.

With two of us spending all of our free time – which is to say all of the time we were awake – thinking about the logistics, we'd come to some interesting conclusions about the possibilities of nomadic living. Robert in particular had taken it upon himself to see how much further my arbitrary £50-a-night budget could be pushed. Realising that I knew hotels better than he did, he'd focused on other types of accommodation: and the fruits of his research tasted delicious.

Rob had discovered that, for most of the year, there were hundreds – thousands, even – of luxury villas lying empty, all over Western Europe. During the summer months these places – with their heated swimming pools and tennis courts and hot tubs and breathtaking sea views – rented for as much as £4000 a week as holiday homes for rich people. And yet, between September and June, they sat empty, abandoned and unloved – but still available to rent. If you didn't mind the fact that it was slightly colder than normal, or that you had to stay outside of normal holiday time, then owners were more than happy to rent them out for a few hundred pounds a week simply to justify keeping the heating on.

The deals were incredible, as was the range of places available. On just one website – Owners Direct – so called because it allows the owners of the villas to rent directly to people, without paying agency fees – Robert had found a twelve-bedroom château in the French Pyrenees for less than £1000 a week in the off-season. Twelve bedrooms! If we could find more people to join the club and split the rent, that worked out at £12 per person per night. But even that paled in comparison to the next place: for a few hundred pounds more, we could rent an entire hamlet, complete with fifteen houses and its own shop.

Or, to put it another way, if three people split the rent they could rent their own village for less than I was paying for my one-bedroom flat in London. Every day my inbox would slowly fill up with emails from Robert with subject lines like 'This place has its own beach!' or 'Why would a house need a private race track?!'

Eventually he'd settled on a three-bedroom villa in an isolated village called Valle de Abdajalis. High in the Andalucían mountains, surrounded by breathtaking scenery and crystal-clear lakes, the villa had an outdoor hot tub and a mountainside patio with a barbecue and its own bar – and it was less than an hour from Málaga airport. More importantly, it was available until June for the off-season price of £420 a week. If Robert and I went halves on the rent, we'd be paying £210 a week. Or £30 a night, which included weekly cleaning and wifi. EasyJet flights from London were less than £60 return, and we could hire a car for £10 a day. Even with transport, it was still under my £50-a-night budget. The decision took me about thirty seconds to reach.

But Robert's thinking hadn't stopped there. With an extra bedroom, he'd realised that we could offer weekend breaks to our friends in London for, say, £200 for two nights, and cut our weekly rent in half at a stroke. He'd sent out a group mail to his personal and business contacts and had so much interest that we could have filled the place every weekend, and lived there ourselves rent-free, for a year. As a cheeky bonus, he'd added the fact that 'guests would be expected to fill the fridge with food and booze'. That would take care of our weekly shopping bill, too.

Our plan was to take the place for two months at first. Robert had work to do on the business plan for his new venture and I had final edits to finish for *Bringing Nothing to the Party*, ahead of its July publication.

Working in hotel rooms was one thing, but sitting in the mountains of Spain, miles from anywhere, I truly appreciated just how much the Internet had changed how – and where – it's possible to work. With only my laptop and my mobile, I was just as connected to the world up a mountain in the middle of nowhere as someone working from an office in London. But unlike the office worker, I could choose at any time to close my laptop and switch off my phone and instantly be on holiday. Rather than having to make time to work before I could relax, I could spread both of those experiences throughout the day. Half an hour's work – in the hammock, of course – then a beer and a splash in the hot tub, then another half-hour's work. After the first week I realised I was actually working for more than eight hours a day some days, every one of them productive.

I had also become an expert in the emerging art of hammock working. For the first few days I was a struggling amateur – trying to balance my laptop on my stomach as I lazed in the hammock. My neck and wrist soon told me where I was going wrong. Over the next week of trial and error I narrowed down the three most comfortable positions for hammock working:

Position one: the yogi

Trying to work whilst lying flat is crippling to your productivity and your neck. For a start, you're liable to fall asleep, which is a bad idea if you have a laptop balanced precariously on your stomach a few feet above a concrete patio. With the yogi position, you sit upright, in the centre of the hammock, with your legs crossed. The sides of the hammock just touch the edges of your knees. The yogi is actually the least comfortable of the three positions, but it has the benefit of being only a stretch away from lying down. If you're a fan of spontaneous snoozes, this is the position for you.

Position two: the sideways yogi

Of the three positions, the sideways yogi is the most suitable for long stretches of work. Your posture is exactly the same as the yogi, except that, instead of facing forwards, you turn sideways. The benefit of the sideways yogi is that it allows you to swing gently back and forth as you work, and also provides more support for your knees. Experts at the sideways yogi can position their beer just slightly behind the hammock so that it is retrieved on the back swing, swigged on the forward apex and then returned on the next back swing. Warning: after six beers there is every chance you will fall backwards on to the patio and almost snap your spine.

Position three: the straddle

The only two drawbacks with hammock working are 1) after a while your attention can start to drift, and 2) after a couple of beers, dizziness becomes a factor. Both of these problems are solved with the straddle. As the name suggests, the straddle involves sitting up in the hammock, with your legs either side, planted firmly on the floor. This stops the hammock swinging, curing the dizziness, but also forces you to sit up straight, aiding concentration. When I showed it to Robert, he imagined it probably had long-term benefits for posture, but that was just a theory. He's not a doctor.

On this particular day, I'd opted for the basic yogi, which, as the sun had grown warmer, had inevitably led to the snooze. A snooze interrupted by the gentle sound of goats being herded to their doom, and now Robert – talking loudly on his phone.

'With all due respect, Alan, I just don't think that's a reasonable price for an ornamental goose lamp. Frankly, I'm not sure there *is* a reasonable price for an ornamental goose lamp.'

It was a slightly odd argument to wake up to, made no less odd by the fact that Robert had been waiting to have it for the past twelve months.

The argument had been inevitable, really, since the day, back in 2007, when Rob had first moved into his penthouse apartment just off Leicester Square. Along with its roof-top Jacuzzi, the apartment also had a bar, a dance floor and a cinema. An incredible place to live, but also much too large for Robert to occupy on his own. Most people would have looked for some-where smaller. Not Robert. Instead, he'd decided to occupy just one small bedroom and turn the rest of the flat into a twenty-four-hour members' (read: drinking) club for young entrepreneurs and assorted hangers-on. In a nod to its location next to a Chinese restaurant, he gave it the amusing – but borderline racist – name Mr Rong's. So successful was the endeavour that, by halfway into the first year of the lease, the *Financial Times* had run a lengthy profile of Robert and his party flat – they were the ones who called him 'the Hugh Hefner of London' – Channel 4 News had sent round a camera crew and a documentary maker had begun making a film about the people who worked and played there. Of course, running a nightclub out of a private home broke about a dozen laws, as well as being a massive breach of the terms of Robert's lease. And yet, remarkably, he'd got away with it for a whole year, largely because no one in the press thought to check who actually owned the place.

As one of Scotland's most gifted comedy actors, Alan Cumming has played more than fifty film roles including Boris in *GoldenEye*, Piers in *Spice World* and Fegan Floop in *Spy Kids*. He's won both a Tony and an Olivier for his stage work in the West End and on Broadway. He's written a novel, and created his own fragrance and range of toiletries with names like – and this is possibly his finest work– 'Cumming All Over' (a body wash) and 'Cumming In A Bar' (soap). Oh, and he has an OBE.

And yet, in common with an entire generation of twenty- and thirty-somethings, there's only one thing I think of when I hear the name Alan Cumming. And that's his portrayal of the über-camp flight attendant Sebastian Flight in the nineties sitcom *The High Life*. Specifically, his catchphrase 'Oh deary me'. It's hard not to feel sorry for the man.

But his inability to escape a role he played for six episodes of a sitcom in the nineties is not why I feel sorry for Alan Cumming. I feel sorry for him because Robert, me and about two hundred other drunks spent an entire year systematically trashing his flat just off Leicester Square.

It was vital that none of the press that Rong's attracted mentioned

Cumming's name. If a journalist realised there was a celebrity angle – no matter how tenuous – then it was bound to show up on the Internet and Rong's would be busted, as would Robert's five-figure deposit. I was one of only three or four people trusted with safeguarding the owner's identity, which was trickier than you might think given that we kept finding cupboards full of 'Cumming All Over' body wash around the place.*

Now, though, safe at the top of a mountain in Spain, Robert didn't care. Once he decided to become the second member of the Kings of the Road Club he'd sent an email to Cumming's office saying that he wasn't renewing his lease then he'd put the keys in the post and left the country. We joked that putting your keys in the post and leaving the country was the application – and acceptance – process for the club. A few weeks later, all being well, your deposit would land back in your bank account – neatly offsetting your first month or two of travel – and you'd be free. Or at least that was the theory.

Unfortunately for Robert, and his deposit, there was still the matter of an ornamental goose lamp.

902

'Who was that?' I asked, once he'd finished on the phone. It was apparent that he had not been the one to hang up.

'Alan Cumming.'

'Oh deary me.'

Robert gave me a summary of the conversation. Apparently, when Cumming had received Robert's letter, he'd sent a letting agent around to the flat to see if there was anything that needed fixing before he returned the deposit. A broken light bulb or two, maybe some scratches to the paintwork. What the agent had in fact discovered was the aftermath of a 365-day party. The Jacuzzi

---

* Still, knowing such an exciting secret made me feel a bit like one of He-Man's friends. Man-at-arms possibly, or Orco. Not the sorceress.

needed rebuilding, almost completely, as did the entire wooden floor – marked as it was with the holes of a thousand stiletto heels. The list of things that were broken or missing went on and on, ending finally with a missing ornamental goose lamp.

'So that was him calling to say you weren't getting your deposit back then?'

'Oh no,' he said, 'that was him calling to say I'm not getting my deposit back and I owe him an additional twelve fucking grand.'

'You're kidding me.'

'I wish I were – he's sending me a list of missing things.'

For the rest of the afternoon Robert sat in the hot tub, his laptop perched on the side, reading items off the list Cumming had sent through.

'Do you even remember seeing an ornamental goose lamp?'

'No, Robert, I don't recall seeing an ornamental goose lamp.' Ornamental goose lamp was one of those phrases – like 'pineapple chunks'– that became more ridiculous the more you said it.

'Shit – someone must have stolen it on opening night. Wait, what the hell is a 'brushed steel ornamental carrier bag'?'

'I have no idea. Are you going to pay for all of this stuff?'

'I don't know.' He considered the question for a moment, making it clear he thought he had a choice. 'I might. Or I might just spend a hundred quid on a new phone. What's he going to do? Come looking for me up a mountain?'

He closed the lid of his laptop, laid it down on the patio and sank down into the hot tub.

'You're right,' he said, 'being a nomad does give you more options.'

903

I took another swig of my beer and figured I should probably get back to 'work'. The previous day, I'd received a call from Rebecca

Lewis*, courtesy of my publishers, Weidenfeld & Nicolson. The fact that I was being assigned a publicity manager was just about the best news my ego had ever heard, and for the next twenty-four hours I'd been sure to drop it into every conversation I'd had. 'Oh, I'll have to call you back, I think that might be my publicity manager on the other line.'

The truth is that Rebecca wasn't just *my* publicity manager, but the publicity manager for most of W&N's authors, including ones that were actually popular and successful. It was into this deep well of legitimate talent that Rebecca would dip to try to find some famous – or at least recognisable – name to write a promotional quote for the front of the book. Also, once we got nearer to the day of publication, it would be her job to try to get it reviewed in newspapers and to get me on to Radio 4 programmes to pretend I knew what I was talking about.

Until then, though, I was basically on my own. Rebecca was relying on me to use my skills at online self-promotion to get people excited about the prospect of my book.

During our conversations we'd realised that I had a couple of advantages in this area not enjoyed by other first-time authors. For a start, I knew my way around the Internet. I had a blog – which Rebecca had been reading, leading her to characterise my time in Spain, quite unfairly, as 'a holiday'. I also knew how to use things like Facebook and YouTube and even Twitter to build hype. Rebecca hadn't heard of Twitter, something I made her feel bad about, even though I'd only discovered it myself a few months earlier. Making people feel bad for not knowing things is something Internet experts are very good at.[†]

The second advantage I had was that *Bringing Nothing to the Party* was a memoir, which meant that, to promote the book, all I really had to do was to draw as much attention to myself as possible.

---

* Who has since got married and is now called Rebecca Gray. Congratulations, Rebecca!
† Not that I'd expect someone like you to know that.

Between her office in London, and my equally connected one in a Spanish hammock, Rebecca and I formulated a plan. Since South by Southwest, traffic to my blog had continued to grow, with a few thousand people a day following my travels, particularly when I got drunk and did something stupid. With Rebecca's blessing, I would spend my time in Spain expanding the blog into a fully-fledged promotional website, complete with details of the book, extracts, interviews with key people featured in it (starting with Robert, of course). I'd also make sure that I wrote something new for the blog each day in the hope that more posts meant more visitors, which meant more potential book buyers.

To sweeten the deal – as if sitting in a Spanish hammock writing about myself wasn't a sweet enough deal already – Rebecca agreed that W&N would release the final chunk of my book advance, normally due on publication, a few months early to pay for my time while I worked on the site.

When I got off the phone I couldn't stop laughing. For the next couple of months, I was being paid to sit in a hammock at the top of a mountain, building a website about myself and writing daily blog posts about my own brilliant adventures. For an egotist, this was the dream gig.

For the next few months, getting drunk and doing stupid things would no longer be a hobby, a distraction from my day job. It would *be* my day job. My decision in Vegas was completely vindicated. It *was* possible to be a professional drunk, if you were prepared to put in the hours.

I was more than prepared.

904

Of course, having brilliant adventures in Vegas is easy. Having brilliant adventures in Laguna Beach is pretty straightforward too. Even on a train between Dallas and Chicago, you can meet enough interesting people to inspire half a dozen blog posts. But being up a mountain in Spain poses real logistical problems, from a brilliant adventure standpoint. For a start neither Robert nor I spoke Spanish. We hadn't really appreciated how much of a drawback this would be: like most Brits, we'd grown up with package holidays to the Costa del Sol where every barman spoke perfect English and you were never more than ten feet from an expat bar called Knockers. In the Valle de Abdajalis, we couldn't find a single English speaker; not in any of the bars, not in the one local restaurant and not in the shops.

I'd downloaded a beginner's guide to Spanish from the Internet and was embarrassing myself daily. On the first night, I'd ordered what I thought was a bottle of house white wine – '*vino blanco de la casa, por favor*'. Unfortunately, what the bartender actually heard me say was '*fino blanco de la casa*' and after ten minutes of shuffling around in a dusty storeroom he emerged with what he thought I wanted. Robert and I had forced down almost the entire revolting bottle before we realised we were drinking very dry white sherry.

Robert had taken a different approach to overcoming the language barrier, relying on a combination of shouting in English and rudimentary hand gestures. His way of ordering five slices of ham in the local shop was to point at the ham, hold up five fingers and then make a chopping motion with his other hand. I mocked him for his laziness and ignorance until he pointed out that his ignorance had actually resulted in him obtaining five slices of ham, whereas my 'Spanish' had ended with us drinking a bottle of white sherry.

Our inability to meet the locals and discover the first thing about them meant that Robert and I had spent much of our first week enjoying our own company, inventing a succession of ridiculous games to fill the time between drinking and sleeping.*

Most of the games had brilliantly cryptic titles, including my

---

* I was the proud inventor of most of these games, to the point where Robert quickly dubbed me the Gamesmaster. It was a title I wore proudly, even though I'm pretty sure it still legally belonged to Sir Patrick Moore after his TV show of the same name in the early 1990s.

two favourites – 'Water-balloon Dodgeball' and 'Ten Can Orange Bowling'.

The former was the result of a drive to the nearby town of Alora where we found a small kiosk selling ice cream and water-balloons. The latter was ten-pin bowling using empty cans and some oranges which we managed to cajole out of a kindly local farmer. Each game lasts for five rounds, or until the last orange has been smashed to Tropicana.

Then there was 'Kate Nash or not Kate Nash' – a game where players listen to short (five- or six-second) clips from my iTunes library and have to determine whether the singer is London-based singer-songwriter Kate Nash or not Kate Nash. Robert was the undisputed champion of this, having zipped through Kate Nash, Remi Nicole, Kate Nash, Laura Marling, Kate Nash and Kate Nash before being tripped up by Colbie Caillat. A bonus round involving a Victoria Wood clip took him a good minute and a half of internal debate.

There was 'Roof Ball' – a game involving getting a ball stuck on a roof. That was quite a short game.

Finally there was 'Road Frisbee': All of the fun of Frisbee, all of the excitement of being hit by a car coming around a blind corner at high speed.

The games were fun, for sure, but as you will no doubt testify, they don't make for fascinating reading. No, if I wanted to fulfil my obligations to Rebecca, I knew I had to accept reality, no matter how unpleasant. My only option was to spend every single day getting absolutely blind drunk in one of the two local bars – Alejo's and Carpe Diem – in the hope that I would inevitably end up doing something stupid enough to write about.

The plan began well. On the first night Robert and I decided to see if we could drink so many beers that the empties would cover an entire table in Alejo's bar. Even with the relatively strong euro, bottles of San Miguel were still less than 60p each and by 3p.m. we'd drunk at least a dozen each. At this point Alejo realised that we were likely to be his best customers that week and so started offering us even more beers on the house. For less than twenty-five quid, between us we covered an entire table with beer bottles. It was only then that we remembered that the bar was halfway down the mountain, and our villa was right at the top. An amusing blog post about mud and fields and goats and a frighteningly deep leg wound soon followed.

Another night we decided to try our luck with the local women. And by local women, I mean the only two twenty-something-year-olds in the entire village. Every other woman was either under sixteen or over sixty. 'But don't forget the age of consent is only fourteen here,' said Rob. He was joking. I hope.

Our efforts with the twenty-somethings were relatively unsuccessful. Robert wisely gave up after a couple of minutes when he realised that there was no hand gesture for 'if I told you you had a beautiful body would you hold it against me?' Or, rather, no hand gesture that wouldn't get him shot by an angry farmer dad. I pressed on, though, realising that I was at least fluent in the language of booze. Buying girls a drink is the same in any language, right? Unfortunately the girls had figured out another language that was universal: they knew the lyrics to hundreds of English pop songs and were able to repurpose them to explain their lack of enthusiasm for going up a mountain with a drunk Brit. 'Get back,' said the first girl, while the second sang the lyrics of Babylon Zoo's 'Spaceman', to indicate that she wanted space, man. I had to admit, it was a rather neat pun.

The most exciting drunken adventure, though, came at the end of our second week, when Robert's business partner Scott flew out to join us. The three of us spent an enjoyable afternoon getting to grips with the villa's barbecue, thanking our lucky stars that there were no women to be amused by how inept we were at creating fire and grilling meat. Then we headed down to Alejo's where Robert had become adept at ordering vodka and Red Bull by doing a passable impression of a drunken man pretending to be a bull.

Through trial and error, we'd realised that there were no actual licensing laws in Valle de Abdajalis. As long as we were happy spending our money, Alejo was happy to serve us. Generally we'd made it to about three in the morning before stumbling back up the mountain, but tonight Scott decided we should do a proper test – how late could we continue drinking until Alejo insisted we call it a night? You could tell Scott was a scientist.

The experiment – which was actually closer to a battle of wills – began just before 9 p.m., and by 3 a.m. we were trashed. Beers had become mixed spirits, which had become straight spirits, which had become shots. I was wearing a cowboy hat and Scott was occupied at the far end of the bar helping Alejo cut a wooden butternut squash in half with a hacksaw, for some reason. Robert had long moved on from vodka Red Bulls but was still doing his drunk bull impression, just for fun.

'I'm going to call it a night,' Robert slurred, after a few more rounds. 'I can't walk.'

'Moo . . .' he added.

'That's not the point,' I replied as best I could. 'The point is we're experimenting.' The sound that came out of my mouth in no way resembled the word 'experimenting'. There was no convincing Robert of the importance of the experiment – him not being a scientist, and all – and so he headed off on his own, back up the mountain.

And then there were two – well, three – Scott, me and Alejo, who had left Scott to finish cutting the wooden squash and was now rummaging about under the bar. He emerged with a bottle of some kind of green liquid. It looked like toilet cleaner. Looking back now, there's a very good chance it *was* toilet cleaner.

Alejo took three shot glasses off his shelf and set them down on the bar, filling each to the brim with the green goop. He drank the first himself and shuddered, before gesturing to the other two, and then to us. We did as we were told. Even after an entire night of drinking, I could feel the hit of the alcohol. It was like the end of level boss in a drinking game. But – ha! – we'd defeated it. Alejo put the bottle away and then put his hands together next to his face, miming sleep. Victory was ours! It was 5 a.m., and outside it was starting to get light.

We staggered – crawled, really – out of the bar and into the street. There was no way on earth we were going to make it up the hill. According to Scott, who had to remind me of most of this the next day, I was lapsing in and out of consciousness.

'Where now?' I said.

'Home?' said Scott.

'Lightweight,' I said. Again, the word that came out of my mouth almost certainly didn't sound like that.

Just then we noticed two men standing by a white car on the other side of the road. They looked like hit men. They looked at us, and we looked back, and then they spoke.

'Cocaine?'

Another universal language.

905

I don't do drugs.

I'm not just saying that because I'm writing these words in a book and it would be monumentally stupid for me to admit to using illegal drugs in print. If you've got this far and not realised how monumentally stupid I'm capable of being, then you haven't been paying attention.

I've *done* drugs; it's hard to live in London and not have at least once, but I don't do drugs. Drink has always been my vice – and it's served me perfectly well.

The point is, even totally paralytic, I had no interest in buying cocaine from these people. I did have an interest, though, in getting a lift up the mountain in their car.

'Where?' I asked.

They pointed vaguely up the mountain and said something that sounded like the Spanish for 'at our house'.* There is no universe

---

* It's equally possible that they were offering us some white sherry.

in which going with them was a good idea, whatever lay in store for us at their house. But then again there is no universe in which being this drunk and having to climb half a mountain is a good idea.

'OK,' I said.

'This isn't a good idea,' said Scott.

'We'll be fine,' I said. My half-formed plan, I think, was to get further up the mountain and then tell them we'd changed our mind and then get out and walk the rest of the way. It simply didn't occur to me that two hit men drug dealers might have any problem with this plan.

We got into the car, Scott in the front and me in the back with the second hit man. There were no rear doors so I had to clamber in over the front seats. The drug dealer in the driver's seat floored the accelerator and we began to race up the mountain. We must have been doing at least seventy miles an hour, screeching around blind corners and narrowly avoiding spinning off the road to our deaths, when I decided it was a good time for Scott and me to get out.

'Stop the car!' I said, in English. I wasn't sure if the driver hadn't understood my request or he didn't care. Either way, he carried on driving, maybe even accelerating slightly.

'Stop!' I shouted, even louder this time. Scott was now shouting the same thing, but in actual Spanish. Still nothing. Having dismissed all other possibilities, I came to the conclusion that we were being kidnapped. Not simply that we were going to be forced to buy drugs, but rather that Scott and I were being driven to a mountain-top dungeon where we'd be held against our will and forced to perform unspeakable acts, in a combination of English and broken Spanish. Faced with this reality, there was only one sensible course of action. I reached forward between the two front seats and grabbed hold of the handbrake, pulling it up sharply with both hands.

What happened next is exactly what you'd expect would happen next. The car jerked into a flat spin, gravel flying up as we slid, mercifully, away from the mountain edge – but towards a wall built of rocks. The hitman behind the wheel reacted with all the speed of a man with a head full of cocaine, slamming on the footbrake and trying to steer into the spin. We eventually came to a rest in a ditch. Had we spun in the other direction, we'd have fallen at least a hundred feet straight down the mountain into some trees.

That's when the shouting started, and the first punch – thrown by the hit man in the back – almost connected with the side of my face. The window on Scott's passenger side was open and I decided to try to climb from the back, straight out through the window. Unfortunately Scott chose precisely that same moment to get the fuck out of the front of the car, swinging the door open. The result of our uncoordinated actions was that I was left hanging out through the window, swinging on an open door.

Still inside the car, Scott grabbed my legs and pushed me the rest of the way forward, where I fell face first on to the road. The shouting continued as we started to run, scrambling over the ditch and down a small drop into a field. I landed awkwardly, twisting my ankle. Scott would tell me later that he carried me the rest of the way up the mountain back to the villa. Given the searing pain in my ankle for the next three days, and the fact that our clothes were covered in dirt and blood, I believed him.

'Still,' I said as I hobbled from my room the next morning, out on to the patio where Rob was soaking in the hot tub and Scott was trying to sleep off his hangover in the hammock, 'you've got to admit, it's a funny story.'

'Yeah,' said Scott, 'it's a funny story if you don't remember it, and if you don't speak any Spanish. I actually know what they were shouting at you. They were saying that they were going to come back with a knife and stab you.'

'Oh,' I said, making a note to include that detail when I wrote up the story for my blog.

906

It wasn't long after what became known as 'the drug dealer-attempted murder night' that Robert and I decided we needed something other than all-day drinking to entertain us during the rest of our time up the mountain.

Since I arrived in Spain, barely a day had passed without an email conversation with Hannah, who, having split up from her boyfriend, was now throwing herself into a combination of work and drinking. As was only right and proper.

Perhaps it's because I was spending my whole days getting drunk in a hammock, but I was worried about how hard she was working: spending long hours finishing an important new project. No matter what time she emailed – day or night – she seemed to be still in the office. One morning, on a whim, I sent her an email.

From: Paul
To: Hannah

Hey – you should come out to Spain this weekend. If you're going to work hard, you should at least do it from a hammock.

I mean, I knew she'd say no – that she was too busy – but I also knew there was no harm in planting seeds.

A few minutes later she replied.

From: Hannah
To: Paul

You mean it?! I'd love to come out and see you guys. I really need a weekend away from it all, lounging around in a bikini, or less. Lemme check flights, ok?

I stared at the email, assuming I was missing a 'but'. But I wasn't.

'Rob!' I shouted. 'You will not fucking believe what just happened.'

Robert looked up from his laptop. 'From the way you're squealing like a fucking girl, I'd say Hannah replied to your email and is coming out this weekend.' He paused. 'You should invite Eris to come over the weekend after. You're on a roll.'

I laughed. Flying from London is one thing but San Francisco is a bit of a way to fly for a weekend. I did email Eris, though. 'Robert says you should come to Spain next week. x'

An hour or so later, as California woke up and Eris arrived at her desk, she read my email and sent her reply.

I stared at my screen again, trying to decide if I was misunderstanding the list of plane times. I wasn't.

'Rob!'

'You're fucking kidding me.'

907

'So let me get this straight,' Robert said, 'this weekend, Hannah, the girl you have an enormous crush on but haven't actually done anything with is flying out to see you.'

'Yes.'

'And then after she leaves, Eris, the girl who you have actually done stuff with, but decided you were cooling things off with because she lives in San Francisco, is flying out to see you.'

'Well, technically she's flying to see us. She had some holiday time and wants to spend it doing something different. Apparently our nomad lifestyle has inspired her. She says she's interested in being the third King of the Road.'

Robert laughed. 'Everything about this is ridiculous.'

Try as I might to remain cool, I spent the rest of the week unable to think – or talk – about anything other than Hannah's visit.

'I just can't understand why she'd said yes.'

'Uh, she likes you, you fucking idiot,' said Rob.

That couldn't be it. Until just a few weeks ago she'd thought

I was a drunken dick. Surely discovering that I could occasionally write a funny email or a blog post couldn't have changed that. I started to worry that I'd misinterpreted her trip. Maybe she wasn't interested at all; maybe she really did just want to sit in the sun. Oh God, what should I do about beds? Should I give her the spare bed – in which case would she think I wasn't interested? Or should I assume she'd want to share with me, which could lead to all kinds of embarrassment if I was wrong?

'Jesus Christ,' said Robert, 'this is typical you. You treat every other girl like total crap, which of course makes them fall madly in love with you. And then Michelle and I have to pick up the pieces and explain that you're not a total bastard, just *'emotionally unavailable'*, which we all know is a euphemism for 'a total cunt'. But then the moment you meet a girl you actually like, you totally lose your shit and turn into a quivering virgin.'

'It's just that Hannah's . . . I dunno . . . different,' I said.

'Virgin,' said Rob. 'Quivering emo virgin.'

'That's actually going to be the title of my second album,' I said.

By the time I drove to the airport to pick Hannah up, I'd decided that Robert was right. Faint heart never won fair Canadian. If I'd got the wrong end of the stick then I'd just have to live with the embarrassment – there was always the spare room for one of us to sleep in.

To make things more interesting, Robert had invited a girl over as well. Her name was Sally – a South African who had until recently dated Michael. 'Does Michael know she's coming out?' I asked Rob.

'Not entirely,' said Robert, 'best not to write about her.'*

We'd convinced the girls to take the same flight so we'd only have to drive to the airport once. This seemed like a brilliant idea until – on the way to the airport – we realised that there was a chance that they'd have met on the plane and started comparing notes. I'd told Hannah some of the indiscreet things Robert had

* Okey-dokey.

said about his date, and I was pretty sure he'd told Sally about my gibbering excitement over Hannah. These were not details that needed to be exchanged. Fortunately, even though they came through arrivals at almost exactly the same time, it seemed that neither had realised who the other was.

Robert pulled Sally into a long hug before kissing her firmly on the mouth. 'Hello, darling,' he said. I hesitated for a second before hugging Hannah and awkwardly kissing her cheek. I looked into her eyes for clues. Had she been expecting a kiss? No, of course not, that would be weird. I took her bag and we headed back to the car.

We'd been in the villa long enough now to have mastered the art of barbecuing and the girls were, we thought, suitably impressed by our skills at making fire and grilling meat. After dinner Robert suggested that we get into the hot tub, and he and Sally headed off to their room to 'get changed'. This was the moment of truth; the moment where, surely, I was going to make a total fucking fool of myself, and probably get stabbed in the eye with a barbecue fork. Hell, this was the girl who had pushed me across a room for accusing her of being American.

I turned to Hannah. She spoke first.

'So,' she said.

'So,' I replied. And then I kissed her.

The barbecue fork remained on the table.

'About fucking time,' she said. 'Which one's our room?'

908

The day after Hannah flew back to London I walked – floated, really, on a cushion of happiness – into the kitchen to find Robert scribbling on a notepad.

'Working hard?' I asked.

'Fourteen thousand miles.'

'What?'

'Fourteen thousand miles. That's the total distance – including return trips – that women will have flown in order to sleep with you in Spain, once Eris gets here.'

'First of all, Robert, it's horrible that you worked that out,' I said. 'I mean, I take no small amount of pleasure in the number – but it's horrible that you've actually worked it out.'

'Oh, it's worse than that. I was actually going to suggest a game – 'the Google Maps Challenge' – to see if I could beat your total by the end of the trip.'

'Well, I'm glad you thought better of it.'

'Actually, I just realised that to win I'd need to find five girls willing to fly here, just to cancel out Eris.'

'Well, in that case, I accept your surrender. Good game, Rob.' I patted him on the back, and headed to the fridge for a celebratory beer.

Eris's flight arrived at Málaga airport at five o'clock, and we decided to make the most of the sun by heading down to the beach. Eris had been intrigued by the concept of Eurotrash, and we could think of no better place to explain it than the playground of the rich and most wanted: Puerto Banus.

The Ocean Club in Puerto Banus describes itself as 'the most exclusive and impressive setting on the Costa del Sol', a sort of outdoor daytime nightclub, with topless women sunbathing by a gigantic pool, which backs right on to the beach. Access to the bar is limited to models, playboys and their playthings – which meant there was no way Rob, Eris and I were going to get in. Unless, that is, we pulled the lunch trick.

'Hello, there are four of us for lunch.'

The door person – a tanned male model in a black suit and a white t-shirt – looked us up and down. For a start, there were only three of us. And, also, we certainly didn't look like people who were going to spend fifty euros on a plate of Tempur de Gambas Agrudulce. Good eye, door person. But who can tell these days? We might be dot com millionaires; they always dress like scum.

'Do you have reservations?'

'Oh, no,' said Rob, affecting his best playboy-on-shore-leave tone, 'we weren't expecting to moor for another week. Will it be a problem to walk in?'

'No, no, for lunch that will be fine,' said the door person.

'Thank you. We're expecting one more person before we sit down. If we wait in the bar, can you let us know when they arrive?'

'Certainly, sir.'

Of course, our nonexistent friend would never show, leaving us to drink with supermodels for the rest of the day. We sat at the bar and Robert called over a barman.

'Three piña coladas, please.' Robert's playboy impression was taking a turn for the Derek Trotter, but 'in for a euro, in for . . .'

'Thirty-six euros, please. Would you like to open a tab?' Jesus Christ. I gave the barman my card and he began mixing the piña coladas, pouring them into small tumblers.

'Whoa, whoa, whoa,' said Robert, 'what do you think you're doing?'

'This is how we serve piña coladas,' said the bartender.

'No, no, no,' said Robert, 'piña coladas are served in those big piña colada glasses.' Glasses which just so happen to be twice the size of the tumblers.

The bartender sighed. 'We don't have any piña colada glasses, sir.'

'Well, that's not good enough,' said Robert, 'but I suppose we can make do with brandy snifters. They're close enough. Honestly – who serves piña coladas in a tumbler?'

'Our . . . *clientele* . . . prefer it that way, sir.' He said the word *clientele* in such a way as to make clear that we did not fall within the narrow borders of his definition. Rob just shrugged; the customer is always right. Grudgingly, the bartender decanted two of the tumblers into a single brandy snifter and slid it over to Robert before skulking off to make two more very large piña coladas for Eris and me.

Robert called after him. 'And a little paper umbrella, please.'

The three of us had only taken the smallest sip from our drinks – with little paper umbrellas – when a stunning blonde with an all-over tan and no bikini top came and stood next to where we were sitting.

'What are those?' she asked, in a heavy German accent.

'Piña coladas,' said Rob.

'*Nocheinen, bitte,*' she said to the bartender, pointing at our glasses. Robert grinned his victory at the bartender.

'With a little umbrella,' said Rob.

'*Ja, miteinen Regenschirm,*' confirmed the German woman.

Twenty minutes later we looked around the bar. 'This is freaking hilarious,' said Eris. And she was right: at least a dozen of the Ocean Club's clientele were strolling around sipping piña coladas in brandy snifters, each replete with brightly coloured umbrella.

Our work there was done.

909

'Hey, Paul, don't drink this.'

Eris was unpacking her suitcase in our bedroom. I'd taken every possible precaution to remove any trace of Hannah from the room, but still, every time Eris opened a cupboard, a small wave of panic washed over me in case I'd missed a tell-tale hair clip or suchlike.

In Eris's hand was a silver hipflask with an inscription beautifully engraved across the whole of one side. From across the room I couldn't make out what it said, but clearly the contents were important.

'OK, I won't. Why, what is it?'

'It's my mom.'

910

Eris's mother had passed away very suddenly a year or so earlier. This is something I was aware of, but hadn't really pried too much into. In fact, I knew that Eris had lost both of her parents, both very suddenly, and both very recently. I was waiting for her to find the right time to share the details with me, if she wanted to.

What I certainly hadn't known was that Eris had her mother's ashes placed into a specially engraved flask, which she had decided to bring with her to Spain. Her plan – and it was a heartbreakingly lovely plan – was to leave some of the ashes in each of the places she visited around the world; places her mother never got a chance to visit. None of this I'd known. But all of it I had to figure out in the split second after Eris spoke those words.

'It's my mom.'

'Oh,' I said, 'OK.'

Hooboy.

Thank God she'd warned me. That could have been awkward.

911

The last time I tried to keep the existence of one girl from another girl it had ended in disaster when I'd accidentally, and drunkenly, invited both of them to the same London pub at the same time. The two girls, both Americans, incidentally, had spent the rest of the evening comparing notes on what a complete and total shit I was, resulting in their becoming best friends for ever. Or 'BFF's as they – both being American – would have it said.

Another result of that night was that they'd subsequently decided to do everything they could to get their revenge on me; starting by setting up a website explaining why no girl in her right mind should ever date me. Like I said, I love American girls and their fiery ways.

Keen to avoid a repeat of history, I decided that, when it came to the Eris–Hannah situation, honesty was the best policy.

'Eris,' I said – which was about as much of the conversation as I'd planned before I started to speak – 'remember that girl Hannah I told you about at South by Southwest?'

'Of course,' said Eris, 'the Canadian you wouldn't shut up about.'

'Oh, yes, her. Well, I should probably tell you that she came out to the villa last week. I mean, it's not . . .'

'I know.' Eris just carried on unpacking; she didn't even pause.

'What do you mean?'

'I mean, I know. I've been reading your blog.'

'But I didn't mention her on the blog.'

'Exactly, you didn't post anything the whole weekend. Total rookie mistake. It was obvious you were getting laid and didn't want anyone to know.'

'So you're not annoyed?'

'I flew to Spain from San Francisco and am about to climb into your bed. Does any of that say 'annoyed girl behaviour' to you? If I were annoyed I could have set up a hate blog from home and saved the aeroplane ticket.'

Touché.

It was too much to hope that Hannah would be as understanding. As Eris finished unpacking, I walked out to the patio and dialled Hannah's number. She answered on the second ring. Dammit; I was half hoping it would go to voicemail.

'Hey,' I said.

'Paul! Hey! Wait – shouldn't you be boning that Eris chick? Doesn't she arrive today?'

Okey-dokey.

'How did you . . .'

'You told me last week when you drunk-dialled me from Alejo's.'

'Oh,' I said. 'I don't entirely remember the conversation. So you don't think I'm a shit?'

'Of course I do. I think you're a total fucking dick,' replied Hannah.

I started to explain: 'I know, it's just that . . . wait . . . hang on, the last time I was drunk in Alejo's was before you came out. Why didn't you say anything while you were here?'

'Don't be an idiot. You're not a dick for having another girl fly out – that's actually kinda hilarious. You're a dick because she's probably lying in your bed waiting for you while you're on the phone to me. How do you think that makes her feel, you fucking dick?'

I'm really not very good at this.

912

Another thing I'm not very good at is having sex with someone, knowing that their dead mother is in my bedside cupboard.

Not that having sex with someone's live mother in my bedside cupboard would be any easier. Mothers, generally speaking, should not be in bedside cupboards while you are having sex with their daughters. Is all.

And yet, despite these thoughts, and their attendant performance anxiety issues, Eris's visit was one of the highlights of my time in Spain. We'd agreed that casualness was the key – which made me feel less bad about Hannah, and her less bad about flirting outrageously every night with the waiter in the village's only restaurant.

Scott had returned to the Valle for another visit and he, Robert, Eris and I had decided to head out for food and no small amount of wine. We'd opted to take the car down to the village so I was laying off the booze for one rare night, but the other three were more than making up for my temperance. By the end of the meal both Eris and Robert were trashed, with Scott not far behind. Eris's waiter-flirting had become increasingly obvious; she didn't speak the language much more than Rob or I did, but apparently Spanish men aren't as demanding on that front as Spanish women. Scott decided this would probably be a good time to head back to the villa to finish some work.

'I'll come with you,' I said, in what I intended to be a study in nonchalance but which, as Robert quickly pointed out, came out more as a study in how to be a sulky hypocrite.

'Don't be silly,' said Eris, 'let's go and have another drink at Carpe Diem.' Grateful for any plan that got her away from – let's call him – Juan, I agreed.

Carpe Diem was empty – just me, Robert, Eris and the bartender. 'I'll get the drinks,' I said, 'you guys sit down.' Having successfully separated Eris from Juan, it was time for plan B – stop her getting any more drunk so she wouldn't go back and look for him. My plan was as simple as it was foolproof: instead of ordering Eris a rum and Coke, I'd just get her a straight Coke and gamble on her being drunk enough not to notice. Apparently I'd moved on from sulky hypocrite to devious hypocrite.

As I stood at the bar waiting to be served, I considered the morality of what I was about to do. Spiking someone's drink – especially a girl's – is definitely, unequivocally, wrong. But unspiking a drink? Is that still bad? No, I thought; if anything it's the opposite of bad. Unspiking someone's drink is good; a noble, generous act.

I took the drinks back to the table, making sure to give Robert the Coke with the rum and Eris the non-alcoholic variation. It was all very Danny Kaye. Eris was distracted, playing with her phone, as I sat down, so I whispered to Robert, explaining what I'd done. It was his round next and I was hoping he might help me out with my unspiking plan, what with him being my friend and all. Apparently, though, being thrashed at the Google Maps Challenge had left Robert sporting a grudge.

'Errrrriiissss . . .' he sang across the table.

I stared at him. Don't you dare, you bastard. Eris looked up from her phone.

'Paul seems to have deliberately got you a straight Coke so that you won't get any more drunk and run off with' – let's call him – 'Juan.'

Eris looked puzzled for a second, and then picked up her glass and took a sip. She swilled the liquid around in her mouth, searching for any hint of alcohol. Then a smile started to play around the corner of her mouth, which was still full of Coke. She leaned across the table towards me and pursed her lips into a small 'o' shape . . . and then spat the entire mouthful – shooting like a black, sugary fountain – into my face.

Robert collapsed into laughter. He laughed so hard in fact that he almost fell off his chair. Eris, too, by now, was in hysterics. This was literally the funniest thing either of them had ever seen; me, once smug with my unspiked drink plan, now covered with Coke, dripping from my hair and running down my nose. I started laughing too. I mean, it *was* funny.

Of course, this was the exact moment, at the very height of my sugary comeuppance, that – let's call him – Juan chose to walk into Carpe Diem, looking for an after-work drink. Eris stood up, her face a picture of innocence, and walked over to him, before he'd even made it to the bar.

'Hallo,' he said, apparently his only word of English. But he didn't really need any other words, as Eris immediately grabbed both sides of his face and kissed him. For about twenty seconds.

This seemed like a good time for me to leave. I headed back up the mountain, leaving Robert and Eris to their full-strength rum and Cokes, and God knows what else.

913

Two hours later, Robert and Eris finally made it back to the villa, which, given their state, was just as much of a miracle as it was every night that I'd managed it. I was sitting on the patio when they arrived, sharing a bottle of rum with Scott. Robert sat down to join us while Eris headed off, I assumed, to bed.

'Have you forgiven me, darling?' asked Robert, still not having quite finished laughing.

'Fuck off,' I said, filling his glass half with rum.

He explained that, after I'd left, Juan had disengaged himself from Eris's mouth and immediately started to panic, trying, in broken English, to apologise to Robert for 'keesing the lady of your friend'. To his credit, Robert had made the man feel as guilty as their mutual lack of communication skills would allow, suggesting through rudimentary hand gestures that this might be the end of our nightly trips to his restaurant. The fact that we only had a few days left in Spain having more to do with this than anything else. They'd all had a few more drinks before deciding to call it a night, having served me right for my amateur womanising and my stupid jealousy.

'Shhhh . . .' Scott held up his hand, 'what's that . . .?'

We could hear a crunching sound coming from the front of the house. Someone was walking down the gravel driveway. And the sound was getting quieter; further away.

'Where's Eris?' asked Rob.

'I thought she'd gone to bed,' I said.

'Yeah, I think you thought wrong.'

'Well, I'm not going after her,' I said, pouring the remainder of the rum from the bottle into my glass. Then I put the glass down, sighed as loudly as I could – in the hope that Eris would hear it, despite being well on her way down the mountain by now – and trudged round to the front of the house.

I finally caught up with her halfway down the first big hill of the mountain road.

'Where are you going?' I asked, redundantly.

'To find' – let's . . . – 'Juan,' she slurred. Dear God, she was nearly as drunk as I usually was.

'Don't be silly,' I said, putting my hand on her shoulder in the hope that it might at least stop her walking. Which it did, but only for a second. Which was the time she needed to turn around and punch me, as hard as she could, in the face. And then off she ran, down the mountain, back towards the village. It was 3 a.m.

'Fine,' I shouted after her, 'I'm not chasing after you.' And I didn't. I turned around and walked back to the house.

'Bollocks to her,' I said as I stormed back into the patio. 'I'm not her keeper.'

Scott – now the least drunk of us – wasn't entirely convinced. 'We can't just let her run off down the mountain at this time of night. What if she slips – or gets hit by a car.' I was worried, too, now that I'd got off my high horse about someone else behaving idiotically while drunk.

'We'll have to go and find her,' said Rob.

'That's going to be interesting in the dark,' I said. There were no streetlights on the mountain road and seeing more than a few feet ahead was impossible; I'd lost count of the number of times one or other of us had nearly fallen to our deaths on the way home.

'We'll take the car. Which of us is least drunk?'

Given that I'd just finished the last of a bottle of rum, the answer clearly wasn't me. Robert had sobered up a fair amount, but was hindered by the fact that he hasn't driven a car in his life. Which just left . . .

'Fuck sake,' said Scott. 'OK, come on.'

The three of us piled into the rental car, Scott and me in the front and Robert in the back. The person who can't drive has to sit in the back; that's the rule. Scott drove slowly down the mountain; hitting Eris with the car would have been counter-productive. Robert and I scoured each side of the road for any sign that she'd veered off into a field or fallen in a ditch.

By the time we arrived at the outskirts of the village, still with no sign of Eris, I was starting to get frantic. Why hadn't I followed her? Just because I was in a strop and my ego wouldn't allow me to beg her to come back to the villa, and safety?

'Look!' shouted Scott, pointing over the steering wheel, towards the village square. And there she was, standing right in the middle of the square, looking completely lost. Scott switched off the headlights and began to creep the car slowly towards the square. We knew there was every chance she'd set off running again if she saw us, probably down one of the four or five narrow, car-proof alleyways that lead off the square.

The car reached the edge of the square, which is when Eris spotted us. She stared at us, or at least towards the dark outline of the car, presumably trying to figure out if it was us or not; we stared back.

And then she was running.

Scott – and I still don't know where he learned to do any of what followed – slammed his foot on the accelerator and the car surged forward, overtaking Eris in a second, just before she had the chance to make it to the alley. Then, with a deft twist of the steering wheel and a little help from the handbrake, Scott spun the front of the car ninety degrees, blocking the space between her and the alley.

Before we'd even come to a stop, I jumped out of the front door, grabbed Eris around her waist and threw her – I mean, physically threw her – through the back door that Robert had swung open. I jumped back in the car, Robert took over the grabbing and we were away.

It took a full twenty minutes of cajoling back at the villa before we finally convinced Eris that going to bed would be a much better use of her time than running back down the mountain to see a Spanish waiter who had probably been in bed for hours.

Calm restored to the Valle de Abdajalis, I went back to the patio, saw the empty bottle of rum and sighed.

'Don't worry,' said Scott, following behind me and reading my mind, 'I saved a spare bottle in my room, just for this kind of eventuality. You want me to go and get it?'

'*Por favor,*' I said.

'You know,' said Robert, as Scott headed off to recover his emergency booze supply, 'I still don't know what that means.'

'What what means?' I asked. '*Por favor*? How can you not know what that means, you must hear me say it a dozen times a day, everywhere we go . . . It means 'please'. As in '*Uno San Miguel, por favor.*' Come to think of it, I've heard you use it too.'

'Oh,' said Robert, 'I just assumed it meant "for me".'

Eight weeks in Valle de Abdajalis – an entirely non-English-speaking village – and Robert hadn't learned a single word of Spanish. Which might make things difficult for him when the police inevitably turn up tomorrow to interview us about the very loud kidnapping we had just staged in the middle of the village square.

Scott returned with the last bottle of rum of the trip as the sun started to rise over the top of the mountain.

Chapter 1000

Like I've Never Been Away

It felt funny arriving at Gatwick as a visitor. Previously, I'd always associated the immigration halls at London airports with home-coming. Finally being able to climb back into my own bed, and to catch up with all my friends. But this time it was just another airport; another taxi journey to another hotel.

After two months of preparation – responding to questions from libel lawyers, checking final proofs and hyping the hell out of myself on my new site – the month of publication had arrived. The first copies of the book were due to appear in shops on the last Friday of July and I'd flown back to London to conduct some more video interviews with 'characters' from its pages, as well as to organise my own book launch party.

One of the things that first-time authors most look forward to when they get a book deal is the glamorous launch party to mark the day of publication. In fact, due to the vast numbers of books that large publishing houses churn out each year, there's almost never a budget for anything more than a nice lunch for the author.

Throughout the writing process, though, I'd been using the promise of an invitation to the launch party as a bribe for friends to allow me to write embarrassing stories about them. 'You'll be guest of honour,' I promised about a hundred people, including at least two cab drivers.

Fortunately, as it turns out, the same trick works for venues. I looked through the book manuscript and made a list of all the bars I'd written about. There were a lot, and most of them were in central London. I sent them all the same email, just dropping them a line to let them know that they were 'the key location' in my new book and wondering if, by any chance, they'd like to host the launch party. What I hadn't realised was that two of the venues – the International Bar* on Trafalgar Square and the Gardening Club† in Covent Garden were both owned by the same company, and therefore had the same PR person, who got the same email from me twice. Fortunately, though, he had a sense of humour about my blatant, and clumsy, attempt to blag a free party venue. He offered the International for the party itself, and guest list entry to the Gardening Club for the after-party. The latter being easily the best place in London to pick up American student girls, it wasn't a difficult offer to accept.

A month back in London also fitted perfectly with my nomadic experiment. I had always planned to spend at least some time 'back home' during the year – to catch up with friends as well as sorting out silly administrative things like going to the dentist and catching up with my bank manager. I'd managed to free myself of most bills when I left my flat behind, but there were still some things that needed face-to-face attention. Also, I wanted to come back to remind myself why I'd left in the first place.

Hotel rates in London have surprisingly little seasonal fluctuation. January and February are a tiny bit cheaper, and there tend to be fewer deals available at hotels popular with tourists, but, apart from that, you can pretty much stay for the same price at the height of summer as you can the rest of the year. That's the good thing about staying in hotels in London.

The less good thing about staying in hotels in London is that the average nightly rate is about a billion pounds and, outside of five-star places, the standards are generally appalling.

In fact, even at five-star level, it's a mixed bag. On my first night back in town, I decided to stay at a five-star hotel near Green Park, one of the most prestigious in the capital. When I opened the

---

* Described in chapter three of the book when I'd managed to get myself thrown out of my own party there.
† I quote: 'A fucking dive – a tiny sweaty nightclub where the drinks are cheap and the women are available on draft.'

wardrobe, I discovered that someone had written, in huge pencil letters, inside the door: 'this place is a shithole.' It was a pretty accurate review: the room was tiny, the shower didn't work and when I tried to call reception to complain, in the hope of getting an upgrade, I was foiled by the fact that the phone didn't have a dial tone.

There lies the problem with the hotel star-rating system in the UK: it's complete bullshit. As with most countries, including the US, there is no legal obligation for hotels to be independently assessed. Yes, many of the star ratings you see on the side of British hotels have been awarded by the AA or VisitBritain (what used to be the British Tourist Authority) which are the only two really reliable ratings organisations in the country, especially since they recently synchronised their ratings criteria. But both of these organisations charge hotels to be rated and many, including huge chains like Hilton, simply choose not to sign up. Aside from legislation designed to prevent grossly misleading advertising, there is nothing to prevent a hotel from self-assessing: a homeless person could draw five stars on the side of his cardboard box and call it a five-star property. Indeed, many hotels will describe themselves as 'four-star standard' or 'five-star standard' despite being – as the wardrobe reviewer put it – 'a shithole'. That's just another reason why I tend to rely on Internet reviews from actual guests before making a booking.

But on my second night back in London even a four-star standard shit hole would have been a step up. In the interests of research, I had decided to stay for a couple of nights at a £50-a-night hotel. I was curious to know what standard of room I'd get in London for my normal budget which, let's not forget, had covered a spa suite in Vegas, a classic movie set in San Francisco, one and a half rooms in a villa in Spain and about five minutes in a 1978 Dodge Challenger.

After paging through literally dozens of pages of hovels on Trip Advisor – sample review: 'Dreadful hotel. I'd be embarrassed to offer the room to anyone!' – I finally found the only place in London which seemed to fit my basic criteria. Namely: do the rooms look decent, does it have wifi and is it central? The only place answering all of these questions in the affirmative, despite not even pretending to have any stars, was the Easy Hotel in Victoria.

There are actually five Easy Hotels in London,* and, while they're not actually owned by the people behind low-cost European airline EasyJet, they do license the company's branding and colour scheme. As a result, the rooms are decorated in the same vivid orange that makes EasyJet planes so easy to spot, even from 36,000 feet. Close up, that's less of a selling point.

The hotels also share EasyJet's business model, which makes a lot of sense given that airline seats and hotel rooms are both highly perishable. Like EasyJet flights, Easy Hotel rooms are only sold online, at highly variable rates. When demand is high, the price goes up, when demand is low, it goes down.

If you're savvy enough to pay for your Easy Hotel room months in advance then some splendid deals can be had – as low as £20 for a double room. Given that the hotels are small – fewer than fifty rooms in each – and centrally located, they are sold out most nights, so if you leave it till the last minute you'll pay through the nose – maybe even over £100 a night.

With such low revenue per room (RevPAR† as it's called by hotel managers) it's hard for a budget hotel chain to afford to invest in decent standards of decoration and comfort. Easy Hotels solved this problem by making their rooms entirely functional, and totally standardised. Every room is exactly the same: a double bed, built into a wooden base fixed to the (laminate, wipe-clean) floor, and an entirely self-contained shower and toilet unit. Add in two coat hooks and a flatscreen TV on the wall and that's it. Servicing an Easy Hotel room could be done with a single maid, a fresh set of

---

* Six if you include the one that's a few miles from 'London Luton Airport' which is in London like Belgium is.

† Revenue per Available Room: the hotel's total revenue in a given period, net of tax and food, divided by the number of rooms available. The higher the better for the hotel. RevPAR is also a fun word to use casually when talking to hotel managers as it fools them into thinking you know what you're talking about. The equivalent in the airline industry is Revenue per Available Seat Mile (RASM), which is much less fun to say.

bedding and a hose. The beds are perfectly comfortable; and, given that's the only furniture in the room, there's really nothing left to complain about. Unless, of course, you decide to invite a girl back.

1001

'Fucking hell,' said Hannah.

'Yes, I know,' I said, 'but I needed to see what it was like – it's part of my experiment.'

'And bringing me back here was part of the same experiment, was it? To test my tolerance of bright orange walls? Jesus Christ, Paul, I'm a designer; this is like torture.'

'It could have been worse,' I explained, 'at least there's a window.' I pointed to the small sliver of glass right at the top of one of the walls. Through it we could just about make out people's feet walking past on the street above.

'Yes, well, I'd hope there was a window.'

'I'm not kidding,' I said, 'the window was an optional extra. I had the choice: £35 for a standard room, £50 for "standard room with window".'

'Well, I have to admit, design aside, this place was a smart tactical move on your part – I mean, all there is to do here is go to bed or else watch crap British television.'

'Actually . . .'

'What?'

'If we want to watch crap British television we'll have to pay five pounds at reception to rent the remote control.'

1002

The next day I met Robert. He too had decided to come back to London, partly because he didn't want to miss my launch party – he was guest of honour, after all – but mainly because he was determined to prove it was possible to stay in London on the Kings of the Road Club budget.

After my Easy Hotel experience, I'd basically resigned myself to the fact that I'd be paying through the nose for my short stay in the capital. At least it proved my point about the cost of living in London, and made me excited about the prospect of leaving again.

Robert on the other hand seemed to be taking the whole experiment much more seriously than I was, which was frightening, but also slightly gratifying. Just about everyone who I'd told about my new nomadic life had been fascinated by the idea and many of those had expressed an interest in trying it out. Robert's enthusiasm, and his success in making the budget work so well in Spain, proved that living on the road wasn't something that only a person who grew up in hotels could do. It was actually a lifestyle choice that anyone could make, provided they were willing to throw themselves into it feet first.

But while Robert was going overboard in trying to find a fun place to stay in London for £50 a night, I had seized on an opportunity to take a more relaxed approach to the rules – if only for a couple of days. My friend Anna and her boyfriend were going to be out of town for a couple of days to look after her parents' dogs. Anna knew I was 'doing that whole living in hotels thing', but if I was interested in staying at their house in north London for forty-eight hours I'd be very welcome. Unless I thought that would be cheating.

I'd accepted in a heartbeat.

'That's cheating,' said Robert over lunch.

'No it isn't,' I said.

'Yes it is. Anyone can survive on an accommodation budget of £50 a day that way: just sleep on your friends' sofa for a year. Job done. But if you can live with yourself . . .'

'Yes, Robert, I can live with *myself* – which is why it's not cheating. I'm not sleeping on their sofa while they're still there. I'm sleeping in their proper bed, while they're not. I'm just renting the place for a couple of days, for free. There is nothing in the non-existent rules banning that.'

'Hmm,' said Rob.

'Anyway, you didn't see the Easy Hotel. There's just nowhere practical and central in London where you can stay for less than fifty quid a night.'

'Hmm,' said Rob.

'What do you mean 'hmm'? Where are you staying?'

'Pimlico, just down the road from the Easy Hotel, actually, but far enough away from Victoria so as not to actually – you know – be in Victoria. Thirty-five quid a night. And it's full of beautiful women.'

Bullshit. I used to live in Pimlico. It's a nice part of London; one of the best, in fact. My rent was somewhere north of £2500 a month for a one-bedroom flat. There were some pretty cheap guesthouses on the outskirts, but nothing for £35 a night.

'I don't believe you,' I said. 'There's no way you've found a hotel for £35 a night in Pimlico.'

'And there's your problem,' Robert continued. 'You're obsessed with hotels. You don't think laterally. What do we know about June and July?'

'It's summer. But that doesn't matter in a London hotel ... OK, so you're not in a hotel.'

'Correct. The key is to think who leaves town in summer, and so what's going to lie empty. It's like the villa.'

It took me two courses and the best part of a bottle of wine before I got it.

'Students. That's who leaves London during the summer.'

'Well done, mate – only took you half an hour. I'd figured it out before I'd even landed back from Spain. Student halls of residence all lie empty over the summer; the first years have all moved out at the end of May and the new influx doesn't come until September. I made some calls and it turns out all the halls become hotels during the off-season. They're not luxurious, but they're much better than when we were at uni. They put in proper hotel bedding and shampoos and stuff; and there's free wifi. Also, the only people left behind are foreign exchange students. My place in Pimlico is full of hot Italian girls.'

'Thirty-five quid a night?'

'Yep.' A smug smile covered much of Robert's face. 'Beers are on me for the rest of the day. I can afford it.'

1003

Had circumstances been different the next morning, I too would have felt smug. I would have called Robert and I would have said something along the following lines.

'Ha! Guess what, Robert, I'm even better at this game than you. I've found somewhere in London that's central, not somebody's house, and available for less than thirty-five quid a night. In fact, it's totally free.'

Circumstances being what they were the next morning, though, calling Robert wasn't an option. For a start, I didn't have my phone. It was in a different room, a few feet down the corridor in a little plastic bag with my name written on it in ballpoint pen. My shoes were in a bag too, as was my belt, my wallet and the keys to Anna's house, where I'd finally made it after spending the rest of the afternoon and evening drinking with Rob.

We'd finished our second bottle of wine, I'd met Anna to pick up her keys and then Rob and I had headed off to meet our friend Angus for a few more drinks. Those drinks had led us back to Angus's house where we'd opened a couple of bottles of champagne. The night had ended with me deciding to take a cab to Adam Street, a members' club – of which I wasn't a member – just off the Strand. At some point I'd realised that Robert wasn't with me and decided to go home. And that's where things had gone terribly, terribly wrong.

For all of my drinking, particularly during the last few months I'd actually lived in London, I'd never ceased to be surprised at my ability to get home while plastered. No matter what ridiculousness I'd indulged in the previous night I'd always, regular as clockwork, woken up in my own bed the next morning, like Bill Murray's character in *Groundhog Day*.

Even when alcohol had forced the shutdown of every other part of my brain, there was – apparently – a little fail-safe part at the back that contained my address and whatever instructions were required to make my legs carry me into a taxi and my hands pay the fare.

Sure enough, I'd stumbled out of Adam Street and tumbled into a cab, £20 note in hand, and given the driver my address. Unfortunately, it seems I'd forgotten to update the address details at the back of my brain and so, after about twenty minutes, I realised that I'd sent the cab heading towards my old flat in East Dulwich. We were just passing the Elephant and Castle roundabout when my mistake became apparent.

'Sorry, mate,' I said to the driver, 'I've just realised we're going the wrong way. I'm actually staying in Crouch End.'

The driver groaned, in the way that only a London cab driver would when he's just learned that he's going to have to do something that will earn him an additional fifty quid, but soon we were headed north. The only problem now was that the meter was already nudging towards £20: we'd have to stop at a cashpoint, which was sure to elicit another groan. No! Wait! I still had fifty quid in my travel wallet back at Anna's, a precaution I'd taken in every city – one night's accommodation budget in local currency – just in case I lost my actual wallet and needed to spend an extra night sorting it out. Pleased at my brilliant foresight, I celebrated by passing out.

I recall waking up outside Anna's house. 'I'll just be a minute, mate,' I remember saying, as I fumbled for my keys and headed inside.

I remember finding my travel wallet and being relieved that the £50 note was still there. I remember being distracted by my phone vibrating in my pocket. It was Hannah, calling me back after the half-dozen times I'd called her from the back of the cab. That's really all I do remember.

Piecing everything together the next morning, here's what must have happened. I must have started talking to Hannah. From my slurring and my slipping in and out of consciousness, she would have quickly deduced that I was drunk and offered to call me back in the morning: these are facts that Hannah confirmed the next day. Then, still absolutely paralytic, I must have headed off to bed, completely forgetting that there was a taxi driver sitting outside Anna's house, meter running, waiting for his money.

1004

A quick flashback. Two years earlier – almost to the day – I had a similar incident with a cab driver. I had spent the night out with, among other people, my ex-girlfriend, who also happened to be my business partner. Concerned that she'd be able to get home safely, I'd insisted that she take one of my two credit cards in order to pay for a taxi. I kept the second card to pay for my own journey home. Unfortunately, what I hadn't realised was that the card I retained had expired the previous day, leading to an amusing impasse when the driver refused to let me go into my flat to get another method of payment, fearing that I was planning to run off. He instead drove me to a police station where, as a direct result of my getting lippy with the desk sergeant, I was arrested and held for a night in the cells. After that I vowed never to rely on a credit card to pay for a cab again, but, rather, to ensure that I always had at least twenty quid in cash in my pocket, no matter how drunk I got. Twenty pounds being more than enough money to get home, unless of course you send the cab driver in the wrong direction for twenty minutes.

1005

'Get up!'

Being woken up with those words is always bad news. Being woken up having those words shouted at you by three policemen standing over your bed, one of whom has an extendable baton poised to hit you, is really, really bad news.

As I would later discover, the cab driver had called 999 after waiting an hour for me to return with his money. The police had tried ringing the doorbell, but I hadn't answered, by reason of being passed out. It's at that point they'd racked their brains for a lawful solution and realised that there are only a small number of occasions when it's justifiable to kick someone's door down.

The belief that a crime is in the process of being committed is one such occasion. That wouldn't really wash as technically my 'crime' had been committed over an hour ago. Another occasion is if the police genuinely believe that a third party is in imminent danger. They had no reason to believe anyone but me was in the house, so that was a non-starter as well.

Which just leaves the third time when kicking a door in without a warrant is justified: a genuine belief that someone inside was ill or seriously injured. Ding! The fact that I'd been very obviously drunk when I went into the house and was now not answering the door could only mean one thing: I had choked on my own vomit and died. There was nothing else for it; using one of those metal battering ram things you see on cop shows, the police had smashed the living shit out of Anna's front door to 'rescue' me.

You'd have thought that discovering me alive and well, but asleep, they'd have been delighted. Apologised for the door, even. 'We're just glad you're OK.' But no – by the time my eyes were open and I'd started to process where I was, they'd hauled me out of bed – mercifully still wearing my clothes – handcuffed me and thrown me into the back of their van.

1006

Welcome back to London, I thought, when I woke up for the third time in twelve hours, this time lying on a wooden bench inside a cell at Marylebone police station. I'd already been fingerprinted and had my DNA taken; they'd been thrilled to discover a match with my previous arrest record – and even more so when they found it was for exactly the same crime: making off without payment.

Unable to interview me while I was still drunk, they'd thrown me into a cell until morning.

The first time I was arrested, I was terrified – worried what it would mean for the company I was then in the middle of starting, worried about what the consequences generally would be for me getting a criminal record, and just generally terrified at being locked in a police cell for the first time in my sheltered life. This time, though, I just felt bored. I knew that I would be interviewed in a few hours by two policemen who would probably be about nineteen years old and who would either slap me on the wrist in a 'we've all had a drink, you idiot, don't do it again' way, or would take a dislike to me on the basis that I'm a smart-arse middle-class twat with a law degree, and would decide to charge me.

That second possibility is what had transpired the previous time. I'd avoided court, and a criminal record, only by calling the Crown Prosecution Service and convincing them to drop the charges, which I'd managed to do because – after all – I'm a smart-arse middle-class twat with a law degree.

Whichever route the police decided to take this time, I knew nothing terrible would happen to me and that I wouldn't end up in jail. More importantly, I knew that I'd have an amusing story for my blog – or maybe even a freelance article – which would in turn help promote my book. I had turned into an accidental career criminal, in so far as accidentally committing crimes now directly benefit my career.

Another hour passed and finally, as expected, came the clanking before the door swung open. The custody sergeant marched me down to the interview room where, as expected, sat two policemen and a tape recorder. They explained my rights, I explained that I didn't want a lawyer, and then I began to tell them the whole story. They laughed a couple of times, and I made a mental note to include those parts of the story in the blog post. And then came the moment of truth.

'As this is your second offence,' said one of the policemen, 'but the last time the charges were dropped, we're happy to let you go with a caution.'

'Hmm,' I said. A caution is one of the more misunderstood punishments in the English justice system. Although people often talk of 'getting off with a caution', accepting one does actually have some consequences. For a start, to be eligible for a caution, you have to admit that you're guilty of a crime. Even though a caution isn't technically a conviction, this admission forms part of your criminal record, which means it will appear if you're ever subject to a background check. Also, you're generally only allowed one caution – next time it's straight to court.

Knowing all of this, I knew that the smartest thing for me to do would be to do what I'd done the previous time: refuse to admit any guilt, agree to be bailed to appear in court in a month's time and then try to sweet-talk the CPS into dropping the charges in the meantime. It would probably mean having to go to court for an hour or two to set a trial date, but hopefully things would go no further. Yes, that was the smartest thing to do.

'Would you like to accept the caution . . .'

Had I been sober then the problem would have hit me far sooner. Instead, it was only when the interviewing officer asked me the question for the second time that I finally sobered up enough to realise the jam I was in.

If I accepted the caution, and the accompanying criminal record, then I would almost certainly experience problems if I tried to apply for a visa to travel or live anywhere outside Europe. Given how much travelling I was doing, I really, really didn't want a criminal record.

But if I *didn't* accept the caution then I'd be given a court date that could be anything up to two months away. And given how much work I'd have to do – dealing with the CPS, writing letters, making phone calls and all that crap – I'd be basically stuck in London all that time. Then if things went badly with the CPS, I'd have to wait for a second court date, during which I'd actually be fined, or – Jesus – given community service. If I didn't accept the caution then my nomadic experiment was over, in the short term at least. If I did accept it, the experiment was very likely over in the long term.

Suddenly having an amusing story to tell about being arrested again didn't seem like such an upside.

I took a deep breath, which still tasted of rum.

'Yes,' I said, 'I'd like to accept the caution.' I had no real choice: I could hardly bear to stay in London for two more weeks, let alone two months.

The custody sergeant slid the piece of paper across his desk for me to sign. I was being given a 'conditional caution', which is like a normal caution but with the added demand that I pay the cab driver the fare I owed him; the total on the meter by the time he eventually drove off was £135. He also handed me a sealed plastic bag containing my phone, my belt and Anna's keys. 'Probably not much use now,' he said, 'they'll have boarded up the door after you were arrested, but it'll definitely need to be replaced.'

Of course: the bloody door. Anna was due back in less than twenty-four hours and I had to get it fixed before then. I'd probably have to pay an obscene call-out fee for an emergency door replacement company but at least that was better than having her arrive back to a missing door.

Truth is, it wasn't Anna's reaction that scared me – we're old friends and, as a fellow writer, she would probably see the funny side of it. Hell, I should probably give her first dibs on pitching the piece to her editor: 'the night my friend got my door kicked in by the police'. No, the person who scared me was Anna's boyfriend, Drew, who worked for a 'private security company' in Iraq. I'd only met him a couple of times and he seemed like a thoroughly nice guy but – let's be honest – he was basically a hired mercenary; God only knows how he'd react to the drunken idiot who'd got his door kicked in. I really had to get back and fix that door.

Finally the custody sergeant was ready to let me go. He gave me my copy of the caution and reminded me that if I didn't pay the cab driver within ten days, I'd be arrested again and sent to court.

Likewise, if I got arrested again in the next six months, I'd definitely be sent to court. He swung open the big metal door that led out to the main reception. 'Oh,' he said, 'and your friend is waiting for you in the car outside. She couldn't find anywhere to park.'

'My friend?'

'Yeah, I have to say, the bloke she was with didn't look happy at all.'

'My . . . what friend?' I murmured.

'The girl who owns the house, I think. She called earlier to say she'd come back and found the door boarded up. We usually leave a number on the door for the homeowner to call.'

Oh. Fuuuuuck.

'And you said she's with her boyfriend?'

'Looked like it. I wouldn't like to be the one who got that bloke's door kicked in. Good luck, mate.'

1007

To Anna's, and particularly Drew's, credit neither of them killed me. In fact, they both thought my night in the cells, and my grovelling apology were hilarious. 'It was kind of a shitty door anyway,' said Drew, 'we were going to get it replaced. And now we have an excuse.'

'And I'm paying for it,' I said.

'Exactly. Win-win.'

I looked down at my caution and the £135 underlined on it; I made a stab at guessing how much the door would cost – a couple of hundred quid at least – and then added on the price of the wine and flowers I should probably buy Anna and Drew to say sorry. My one night free stay was going to cost me at least £500, plus my new criminal record.

Yeah, win bloody win.

1008

After replacing Anna and Drew's door, I decided that I should probably avoid friends' houses in future. At least in a hotel, the police don't need to kick down doors – they can just ask reception for a key.

I headed a mile or so up the road to the Raglan Hotel in Muswell Hill. The Raglan is a really nice place – the rooms are modern, the service is good and I was able to blag a rate of £75 a night, which was an absolute bargain for London. All of which could only mean that there was a huge catch. And there was: Muswell Hill is several miles from the centre of town, almost an hour, in fact, by a variety of trains and busses. Realistically that meant adding £50 a day just for cabs, putting the total per night at almost three times my budget. In London that still constitutes a bargain.

Still, at least money would soon be no object. The closer my book publication date came, the more keenly I could taste my impending fame and success. Thanks to some advance press, and my drunken travelogues from Spain, people had actually started to pre-order the book on Amazon.

I've never understood why someone would want to order a book before it's out, any more than I've understood people who queue outside shops the night before things go on sale. But just because these people were obviously mentally ill didn't mean I didn't want them as readers. Even if, as Robert said, 'it's probably just all the people who hate you ordering copies for their lawyers'.

Still, whatever the reason, a week before publication, mine was officially the 97,000th most popular book on the site. When you take out all the books about wizards and vampires that was almost certainly the top ten.

Rebecca had been working hard too. She'd lined me up an appearance on Sky News to review 'this week's big stories on the Internet'. The fact that I had no idea – or interest in – what people on the Internet were talking about (unless they were talking about me) was irrelevant. On the day of the programme, the producer emailed me a list of stories about which I'd be expected to opine. My favourite story concerned a new company that rented dogs to rich people in New York. I made a joke about them being just 'for Christmas, not for life'. The host and I shared a fake laugh and then it was back to proper news for Sky and back to my hotel for me.

On the way 'home', I checked my Amazon pre-sales rank and discovered, to my delight that, on the basis of my performance, the popularity of *Bringing Nothing to the Party* had dropped by about 10,000 places. Had people actually cancelled their pre-orders after seeing me on television?

Rebecca was also doing a sterling job in drumming up well-known names to provide positive quotes about the book that could then be used on the cover and in marketing materials. She'd asked if I knew any successful authors and, as well as Zoe, I suggested that she should try Mil Millington, the comic novelist who wrote *Things My Girlfriend and I Have Argued About*.

I suggested Mil for two reasons: one, I've always enjoyed his writing and, two, we'd met a couple of times, including once at the launch party for a company I co-founded. Mil had taken great pleasure in mentioning my drunken behaviour at the party in his column for the *Guardian*'s weekend magazine. In fact, he wrote the episode in such a hideously libellous way that his editor had actually emailed me to check that I wouldn't sue. I'd assured the editor that I'd be on thin ice suing anyone over my drunken behaviour and the thing went to press unedited. Mil owed me a favour, and I sent him an email telling him that I was calling it in, in the form of a quote.

From: Paul Carr
To: Mil Millington

Hi Mil,

You know how ages ago you wrote that column in the *Guardian* about me being a flirtatious drunk? And you know how I was *outrageously* decent about it?

You've probably been feeling for these past years that you probably should do me some kind of enormous favour to make up for how *outrageously* decent I was that one time.

Well, good news! I've written this book about my failed attempt to become a web billionaire and it's going to be published by W&N in July and my publicist has asked me if I know any *A-list authors* who might flick through it with the view to possibly giving me a quote if it's any good. It's called *Bringing Nothing to the Party* and I'm quite proud of it.

What do you think? Can I get W&N to send you one? You can always burn the damn thing. No pressure.

Paul

Mil's reply was grudgingly accommodating . . .

From: Mil Millington
To: Paul Carr

My next book is also out in July. Way to dissipate their energy, Carr. You wanker.

My absolutely unshakeable, long-standing policy about quoting is that 'I don't quote on fiction.' Which you appear to have cynically avoided by doing something that's non-fiction. So, I suppose I have no choice but to read the damn thing, have I? Oh well, at least that'll give me the chance to rubbish it more authoritatively.

Mil

I later learned that I'd wasted a perfectly good favour: Mil is published by W&N and Rebecca is his publicity manager too. She could have ordered him to write the review. Still, a few weeks had passed since he'd received the manuscript and I was starting to wonder if he had indeed burnt it. For all my levity, Mil was someone whose opinion mattered to me. Various copies of the book had been floating around W&N and the majority of the feedback had been positive, but like most people who get paid for writing words I'd always suffered from hideous imposter anxiety; why on earth would anyone pay to publish my words?

Mil is a proper writer; if he liked the book and agreed to provide a quote for it then I could feel like I'd earned my place on the bookshelves next to him. If he hated it, then all my anxieties would be justified.

Finally, an email arrived from him. I could hardly bear to open it . . .

From: Mil Millington
To: Paul Carr

Well, Carr, I've finished reading your manuscript now. I have to admit that I was surprised and quite impressed at your partial success in faking a sensitive side – though this accomplishment will, of course, be lost on those who've never met you. Anyway: a quote.

Off the top of my head, I'm inclined towards: 'Carr's book astonishes with its seemingly pathological delight in defaming Islam.' The trouble with that is, I suspect you'd bury it somewhere inside rather than using it for the cover/posters/promotional button badges.

Alternatively, then, there's this: 'Made me want to vomit for all the right reasons.'

Now, I think that's great. I'd fellate someone through a hole in the wall of a public lavatory for a quote like that. It's arresting, usefully unlike the majority of the other quotes on the other books that will be all around it, and – best of all – is just unclear enough to be intriguing; one might be tempted to pick up and glance through a book with that on it simply to try to see what it might mean, exactly. But, I fear Weidenfeld & Nicolson – with its history and its book publishing mentality and its offices opposite the world's least prestigious nightclub – might find it 'too Internet'. I mean, if the book were a webpage it'd be 'Paul Carr: He's a Cunt' and everyone would snicker with approval. Paper publishing isn't like that, yet. Perhaps W&N wants a quote that's more straightforward, and less likely to get the book misfiled in Waterstone's under 'bulimia'.

So ... um. Maybe:

'Like Dragons' Den in a threesome with a society gossip page and the IT Crowd.'

Publishing loves things from off of the telly, and that mentions *two* things from off of the telly. Plus the word 'gossip'. It might be more to Orion's liking, therefore.

There you go, then. Except, it does occur to me that none of those quotes explicitly says it's amusing. If you wanted to go that way, there's:

'Carr is funny enough that you can almost forgive him.'

This also hits the 'intriguing' target mentioned above, but might be thought unsatisfactory for exactly the same reasons I mentioned, above.

Hell, just use them all; three attributed to made-up names deceptively close to actual ones – 'Steue Jobs', 'Marti N Amis' and 'Ricky Gervias', say. Whatever you fancy – I've got to mow the lawn. If I gave you more quotes would you come round and mow my lawn? No, you bleeding wouldn't, you indolent, garrulous fop: so – that's your lot.

Mil

Allahu Akba!

1009

As the book launch got closer, I decided to check out of the Raglan and move into somewhere more central. Having exhausted every option on Trip Advisor, I knew if I wanted to find a decent place in zone one, without paying more than £200 a night, there was only one possible trick left. Secret hotels.

Even the most popular upscale hotels have nights where they can't sell all of their rooms, but for obvious reasons they don't want to advertise that fact to the world. Instead, they offer the rooms for sale through 'secret hotel' sites, like Hotwire.com. Potential guests can search for hotels by general area ('central London, near Oxford Street') and by feature ('five-star quality, with gym') but until you confirm your booking, and pay for it up front, you don't find out the name of the place you're staying.

The nature of the secret sites, though – hotels use them only as a last resort – means that you can usually only book a room for one or two nights at a time. As a result, I found myself hotel-hopping like a madman for the next couple of weeks, moving to a new place every day – the Holiday Inn Bloomsbury one night, the Copthorne Tara Kensington the next; anything to avoid returning to the Easy Hotel.

One night I lucked out and ended up staying at the five-star Park Lane Hotel for £85. My average nightly rate over the fortnight was just north of £100, still way off budget. But at least I was staying in nice places – every day was an adventure, not knowing where I was going to end up.

Which is how I came to end up staying across the road from Karen's house.

1010

Karen was one of my reasons for leaving London.

She was the girl who, after the incident where she became BFFs with my other ex-girlfriend, had created an entire hate blog about me. More than that, to help with her plan to destroy my life, she was the girl who had spent weeks recruiting as many more of my ex-girfriends as she could find, as well as disgruntled former employees, people who I'd accidentally spilt drinks on in bars, people who thought I'd looked at them funny back in kindergarten; basically anyone who might still be holding a grudge against me and who might want to contribute to the blog.*

Let me be absolutely clear: I was a complete shit to Karen and I deserved every bad thing that she tried to do to me. In fact, over time, after I came out of witness protection, I had come to grudgingly admire her for taking such perfect revenge: going straight for where I would hurt the most – my ego.

But for all that admiration, I still had no desire ever to see her again. When I lived in London, even with eight million people in the city, I remained in constant terror any time I walked into a pub, or a shop, or a restaurant, fearing she'd be there. The girl had eviscerated me online; God only knows what she'd do in person.

Returning to London for a visit, though, I'd started to think differently. For a start, it was ridiculous that I was walking around the city in fear. Karen was a pissed-off ex-girlfriend, not a ninja assassin. Second of all, any anger she had towards me would probably have dissipated now; she'd stopped blogging abruptly a few months earlier, leading me to suppose that she'd found a new boyfriend and decided to give up her campaign against me. And thirdly, the whole thing was my fault. I'd hurt her. Hell, maybe it would be good if I did run into her; maybe it would give me a chance to apologise properly, to her face, like a man. To say 'Karen, I acted like a dick and I got the comeuppance I deserved. I'm truly sorry for the hurt I caused you.'

So, when lastminute.com's secret hotel booking system sent me the email confirming the name of my next secret hotel, and it turned out to be right across the street from Karen's house, my initial horror quickly turned to resolution. Clearly fate, and lastminute.com, had sent me some kind of sign. It was time to face my demons.

Unlike most of my ideas, the more I thought about this one the more certain I became. Rather than waiting for the inevitable accidental meeting, I should send Karen an email, telling her that

---

* The email right at the front of this book? Yep, that was from one of her contributors.

I'd accidentally ended up staying nearby – not across the street, that would just look mental – and suggesting a coffee. No, not an email – that was cowardly. I'd call her: I'd deleted her number from my phone but had kept it written down, just in case.

Yes, I concluded, calling Karen is the right thing to do. And had I been stone cold sober when I'd concluded it – and had it been, say, the middle of the afternoon, then I would probably have been right. But it wasn't the middle of the afternoon: it was midnight and I'd just got back to the hotel having spent the evening drinking with Robert.

She answered on the second ring.

'Hello?' The voice was instantly familiar. I was worried that she'd see my number and not pick up, but judging by her tone – curiosity, rather than concern – I wasn't the only one who had purged our relationship from their phone.

'Hi, Karen, it's Paul Carr,' I said, with possibly a little too much formality.

'Oh, hello,' she said.

This was a good sign. Anything less than 'go fuck yourself' was a good sign.

The conversation started out slow and stilted, as befitted a girl who had created a hate blog having just answered the phone to the object of her hate, at midnight. Oddly, though, once I explained that I was calling to apologise, she became surprisingly civil – chatty, almost.

'Are you drunk?' she asked.

'No,' I almost lied. The truth is, I'd sobered up the moment she answered.

We talked about her blog, and how it had succeeded in embarrassing me and making me feel ashamed of how I'd behaved. She seemed pleased by that, but not in the gloaty way I'd expected. If anything she sounded grateful. Grateful that I'd learned my lesson and that I'd been forced to think hard about the hurt I'd caused.

'Thank you for the apology,' she said, 'I appreciate it.'

I paused, knowing I should end the conversation there. I'd said what I needed to say and now she could go back to her life with – presumably – her new boyfriend and all would be slightly more right with the world than it had been a few hours earlier.

And had I been thinking about it stone cold sober in the morning, then that's probably what I'd have done. But I wasn't sober – not really – and it wasn't the morning.

'I'd really like to see you,' I said, 'I've missed you.' I really had.

'I don't think that's a good idea,' she said.

She was right. I pressed on.

'How about if I came round tomorrow and we had breakfast? I'd really like to apologise properly, to your face.'

'I really . . .' then a pause. 'OK, if you're really not drunk and you're not going to wake up at noon and forget this. Which is to say if any of what you've just said is true, then come over at ten. Bring bagels. And I'll listen to your apology.'

I could have cried.

'OK,' I said, 'I'll be there, I promise.'

I hung up. And then I cried; tears poured down my cheeks and I slumped to the floor in a mixture of relief, panic and a weird sense of joy at the possibility of making things better. I walked over to the minibar and poured myself a whisky out of one of the tiny bottles. My hands were shaking. It hadn't occurred to me that I'd ever be able to make things better with Karen, and now I had a second chance. All I had to do was make it to her house by 10 a.m. I drank the entire mini bottle of whisky in one gulp.

1011

I woke up to the sound of my phone ringing. I squinted at the screen. It was Robert.

'Hey, mate,' I said, 'how you doing? You'll never guess what I did last night?'

'Tell me over lunch,' he said. 'Ten minutes, at your hotel?'

'What?' I sat bolt upright in bed. 'What time is it?'

'About half twelve, why?'

Fuck.

'FUCK'.

1012

'You're unbelievable,' said Robert as we sat down to lunch at a French place a safe enough distance from my hotel. I'd tried to call Karen twice but, unsurprisingly, the calls had gone to voicemail after a couple of rings. How could I have been so stupid? I had drunk half the contents of the minibar to 'steady my nerves' before finally stumbling into bed and forgetting even to set an alarm.

'This is it,' I said, 'the final straw. I have to stop drinking.'

'After this bottle,' said Robert, filling my glass.

'After this bottle.'

1013

'OK, gents, time to make your way outside, please.'

The landlord of the Albert pub in Victoria had already stacked the barstools on the tables and was now getting twitchy. It was 11p.m. and Robert and I were the last to leave. The pub was near to Robert's halls of residence – we'd decided to head there after lunch so Robert could show me around – but we hadn't quite made it there, having been distracted by the pub. We'd spent the whole day talking about Karen and my idiocy. Specifically, I'd spent the day coming up with plans to try to fix things, while Robert had spent the day telling me why each of them was less brilliant than the last.

He was right – this was now definitely an unfixable situation, and one entirely of my making, again. Karen had given me a window of opportunity to make things better, and I'd got drunk and thrown a rock through it. The only thing left for me to do was to give up.

And had I been stone cold sober, and had it been the morning, then that's what I would have done.

1014

'Mate, this is the worst idea you have ever had. I'll say this again: I'm only here because I know you'll do something even more dumb if I leave you alone. But this — what you are doing now — is the dumbest thing you have done in your entire life.'

'It's fine,' I slurred. 'I need to do this.'

Robert was still appealing to my sanity by the time we got out of the cab, and, by the time I reached Karen's front door, he was all but physically restraining me from pressing the buzzer.

No answer.

I buzzed again.

Nothing.

'Come on, mate, let's go.'

But I was determined now, in that way that only the world's most drunken idiot could possibly be. Behind Karen's house was an alleyway, except that in the part of London where she lives alleyways are considered terribly common, so behind her house was a 'mews'.

I remembered that her living-room window backed on to the mews and figured that, maybe, if I knocked on that, she'd . . . well, I don't know. I wasn't exactly thinking straight.

I walked down the mews — Robert following behind — yelling now — 'THIS IS A TERRIBLE IDEA, STOP'. I knocked on the window.

Suddenly there she was. The back door of the house swung open, and there was the girl who for the past year had been my digital nemesis, but also the girl to whom I owed this apology.

'I . . .'

'What the fuck do you think you're doing?'

'I'm . . .'

'Just leave. Now. I mean it.'

'But, I . . .'

'And as for you . . .' she glared at Robert, 'I mean, him — *him* —

I expect this drunken bullshit from, but you – you should fucking know better.'

'I tried to stop him,' shrugged Robert, deciding that this would be the appropriate time to walk back to the main street and have a cigarette. He'd done everything he could.

'I just . . .'

'Leave now or I'll call the police. I really mean it.' She walked back inside, slamming the door. I knew she wouldn't actually call the police – she was just making a point – but I'd had my chance and I'd blown it. I stood in the mews for a few more minutes, calling through the window. She didn't reply. She'd probably gone to bed.

I started to walk back down to Rob. Which is when I saw the blue lights.

She'd called the police. Of course she'd called the fucking police.

I sobered up, or at least I thought I did, and decided that the best course of action would be to keep walking, and not to react in any way to the police car that was now slowly driving down the mews towards me. Hopefully, like in films, they'd assume I was just a drunk and cruise right past me. I still hadn't learned that the way things happen in films is rarely the way they turn out in real life: and, anyway, in this case the police were actually looking for a drunk.

The police car stopped right in front of me, and two policemen jumped out. Between the flashing blue lights and the speed with which they got out of the car, the police clearly take crazy drunk ex-boyfriends standing outside the houses of girls who live on their own very seriously. That fact actually made me happy, for a second, until I remembered that the crazy drunk ex-boyfriend in this situation was me. And that less than a week earlier I'd been given a caution. This was a complete and utter fucking disaster. Why hadn't Robert stopped me?

'Are you Paul?' shouted one of the policemen, even though he was less than five feet away.

'Uh, Paul?' I said. 'No, officer. My name's Bradley.'

A half lie: Bradley is my middle name.

'Do you have any ID?'

I reached into my pocket and took out my driving licence. My still-actually-quite-drunk-it-turns-out logic kicked in. 'See,' I said, pointing at my middle name on the licence. 'Bradley.'

The policeman looked at the licence and then looked at me. He'd seen some dumb lies in his time. 'Yeah,' he said, 'Paul Bradley.'

While I was being busted by the first policeman, I noticed Robert was talking to one of the others. They were both nodding, and I swear I saw the policeman laugh. My policeman wasn't laughing, though, he was on his radio. 'Yes, Charlie. Alpha. Romeo. Romeo. Paul Bradley. Date of birth 7 December 1979.'

A pause. His head was tilted towards the radio, waiting for the reply that would seal my fate. I couldn't make out what the radio operator said but he turned and walked back to his colleague who was now – definitely – sharing a joke with Rob. The three of them stood in their little huddle for maybe half a minute as I just stood forlornly, waiting.

Finally, my policeman came back. 'OK,' he said, 'your friend has explained the situation. Sounds to me like you do owe the poor girl an apology, but this isn't the way to do it. I've spoken to the station and they say there's no record of you, so as this is your first cock-up, and because Robert has promised he's going to take you home, we'll leave it there.'

I couldn't believe it. No record of me. Obviously the police hadn't had time to update their records since my arrest. Thank the lord. 'Thank you, officer,' I said.

'Come on, mate, let's get your stuff from your hotel,' said Robert. 'I'm checking you in at the student halls. I'm not letting you out of my sight until you leave London.'

1015

With the book launch just two days away, I decided that Robert was right: it would probably be a good idea to move into his halls. For one thing I was keen to see for myself what £35 could get you in London, but more importantly I was hoping that Robert would be close enough at hand to stop me should I get any more silly ideas about showing up at Karen's house.

As it turned out, the rooms weren't bad at all – nowhere near up to the standards of a hotel, but far better than I'd expected for £35. Still, having seen Hannah's reaction to the Easy Hotel, I'd have to remind myself not to bring any girls back from the Gardening Club after-party.

Hannah, at least, was unlikely to be the girl I brought back. After I'd drunk-dialled her ten times before being arrested, she'd decided that perhaps her initial assessment of me as a drunken dick might not have been entirely off the mark. We hadn't fallen out exactly, but nor did she have any desire ever to sleep with me again. We settled on being 'just friends'. Hard to blame her, really.

I considered writing a post on my blog about how London had forced me to make a brief transition from luxury hotel living to living like a student, but I decided not to. Part of the popularity of the blog, at least according to the people who emailed me about it, was the fantasy element. It's fun to read about someone travelling the world and living in amazing hotels and having madcap adventures. A £35-a-night student bedroom doesn't really fit into that narrative.

I mentioned this to Robert the night before the party, as we sat sharing a bottle of vodka in the student dining room. He was clearly concerned that I was starting to take myself a little too seriously.

'Jesus, mate, when did you start to care about "narratives"? I thought the whole point was you didn't think about things in advance. That certainly seems to have been the theme for the past couple of weeks.'

'Well, yes,' I said, 'but somewhere along the way I seem to have become some kind of cartoon character. People are reading my blog waiting for the next ridiculous fuck-up; that's what people keep commissioning me to write about too; the hotels, the drinking and the inevitable train wreck. That's what keeps my readers interested.'

'Your readers?' Robert handed me the vodka. 'Just for future reference, do you want me to draw attention to every milestone on your journey towards being a pretentious cock?'

'This is a case in point,' I continued, gesturing with the vodka bottle before taking a huge swig, 'I know logically I should give up drinking. It ends in disaster every time. But that's precisely why I can't – tomorrow night a bunch of people are going to come to a party celebrating the launch of a book about my disasters. It's the only thing I've ever succeeded at. I can hardly give it up. What would I have left then?'

'Your liver?'

1016

The launch party was a huge success, even if I do write so myself. Almost all of the fifty or so guests of honour from the book – those who were still talking to me – turned up, as did a smattering of journalists, my agent and at least fifty people I've never seen before in my life. Copies of the book were scattered around – and by the end of the night they had all been stolen, which I took to be a positive sign. On a giant screen, photographs of the various incidents recounted in the book rotated in a slideshow. I was drunk in every single one of the photos.

Towards the end of the night, my agent – who I suspect was there out of a sense of duty, rather than because I'm a particularly valued client – took me aside.*

'Good party,' he said, 'so, what's next?'

'Well, a few of us are heading to the Gardening Club to try to find some girls,' I said.

'That's nice,' he said, 'but I actually meant what's the next book idea?'

'Oh.'

---

* He's also called Robert, but I'll just refer to him as 'my agent' to avoid saddling you with another Robert.

This was actually a question that I'd been giving a lot of thought to; not least because now this book was published, I needed something to do with my life. I was making reasonable money from freelance gigs but I'd got a taste for being an author now – all Sky News appearances and quotes from Mil Millington – and was keen to stick with it. I had no shortage of ideas – a novel about British men and American woman, a guide to living in hotels, a cutesy observational book about Brits abroad – but most of them were terrible. I decided on the spot to combine them into one big idea and see if my agent thought any part of it had potential . . .

'Well, I've been travelling around for the past few months, living in hotels – and I've spent quite a lot of that time in the US. I thought I might write a novel about the differences between the US and the UK, with a special focus on American women versus their British counterparts. Maybe based in a hotel.'

'Hmm,' said my agent.

And he was right; every part of the idea was bad. That's why I hadn't sent him a proposal; I knew it still needed work. I needed a fresh angle.

'Wait,' he said, 'you've been living in hotels? Why? How?'

I began to tell him about the previous five months. 'It started when I got a letter from my landlord . . .'

. . . and then I woke up in the corridor . . .

. . . a suite in Vegas for $100 a night . . .

. . . just pretended we were hairdressers . . .

. . . got in free . . .

. . . thought Kate Bosworth was a waitress . . .

. . . doesn't work in London, though . . .

By the time I finished the story, he was laughing. Hard.

'That's great. Can you write it up as a proposal?'

'Write what up?'

'Everything you just told me – a guide to living in hotels and blagging your way around the world. All the crazy drunken stuff and the women and the fast cars – the works. Do you think you can keep up the pace for the rest of the year?'

I looked down at the glass of wine in my hand.

'Absolutely,' I said.

'Great – then get me the proposal together and I'll send it to W&N. Let's strike while the iron's hot.'

And that was that. The booze, the madness, everything: assuming W&N liked the proposal then for the next twelve months at least – perhaps even permanently – it would be my job to ensure it continued. I necked my whole glass of wine. I was destined to be a professional drunken dick. Give the people what they want, right?

'Oh,' said my agent, putting his coat on to leave, 'have you seen the publicity material Rebecca has put out about your book? It's rather good.' He handed me a piece of paper from his attaché case. I read the first line out loud.

'If Paul Carr didn't exist, Douglas Coupland would have to invent him.'

I laughed.

Douglas fucking Coupland.

Chapter 1100

A Finely Oiled Machine

December 2008. Five and a half months later.

'Are you here for the nature ... or the exchange rate?' asked the sign in the arrivals lounge of Keflavik airport.* To which the only sensible reply was: 'It's two days before the winter solstice, there are four hours of sunlight, it's minus three outside and you eat puffins. Yeah – I'm here for the nature; pass me a fork.'

I'd ended up in Iceland for a couple of reasons. Firstly, I'd just got back from another visa waiver-busting stay in the US and wanted to spend the couple of weeks before Christmas exploring a new place. Secondly, the country's banking system had crashed a month or so earlier, and every travel writer and her dog was hyping it as the place to go for a cheap weekend break. Sadly this information hadn't filtered through to Iceland itself, and the twenty-five-minute taxi ride from the airport into town cost me the best part of £70.

At least my hotel was cheap. There's little enough to do in Reykjavik at the best of times and as I was arriving during the week – so missing the weekend-break crowd – I was able to get a room for just slightly over my £50-a-night budget which, when you consider the costs of taking cabs is even higher than in London, represents amazing value. Another factor in reducing my rate was the fact that it was the eve of the winter solstice: Iceland's shortest, most miserable day.

---

* Actually, they should have signs like that in all airports: 'Welcome to Riyadh. Are you here to be beheaded over a minor drug offence or for the highly paid jobs?' Or: 'Welcome to Nottingham! Arson or old lace?'

No one said that writing a book about living in hotels would always be sunshine and roses.

1101

In the six months since *Bringing Nothing to the Party* had been published, my life had changed immeasurably. I'd gone from being Paul Carr, the failed business person, loser in romance and struggling journalist, to Paul Carr, the failed business person, loser in romance and struggling journalist who had written a funny book about it. That sounds like a tiny change in circumstances, but the effect had been dramatic.

Two days after the book arrived in the shops, I received my first piece of feedback from a total stranger: a woman called Ellie who had read it in one sitting, on a train journey from London to Edinburgh. Ellie had some questions, most of which concerned my relationship with my ex-girlfriend.

Up until that moment – and I realise how ridiculous this sounds – it simply hadn't occurred to me that anyone would read the book. And it certainly didn't register with me that many of the people who did read it would be total strangers. Thousands of total strangers, reading about my life.

Just before I left London after the launch, the head of a PR agency invited me to lunch. She wanted to pay me a small fortune to talk to her staff about how to use the Internet to make their clients look good, presumably on the basis that if I'd been able to – what was it Mil said? – partially fake a sensitive side, then my secret would probably work wonders for their clients. We arranged to meet at her office and the first thing I saw when I walked in was two neat stacks of my book – maybe ten or eleven copies in all – sitting on her desk. I must have cringed when I saw them because the agency head immediately apologised – 'sorry, I meant to hide those before you arrived. I've bought a copy for everyone in the company to get them up to speed with your story. Those are the spares.'

And so she had – I met maybe half a dozen of the agency's employees and every single one of them had reached a different part of the story. 'You've just left The Friday Project', 'you're hanging out at Adam Street', 'you've just split up with . . .' At lunch, every time I mentioned a friend by first name – Robert, Zoe, Michael – the agency head knew exactly who I meant. The guy with the flat in Soho, the outed sex-blogger, the tousle-haired candy guy.

It's hard to explain how that feels – meeting a group of people for the first time who already know everything about you including your friends, your arrest record and the tragic-comic circumstances in which you split up with your ex-girlfriends. Flattering, in a way, that they'd cared enough to keep reading. But also fucking terrifying. I suppose bloggers like Zoe must feel like that too, but it was genuinely new to me: I'd always been careful not to talk about anything on my blog that affected me emotionally, but for some reason I hadn't applied that filter to the book.

I'm not really sure why I felt more able to express myself honestly in print than online. The closest I've come to an explanation is that when I write online I get instant feedback in the form of emails or people posting comments. This drives home the fact that lots of people are reading and so makes me more likely to steer clear of touchy subjects. When I write for print, though, there tends to be a decent-length gap between writing and publishing, making it much easier to forget that there's a real audience. Because of that, I tend to write books with one person in mind; either an actual person or a fictitious reader.* It probably makes for pretty arrogant prose (my fictitious person always gets my jokes, no matter how 'in') but it's the only way I can avoid being crippled by uncertainty about what to include and what to leave out. The problem with that approach is that it makes it really fucking weird when someone who isn't that reader corners me and tells me that they've read the

* Of course, with this book, that reader is you. Unless you find that creepy, in which case it's the guy standing behind you. Don't look!

book. It wasn't meant for them. It was meant to be a private conversation, between me and my fictitious reader.

But here's the even weirder thing. After a few weeks, the weirdness – those daily surprises – had started to feel normal to me. The idea that my life – failures, fuck-ups and all – was literally an open book. I'd even got used to people I've never met feeling qualified to psychoanalyse me.*

Being aware that everyone knows all the embarrassing details of my life became incredibly liberating. For a start I stopped giving any thought to the consequences of telling the unvarnished truth on my blog; the more terrible the confession, the more people tuned in, and subsequently bought the book.

The same was true with my drunken behaviour in the months that followed the book launch. I'd always been a dick when drunk, but there had been consequences to that dickishness the next day: people who met me while I was drunk tended never to want to see me again. But after the book was published, all that changed: it didn't matter how outrageously I behaved, or how offensive or arrogant I acted, people would just laugh. 'You're such a dick,' they'd say, 'just like in your book.'

The weirdest example of that was when an editor from the *Guardian* had asked me to write a weekly column about my drunken travels through the world of technology. Or, more accurately, when I told an editor from the *Guardian* that I was going to write such a column, and he agreed to pay me for it.

Before the book, I'd had to beg for every single newspaper commission I got, and even then most of my ideas were turned down. But a few weeks after publication, I was ego-surfing for my own name on Google and I noticed that Charles Arthur, the paper's technology editor, had written about me. He'd read *Bringing Nothing to the Party* on holiday and had subsequently read a post on my blog about me crashing a major Internet conference, getting

---

* Nearly. Every time someone tells me that, actually, I'm wrong in describing *Bringing Nothing to the Party* as a business book when 'actually it's a love letter' to my ex-girlfriend, I still want to run screaming from the room.

blind drunk and setting up an impromptu drinking party in a promotional double-decker bus in the middle of the conference centre.

It was a story of dickish behaviour by any metric you care to use – I was eventually ejected when I decided to set fire to a straw hat – but, for Charles, it had made hilarious reading. In his review, he likened me to Hunter S. Thompson which made my now spiralling ego nearly burst out of the top of my head. I emailed him, thanking him for the review and telling him, in effect, that it was his lucky day. I had an idea for a weekly column about my 'gonzo adventures at technology conferences around the world' and I'd chosen the *Guardian* as my outlet. Amazingly he said yes.

We decided to call the column 'Not Safe For Work', both as a warning about its content and also as a reference to the fact that I had been fired from every job I'd ever had, including an earlier stint as a *Guardian* media columnist.

1102

Since starting the column, I'd been travelling non-stop, visiting a new place almost every week and waltzing into just about any conference, festival, party or event I liked. For the first time in years, I could use the *Guardian*'s name to get me into things, and not be lying.

I went to Paris for LeWeb, Europe's most prestigious Internet conference, where technology entrepreneurs and European leaders come together to educate each other about how the world works. It's a two-day event, but unfortunately my deadline fell at the end of day one. Unfazed, I simply wrote 1000 words about how I'd found the venue too cold, the speakers too boring and the wifi connection too spotty to bother sticking around. The correct response of Loic and Geraldine Le Meur, the husband and wife team who organise the conference, should have been to ban me from the event for life. But I was *that guy*: the technology columnist from the *Guardian* who got drunk, went to conferences and insulted everyone, so, instead of adding me to his *liste noire*, Loic invited me to come back the following year as a speaker.

Readers, too, who had every right to feel short-changed by my half-assed review that failed to cover a single minute of the scheduled programme, instead emailed me in their droves to say how brilliantly irreverent I was. Incredibly, rival conference organisers even emailed me to invite me to tear apart their conferences.

I made my second trip to San Francisco for TechCrunch 50, an annual conference organised by TechCrunch.com, the world's most influential technology news site. Entrepreneurs from around the world flock to the conference to pitch their business ideas to a panel of experts and investors. The best pitch is awarded $50,000 and is also heavily promoted on TechCrunch.com. The promotional attention is actually worth more than the prize money, given how TechCrunch is essentially the news site of record for Silicon Valley.

But instead of actually covering the conference, I decided to rent some space above a bar and put on my own event. Called Smack My Pitch Up, the idea of the event was for entrepreneurs – and anyone else who felt like it – to come on 'stage' and pitch the worst idea they could think of, to a panel of drunks. The event was a huge success, and my reputation as a traveling drunk was further assured.

Next I headed to Las Vegas for BlogWorld, an in-no-way-dorky-sounding event that brought together bloggers from across the world for a couple of days of ... well, I actually have no idea. I didn't in fact attend the conference. Rob and I had just decided to fly in for two days of sponsored parties.

An added bonus of BlogWorld was that Sarah Lacy was in town, hosting a promotional event for her book. Since our evening at Homestead the previous April, we'd kept in touch by email, regularly comparing notes on book sales and the weirdness of sudden semi-infamy. Since her South by Southwest interview, and the subsequent publication of *Once You're Lucky, Twice You're Good*, Sarah had been on a non-stop book tour – appearing at industry events, doing readings and generally being celebrated as the person who wrote the definitive book on Silicon Valley. Amusingly, whereas a few months earlier she'd been the interviewer at Mark Zuckerberg's keynote in Austin, now she was frequently the star of the show – being paid thousands of dollars to share her wisdom with attentive crowds.

I wasn't quite at the stage of being paid thousands of dollars to share my wisdom – largely because I had none – but, thanks to my column, I was certainly enjoying a growing level of online infamy for my irresponsible behaviour.

The inevitable meeting of worlds – Sarah's increasingly successful professional one and my increasingly successful unprofessional one – came at BlogWorld when I was invited to a party at the MGM Grand, hosted by a Silicon Valley PR man called Brian Solis. Sarah was guest of honour.

I, of course, had spent the entire day of the party drinking champagne in my hotel room, diligently not covering the conference. By the time I finally arrived at the MGM Grand, I was blind drunk; the kind of drunk which can only end in disaster. The party was outdoors, around a gigantic swimming pool. I remember staggering through the door and slumping down on a banquette underneath some kind of fabric tent. Waiters were milling around, carrying trays of champagne, but I decided to order an entire bottle for myself before thinking better of it. 'Make that two,' I slurred instead. Given that bottles of house champagne were $250, it's probably a good thing that Robert arrived when he did.

'He's probably had enough,' said Robert, cutting off the disappointed waiter, who had just been cheated out of – at least – a $100 tip.

'You're trashed,' said Rob.

'That I am, Robert. And I'm getting paid for it,' I said.

'You're also going to really piss Sarah off. This is her party.'

'Oh, shit, you're probably right' I said, reaching for the half-empty glass of champagne that someone had left on the table. 'Has she realised I'm drunk?'

'I imagine so. You spoke to her when you came in,' he said; 'you told her she looked nice and then asked where Sarah was.'

'Oh,' I said. 'That's not good.'

'No, it's not. Seriously, mate, you have to go somewhere and sober up.'

'I'll be fine.' I necked my glass of champagne as Robert walked away. A couple of minutes later I saw him talking to one of the bouncers.

Two men in black suits with plastic wires trailing from their ears appeared either side of me. 'Sir, can we speak with you for a moment?' said one. 'Just over here,' said the other, guiding me forcefully by the arm towards the exit.

As we neared the door, my drink-addled brain finally figured out what was going on. I saw Robert watching from beside the pool.

'You bastard,' I shouted, 'you asked them to throw me out? Are you serious?'

'It's for the best, mate,' he shouted after me as I was forcibly ejected on to the Strip. 'You'll thank me in the morning.'

'Like fuck I will – you fucking bastard. Judaaaaasss . . .'

Of course, I did thank Robert in the morning. Not only had he ensured I'd been thrown out of the party before I'd drowned myself in the pool – or debt– he'd also spent half an hour smoothing things over with Sarah.

She'd been, quite reasonably, upset at me turning up drunk in the first place, let alone having to be thrown out, but Robert had explained to her that I was just being 'Drunk Paul' – which is how he'd started referring to my most epic drunken behaviour. I was still a nice person when I was sober and, given this was a one-off incident – in Vegas of all places – Sarah should probably give me a pass, he argued. Just this once.

Fortunately Sarah and I had become good enough friends by this point that she agreed, although my behaviour would still cost me an apology lunch, champagne and a promise not to drink for the rest of the time she was in town. I agreed and, if anything, the incident actual made us even better friends, in the way that only twenty-four hours of grovelling apologies can.

Still, I knew I'd dodged a bullet: Sarah was one of the few people who didn't find my drunken behaviour hilarious. 'I mean,' she said, over our apology lunch, 'I just don't get why people encourage you to behave so badly. You're great fun sober, but it's like you feel that you need to get drink and act like a dick to keep up some image.'

'It's not like that at all,' I said, knowing full well that it was precisely like that.

1103

'We haff your room ready for you, Mr Carr,' said the receptionist in Reykjavík, with only the slightest hint of an accent. 'On the sixth floor. Would you like help with your bags?'

I gestured at the single small suitcase parked by my feet. 'I'll manage, thank you.'

She handed me my room keys and I headed to the elevator.

Once you've lived in hotels for a year – which in my case meant over fifty separate check-ins – you get the process down to a science. In the elevator I remove my keycard from its small cardboard folder. The room number is usually written in pen on a small flap inside, which I tear off and tuck into my wallet, behind my driving licence. Always in the same place.

Between the elevator and the room, I decide on a mnemonic to remember my room number, just as a back-up. There's nothing worse that getting back late at night and having either to fish around in your wallet for the scribbled number or – even worse – having to ask reception to remind you.

Room 689. Six eight nine. Heh; that's an easy one. With mnemonics, it helps to have a dirty mind.

I open the door of my room and put my suitcase on my bed. It looks like any other small bag on wheels, but it measures exactly forty-five linear inches, the maximum size for carry-on bags on most major airlines.

I'd dumped my old, much larger suitcase in London back in July.

I was bored of waiting at baggage reclaim for my gigantic case and I knew it was only a matter of time before an airline mislaid it. Given that I carried my entire life in that suitcase, losing it would be pretty disastrous.

Finding the perfect carry-on bag – small enough to fit in overhead lockers and yet with enough pockets and space inside that it would fit everything I needed – took the best part of a week of trawling the web. I read literally hundreds of reviews on travel websites before finally settling on one made by Samsonite.

While I waited for the bag to be delivered, I started the process of even further streamlining my life. I'd already been pretty ruthless when I moved out of my flat, selling or throwing away everything that I could possibly live without, no matter what its sentimental value. I'd kept – so I thought – only the bare minimum I needed to survive: clothes, toiletries, a couple of books, my laptop, my phone and various chargers, passport . . . But when I looked back at my first few months of living out of a suitcase, I realised that there were even more things that could go. For a start, there were clothes that I hadn't worn at all in the previous six months. I was carrying around a black business suit on the basis that at any moment I might be invited to an important meeting, a formal dinner or a funeral. In fact I had been invited to just one formal dinner since I'd left London, but one of the perks of being a writer – I'd discovered – is that you can turn up at almost any venue wearing jeans and trainers and people will just shrug. Given that the way I was going the next funeral I attended would be my own, the suit could probably go, which meant so could the shiny shoes. I ended up keeping just my one pair of Converse, which are the first thing I kick off and place side by side next to the door before I start to unpack the rest of my clothes.

If you're going to own just one pair of shoes, by the way, Converse are definitely the way to go. For a start they're perennially fashionable, like blue jeans, but also dirt cheap. When one pair wears out you can just throw them away and buy another; either an identical pair, or one in a different colour. Which is easy to do as every shoe shop in the world sells them. Thirdly, for some reason, places that ban trainers don't seem to mind Converse.

Back to the routine. I open the wardrobe and remove all of the coat hangers, throwing them on to the bed. Now I can start to unpack.

First the shirts: six of them, all dress shirts, which can be made to look casual or smart, as the need arises. Five black, one blue. I remove each one, unroll it (rolling is far better than folding) and place it on a hanger, before laying it on the bed.

Next I remove my two black cashmere jumpers – one V-neck, one polo neck – and my dark blue suit jacket. Like the shirts, these can all be made to look smart or casual. I hang the jacket on one of the hangers and put it in the wardrobe where the folds will quickly drop out; the jumpers stay rolled and I put them on the shelf inside the wardrobe, along with my four black and one grey t-shirts.

Socks: six pairs. Skimping on socks becomes annoying very quickly when you have to find a place to wash them. By having the same number of pairs of socks as you do shirts, you can always launder them at the same time.

One of my biggest clothing realisations was that I really didn't need more than two pairs of trousers: just a pair of jeans to wear every day and a second pair of light water-resistant trousers that could be worn on a beach, or while I was washing my jeans. I'm already wearing the jeans and I leave the beach trousers in the suitcase. I'm unlikely to need them in Iceland.

And that's it for clothes. As I packed them all into my small bag for the first time in London, and handed the rest to the woman in the charity shop down the road from Robert's halls, I felt a twinge of panic. Surely I'd regret this; surely I'd realise that I was missing something from my extreme capsule wardrobe. And yet, six months later, I'd never once found myself in need of any extra clothes. And if I did? That's what shops are for.

My laptop and chargers plus pens and notebooks and the other tools of my trade are packed in a separate laptop bag: a sturdy leather thing but one that is still light enough to act as a day bag.

On travel days, the bag also contains my leather passport wallet.

My MacBook Pro laptop takes care of all my work and entertainment needs – word processor, DVD player, stereo, television; all packed into one handy device. I don't store anything on the laptop itself though – I have a nasty habit of losing or breaking electronic equipment. Instead I use Google Mail for my email and Google Docs – Google's online office suite – to store all my files. If I lose or destroy a laptop, it doesn't matter. All of my files will still be waiting for me online when I buy a new one. I take a similar approach to entertainment too: using online music services like Last.fm to give me access to my music library from anywhere in the world, Netflix.com for movies and so on. Internet experts refer to a reliance on this kind of storage as 'living in the cloud', a phrase that has always appealed to me. Most normal people stopped at documents and music but by living in hotels, renting cars as I need them and generally having no ties, I was basically living my entire life in the cloud.

The only concession I make to the analogue world is books. I still like to read on paper, rather than on my laptop screen – but I have a rule that I never carry more than one at a time. Instead I'll buy a new book, read it and then, after scribbling a short message in the front – 'hope you enjoy this book. Chapter three is a bit crap, but it's worth sticking with', that kind of thing – I'll leave it behind, either on a train or at an airport or even in a restaurant for someone else to enjoy. Often I'll include my email address in the front, just to see if anyone replies. Someone did once; a man who picked up my copy of Christopher Buckley's *Boomsday* at Chicago O'Hare airport emailed to say it had helped him while away a four-hour delay. That made me happy. Still, at some point I'll probably relent and buy an Amazon Kindle or some similar ebook reader that reproduces the experience of reading paper on an electronic device. They are thinner than books and I've become obsessed with saving space.

The only other things in my suitcase are two waterproof toiletry bags; one containing actual toiletries and the other crammed full of things that I use to keep myself sane: a pack of playing cards, a couple of old notebooks, a spare British pay-as-you-go phone with global roaming for emergencies, condoms, and my one concession to sentiment: a champagne cork that reminds me of an incident with a girl in San Francisco.

I remove the first of the bags – the one containing actual toiletries – and head to the bathroom. I turn on the shower, twisting the controls to the maximum heat setting. (A smell of sulphur immediately filled the room. I smiled, remembering that Iceland runs entirely on geothermal energy. It's actually quite a nice smell when you get used to it, which is lucky as I'm pretty sure I'm going to end up going to hell one day. Room 689 has no bath, which would usually be grounds for an upgrade, but I was in a hurry, and the room is otherwise great so I let it go.)

I never carry shampoo, shower gel or any of that stuff. There isn't a hotel in the world that doesn't provide it. Same with soap and most of the other things that usually go in toiletry bags. I remove my white King of Shaves razor – made entirely of plastic, except for the thin blades: when you carry only hand luggage you can't afford anything that's going to upset the x-ray machines at airports – and place it on the sink next to a tiny bottle of shave gel. Next to that goes my hair wax – again, no big bottles of gel or liquid for the x-ray – and a tiny tube of toothpaste and travel toothbrush. And finally a pair of nail clippers and some tweezers. That's everything. Anything else I might need – headache tablets, spare razor blades, whatever – can be picked up at any shop in any town; there's simply no need to add the extra weight or take up the extra space.

By now, the shower should be boiling hot. I head back out to the room and pick up the pile of shirts from the bed. Cramming everything in hand luggage means that they're creased to hell but a few minutes in a bathroom full of steam will take care of that. I hang the shirts up around the bathroom, as close to the shower as possible.

Finally, I unpack my laptop bag, putting the laptop on the desk and plugging it in to charge. My phone charges via the laptop so

I plug that in as well. I open the laptop and try to connect to the Internet, hoping that the wifi actually works.

Finally, I remove the passport wallet from its zipped compartment and put it in the safe in the room. Along with my passport, the wallet also contains my spare debit card – connected to a UK account with exactly £1000 in it. Along with the £50 note and the $100 bill wrapped around the card, it's my emergency 'get-the-hell-out-of-here' money. The safe, like most modern hotel room safes, asks me to choose a four-digit access code. I close the door, enter the code – the same one I always use – and the lock whirs into place.

I've arrived.

1104

I looked at the time: 6p.m. I was meeting my guide to the city in a bar across the street at 6.30. My entire unpacking process had taken less than five minutes, exactly the same amount of time as it would take me to repack in a few days. That's the beauty of having a system.

I closed the curtains – it had been dark outside for hours already – took off the clothes I'd been travelling in and threw my shirt and socks in the laundry bag that I'd found in the wardrobe. I quickly ticked the relevant boxes: wash and press, next-day return, and left the bag by the door ready to drop at reception on my way out.

Just time for a shower to freshen up after the flight before another evening of madness masquerading as work. I was due to file my *Guardian* column the next morning: 900 words that would justify my entire trip.

The bar was literally across the street from the hotel, and so I was actually a few minutes early. I ordered a drink from the barmaid, who spoke perfect English, as everyone in Reykjavik does. I opened my notebook and began to scribble a few notes. Apart from the fact that Björk is from there, nobody in the UK knows anything about Iceland so I decided to list a few of the facts I'd learned from the guidebook that I'd bought at the airport. That'll be half a column, right there, I thought.

Fact One: the locals eat sharks and puffins. The puffin, by the way, is the only animal in the world that doesn't taste like chicken. By all accounts it's disgusting, but not as disgusting as shark – which emits a smell so putrid that there was a little picture of a gas mask next to it on the bar's snack menu.

Fact Two: almost all of the energy in Iceland is geothermic. This means there's no pollution, electricity is as cheap as water – and the water stinks of sulphur. If Dennis Nilsen had lived in Iceland, he'd never have been caught.

Fact Three: Iceland operates a visa waiver scheme for travellers that was described in my guidebook as 'similar to that operated by the USA'. And, indeed, the empty arrivals hall and unbelievably lax immigrations process at Keflavik International Airport echoes almost exactly that of JFK. If JFK were to be hit with an apathy bomb, planted by Stephen King's Langoliers.

Fact Four: on Saturdays and Sundays, the bars and clubs – each within walking distance of the others – stay open until 6 a.m. This makes me suspect that the reason booze is taxed so highly is to keep British stag weekenders away. After all, it's freezing cold, it's dark and the locals try really hard to speak intelligible English. Take away the ridiculous cost of getting wasted and Iceland is basically Birmingham.

Fact Five: Iceland has a surprisingly large number of Internet companies for a country with only 320,000 inhabitants, roughly the same number of people as live in Cardiff. I had a feeling that there was a fascinating story to be told about the country's growing entrepreneurial class, fuelled by the scores of technically skilled, highly motivated workers being laid off by the banks. To find out more I'd put out a message on Twitter asking whether any locals might be willing to meet me for a drink while I was in town and give me the low-down.

The first to reply was Brian Suda, a displaced Missourian now working in Reykjavik as a software developer, and it was he I was now waiting to meet. Having read all about my penchant for drink, he'd suggested his favourite bar – which happened to be within staggering distance of my hotel – as the ideal meeting place.

Unfortunately, Brian's alcohol-related suggestions didn't stop there.

'Why the hell are you drinking that?' he asked when he arrived, pointing at my beer.

'I asked for something local, and this is what they gave me. It's called "Viking". It sounded Icelandic.'

'They thought you were a tourist,' said Brian.

'I am a tourist,' I said, tucking my Iceland tourist guidebook into my coat pocket.

Brian shook his head and headed to the bar, returning with two small shots of what looked, to my naïve eyes, like vodka. 'This is "Brennivin",' he explained. 'It's a local schnapps that literally translates as "burning wine"' (an alternative name, according to my guidebook, is *svartidauði*, or 'black death').

'It's nice,' I said, necking the contents of the shot glass.

A waitress walked past. 'Two more,' said Brian.

Two hours later and the burning wine had done its work. All thoughts of technology were forgotten and Brian and I found ourselves standing at the back of another bar. Somehow we'd ended up at a gig by Magni Ásgeirsson.

Ásgeirsson, in the unlikely event that you haven't heard of him, is famous – in Reykjavik – as the only Icelandic contestant of the American reality show *Rock Star: Supernova*. In case you missed that too, the show's 'aim' was to find a lead singer for a new rock supergroup featuring Mötley Crüe's Tommy Lee and former members of Metallica and Guns N' Roses. Ásgeirsson made it all the way through to the final, largely because the entire population of Iceland set their alarm clocks for the middle of the night local time to phone America and vote for him. Sadly, as the entire population of Iceland is less than the population of the town of Colorado Springs, Colorado, Magni finished in fourth place and is now back playing gigs in local Reykjavik bars. Bars like the one Brian and I had found ourselves standing at the back of.

The gig was actually rather good, if you like Icelandic hard rock, played at ear-splitting volume in a nearly empty bar on a Tuesday, which – after half a bottle of Brennivin – I did. But after a few more shots of black death, washed down with a pint or two of Viking beer to sober me up a bit, I decided that Ásgeirsson must be fed up with playing his usual rock set every night and wandered up to the stage with a few requests.

'You haff a request?' growled Magni. 'Yes,' I said. 'I'm a journalist from England, writing about Icelandic musicians and I . . .' Magni's face brightened and he reached out and grabbed my hand. 'A journalist! From England! Welcome to Reykjavik – I see you have been enjoying our Brennivin.' Another shot had somehow materialised in my hand. 'I would be glad to play your request. What is it?'

Now, I'm prepared to admit that the fault here was all mine. I should have requested something clever and hard and rocky – but the problem is, I'm not really a hard rock person. I'm more of a middle-of-the-road, dorky guys with acoustic guitars kind of person. I always told myself that it was a question of knowing my enemy: that by liking bands that American college girls like – Matchbox Twenty, Hootie and the Blowfish, REM – I would benefit from some kind of special we-have-so-much-in-common power that I could use to woo those same girls. The truth is, though, I just have really girly taste in music.

My drunken amusement at the idea of interrupting an Icelandic rocker and asking for a song request hadn't stretched as far as actually thinking of what song I wanted him to play. I wasn't expecting him to be so accommodating. Bloody Icelandic hospitality.

'Umm . . .' I said, and then blurted out the first song that came to mind. A favourite song of my ex-girlfriend, unsurprisingly.

He looked at me for a moment, with an expression that clearly said 'are you kidding me?' But then he shrugged. 'Hokay,' he said, 'I try my best.' Satisfied, I went back to Brian.

And so it was that one of my last clear memories of the night is of a shaven-headed semi-celebrity Icelandic rocker clearing his throat, apologising (in English) that 'I'm a little rusty because I haven't played this since school', picking up an acoustic guitar from a case behind a speaker and breaking into the jaunty opening bars of 'Mr Jones' by Counting Crows.

'Maybe we should have pushed his repertoire to "Hotel California",' said Brian before wandering to the bar to see if they had any shark meat for me to try.

1105

Fact Six: unsuccessful 4 a.m. drunk dials to old flames to tell them about how you convinced an Icelandic rocker to play Counting Crows are even more painful to recall the next day when you realise you made them from Iceland, to America, using a UK cellphone.

I woke up in my hotel room; in my bed; and without any strange Icelandic girls. I won't pretend I wasn't slightly disappointed, but I comforted myself with the thought that I at least had enough material for an amusing column about Reykjavik.

I padded over to my laptop and checked my email. It was just after 1 p.m., and outside it was already starting to get dark, which did little to lighten my hangover. Overnight, more Icelanders had emailed to offer their services as tour guides, but my headache told me that I'd probably brush them off and instead spend the rest of my trip recovering in one of the many thermal pools that litter the landscape like hot tubs for giants.

The only other interesting email was from Sarah. I'd last seen her a month or so earlier when she'd made a trip to London to launch the UK edition of her book. As a final act of compensation for my behaviour in Vegas I'd agreed to help Robert interview her on stage at the launch event. Since bonding over their disapproval of Drunk Paul, Robert and Sarah had become good friends too and so she had entrusted him with choosing the venue for the event. Which is how we'd ended up interviewing one the most successful women reporters in a male-dominated industry onstage at the Soho Review Bar – one of London's oldest strip clubs.

Fortunately Sarah, Robert and I share a similar sense of humour so – given my hideously misogynistic comments about her South by Southwest interview earlier in the year, Sarah seemed to think Robert's choice of venue strangely appropriate. 'Maybe you could wear a short skirt and flirt with me?' she suggested.

'Maybe you could fuck off,' I retorted, cleverly.

And now, according to her email, Sarah was heading back to Vegas in January, to appear at the Consumer Electronics Show – the gadget industry's biggest event of the year. Finally prepared to risk another encounter with Drunk Paul, she wondered whether I was going to be there too, given that it seemed like my kind of event: booze, booth babes and cheap hotel rates.

I hadn't planned on being in Vegas, but I was definitely overdue a trip to San Francisco, given that it had been – oh – at least two months since my last visit. It occurred to me that going to Vegas would also provide the perfect excuse for a stopover in my favourite city on earth.

By now I was head over heels in love with San Francisco, partly for work reasons, partly because it's a beautiful city, but also in large part because of the women. As a British writer, covering technology, for a famously liberal newspaper I represented a pretty good trifecta for the huge number of liberal, arty girls who worked in and around Silicon Valley. There was one girl in particular, Kelly, who I'd been seeing quite a lot of on my regular visits; a few days with her in January would be a pretty good way to start the year.

I was looking forward to seeing Sarah again too. After London, she'd just about forgiven me for my behaviour on the first trip to Vegas, and if I could prove that I was able to return to the scene of the crime and actually behave myself, then hopefully the incident could be put to rest for good. It was strange, especially given my occasionally misogynistic attitude towards women, but I really wanted her to respect me.

I took another look out of my hotel window, at the snowy gloom of December in Reykjavik and hit the reply button on Sarah's email. 'Sure,' I wrote. 'Overdue a trip to SF, and Vegas is always fun.'

Chapter 1200

Change I Could Believe In

I flew into San Francisco, after an overnight stay in London, on New Year's Day 2009. I'd decided to catch the 10 a.m. flight from Heathrow knowing that, this being the most hungover day of the year, the plane would be almost empty.

I had a six o'clock wake-up call so had decided to go easy on booze the night before. But — who was I kidding? — it was New Year's Eve in London so I'd finally fallen into bed at about 4.30 a.m., with a Canadian girl called Alana who I'd first met a few months earlier at my book launch. I decided to let Alana sleep as I finally stumbled out of the door and into my cab to the airport at 8 a.m. It was a classy move, taking a girl back to my hotel and then fleeing the country a few hours later.

I wrote her a note on hotel stationery; I have no idea what it said, nor do I remember the cab ride, check-in, security or take-off. In fact, I didn't sober up until I was at 36,000 feet when an angel of a flight attendant shook me on the shoulder. 'Excuse me, sir,' she said. 'There are three free seats up front if you'd like to lie down across them.'*

That's how ill I looked.

Ten hours later, I'd made it through immigration and checked into my usual room at the York Hotel. Except now the hotel wasn't called the York, and my room looked anything but usual. After six months of renovations, the whole place had been restyled as 'Hotel Vertigo', complete with décor themed around the movie. Swirls in the paintwork evoked the look and feel of the opening titles,

---

* A 'ghetto upgrade' in traveller slang.

original movie posters adorned the hallways and, just in case the theme was lost on guests, the movie itself played on a constant loop on the lobby's flatscreen TV. The new rooms were beautiful too, with gigantic king-sized beds and Egyptian cotton sheets, free Voss water and high-end toiletries. Two freakish, but somehow beautiful, porcelain lamps in the shape of horses' heads stood beside the bed. Wrong movie, I thought.

What with the hangover, the early start, the jet lag and the flight time, I couldn't wait to climb into one of those new beds. I unpacked my suitcase – taking exactly five minutes, as always – and checked my email. There was the usual mix: spam, messages from readers of the column, questions about the book – but one email in particular looked like it might be important. Not least because the subject line simply contained the word 'IMPORTANT!' in capitals. It was from Anna, who I hadn't seen since I generously bought her and Drew a new door.

I clicked to open the message, hoping there wasn't a problem with the door. There wasn't – unless you count the fact that a few hours earlier a policeman had knocked on it, asking whether Anna knew of my whereabouts.

Why the police were looking for me, Anna had no idea, nor could she understand why they thought they might find me hiding out at her house.

Still, Anna is a loyal friend and, as it turned out, the perfect criminal's moll, cunningly palming the policeman off with the truth: that I didn't live in her house, that I was out of the country and that she hadn't seen me in months. This failed to satisfy him, though, hence her email. The policeman had left a number. 'If you hear from him, tell him he's in a whole lot of shit' were (Anna swore) his exact words.

Hmmm.

Obviously the police had gone to Anna's because that was the address they had from when they arrested me there – but why in the name of fuck were they looking for me now? I racked my brains for any possible way in which it could be good news. Did the police come round to deliver news of lottery wins? No. Had I lost a dog that they might be returning? No. Also, none of those scenarios would explain the words 'he's in a whole lot of shit'.

Shit.

Shaking with a combination of tiredness, hangover and absolute terror, I dialled the number Anna had given me in her email. It was a mobile number, but as it was already 11 p.m. in London I wasn't expecting anyone to answer.

'Ello ...? Ello?' said the voice on the other end. I swear that's how the policeman answered the phone. If I hadn't been in such a panic, I'd have laughed.

I laughed anyway.

'Ell ... er ... hello,' I said, 'this is Paul Carr. I think you were looking for me earlier?'

'Oh yes, Miiiissster Carr,' said the policeman in a way that reminded me rather too much of my old headmaster just before he was about to give me a detention. There was a rustling of papers. 'My name is DC Jamieson from Bethnal Green police station, and I'm investigating a burglary two weeks ago in east London.'

A burglary? What the hell?

He continued: a month or so earlier, a flat near Liverpool Street had been robbed while the owners were out of the country. The police had dusted for fingerprints and, much to DC Jamieson's evident glee, they'd found mine all over the place. What with me having now fled the country, it was pretty much an open and shut case. Except for the slight detail that I'm not a burglar, and was pretty certain I'd never been to the address he gave me – I don't know anyone who lives near Liverpool Street. Oh, and at the time of the burglary I was in Iceland, getting drunk in the company of Magni Ásgeirsson.

'I'm afraid you've got the wrong person,' I said. 'I've never even been there.' Which in hindsight was exactly the wrong thing to say, given that they'd found my fingerprints on every surface. How, I wondered, could they not find my police record that night outside

Karen's house when they had my full name and date of birth, but apparently they had me bang to rights over fingerprints in a place I'd never been to?

'Well, clearly you have been there,' said the policeman, 'and also, are you sure you're not in the UK at the moment?'

I looked out of the window at the San Francisco bus trundling by. Somewhere in the distance I think I heard a sea lion bark. 'Pretty sure, yes.'

'Well then, how,' – he paused for what I imagine was dramatic effect, but could equally have been a sip of tea – 'do you explain the fact that you're calling me from a UK mobile number?'

I took a minute – more like five minutes, actually – to explain the concept of international roaming to the *detective* constable. He seemed unconvinced at first that one could make transatlantic phone calls on a mobile, but when I finally offered to call him back from the hotel landline he went back to his main line of questioning.

'So if you're so smart, how do you explain your fingerprints being at the scene?'

'I can't,' I said, 'I honestly can't think when I might have been in a flat in that part of London – unless – wait, what did you say the place was called again?'

Another rustling of papers. 'City Reach . . .'

I typed the words into Google Mail's search box, and a few seconds later I laughed again.

'I don't see how this is a laughing matter.'

'I do.' I also knew why the name seemed familiar. Back in November, America had elected Barack Obama as their new President. I'd been back in London on election night and my friend James and I had hosted a live 24-hour webcast covering the voting and results. City Reach wasn't a private flat at all, but, rather, part of the serviced apartment block – a pseudo hotel designed for business people who want a more homey environment than a Marriott or a Hilton – that we'd used as our base of operations. Of course my fingerprints would be there: I'd spent more than twenty-four hours in the place, writing, filming and occasionally sleeping. 'Did the owner happen to mention that their 'flat' was basically a hotel?' I asked the still confused policemen.

More rustling. 'Uh, no . . . he didn't. It's registered as a 'dwelling'. OK, well, if what you're saying is true then all we'll need you to do is come in next week and make a statement so we can check out your story.'

'Uh,' I said, 'I'm about six thousand miles away, and will be for a few weeks, so unless you're planning to come and pick me up by private jet, that's probably not going to happen.'

'Well, until then it's just your word against the evidence. Do you have any witnesses to back up your story about why you were in the . . . dwelling?'

I laughed for a third time. The whole election coverage had been broadcast, for twenty-four hours straight, on the web. Not only did I have the footage on my laptop, but about a few hundred thousand witnesses watching online could back up my story. And then there was the small matter of an Icelandic rock star who could give me a cast-iron alibi for the night of the robbery, a night I'd written all about in the *Guardian*. It was like an episode of *Columbo*, I had so many public alibis.

DC Jamieson wrote all of this down and promised to call me back once he'd checked my story. He never did.

After I put down the phone, I was still laughing. All of this was happening because I'd been wrongly accused – not once, but twice – of deliberately dodging cab fares. Now, because the police had my fingerprints on file, I was being wrongly suspected of burglary. It was a classic story of wrongly accused criminality: from not committing petty crime, I'd graduated to not committing increasingly more serious crimes. In a few years, unless I seriously didn't change my ways, there was a real risk I'd end up not in jail for not committing arson – or perhaps even not-murder.*

---

* I blame the fact that I didn't grow up without a strong father figure, and my lack of not having a decent education. School of soft knocks, that's me.

1201

Two days later, I took the short flight from San Francisco to Las Vegas for the Consumer Electronics Show. It's a two-day event and my plan was to spend the first day avoiding the conference, getting happily drunk and generally doing everything I needed to do to write my column. The second day I'd do the actual writing of the thing, leaving me free the second night to catch up with Sarah for dinner before maybe heading to one of the after-parties. By limiting most of my drinking to the first night, I could safely avoid a repeat of my last time in Vegas, or at least avoid Sarah witnessing it.

That part was critical.

1202

'I was down at the New Amsterdam, starin' at this yellow-haired girl . . .'

I'd been in town less than twelve hours and my cocktail of feelings as I stood in the nightclub at the Luxor Hotel was hard to break down precisely. Perhaps one part *déjà vu*, to one part heartbreakingly nostalgic, to one part trapped, to two parts what in the name of sweet Jesus am I doing here?

'Mr Jones strikes up a conversation with a black-haired flamenco dancer.'

Déjà vu, certainly. It was, after all, the second time in a month that I'd heard someone giving a live rendition of 'Mr Jones' by Counting Crows.

'You know, she dances while his father plays guitar . . .'

As for the heartbreaking nostalgia, as I said, the song is one that always reminds me of my ex-girlfriend. An ex-girlfriend who frequently made it clear during our relationship that if Adam Duritz, the band's lead singer, was to so much as glance at her, she would dump me like a hot shit-covered potato and retire with all haste to his hotel room for the rest of her life. Combine that fact with how badly our relationship had ended and, unless I'm paralytic on burning wine, the merest note of one of their songs is enough to make me want to throw myself off a bridge.

'... *and so, she's suddenly beautiful ...'*

And I was certainly trapped. Whereas in Iceland I was standing at the back of a bar, this time I was right at the front, pressed hard against the low stage and unable to move in any direction. The room was full to bursting point and I was wedged in so tightly that escape was impossible. And as if all that wasn't weird enough, on this occasion, rather than being serenaded by a bald Icelander, the person doing the singing – standing right on the edge of the stage, not two feet in front of me – was my cooler, richer, more talented nemesis: Adam fucking Duritz himself.

Which just leaves the question of what in the name of sweet Jesus was I doing there?

1203

The Luxor is an odd hotel: from the outside it looks amazing – a gigantic pyramid of black glass, with a bright white spotlight bursting from the top: bright enough, they claim, that one could use it to read a newspaper two miles up in space. The shape of the building means the elevators have to travel up and down the sides at a forty-five-degree angle. It's all very impressive.

Inside, though, it's a slightly different story. For a start, the Egyptian theme collapses almost immediately when guests are confronted with the enormous – and I mean enormous – American flag hanging from the ceiling. It's as if the designers were concerned that, without the flag, American guests would stay away, worried they were somehow supporting terrorism by booking into an Arab-themed hotel.

Beneath the flag, a big section of the lobby is taken up with a food court including Starbucks and a McDonald's, each with a line of obese tourists waiting to pay inflated Vegas prices for food they could buy in any other city on earth. The rooms themselves are fine – decent even – but once you take away the fact that you're in a pyramid in Vegas, there's nothing in them that you wouldn't find in a mid-range Holiday Inn. Still, I hadn't chosen the Luxor for its rooms, I'd chosen it because it was the venue for several of the CES after-hours parties, including the main Intel-sponsored one at the end of the first day which – according to the online chatter – was the must-attend party of the conference.

I'd spent the whole of the first day, as planned, doing absolutely no work whatsoever. I'd watched a *Monk* marathon on TV in my room at the Luxor (only $95 a night, even with the conference going on – viva Las Vegas) before ordering room service for lunch and spending the rest of the afternoon drinking champagne while idly checking Twitter updates from actual attendees to see if there was anything I might possibly write about. I'd made a few notes, but I still didn't have anything approaching an angle for the column. Had I actually bothered to go to the conference, I would have discovered that there was actually no shortage of angles: CES was sharing a venue with the Adult Video Network conference – a convention for porn stars. You live and learn.

But, anyway, by the time I left the room it was almost 6p.m. I'd just have to hope I found something useful to write about at the Intel party, assuming I could first figure out a plan to blag my way in. And what better place to come up with that plan – I decided – than over another glass of champagne, in one of the hotel's bars. I put on my party shoes, which is to say my only shoes, and headed down in the forty-five-degree elevator to the lobby.

The party was due to start at 7.30 and by 7.15 I was almost out of ideas. I'd spent over an hour on my phone, emailing every contact I knew who might be able to help – people who I knew were in town, Intel PR people – but an entry wristband remained elusive. If I didn't get a reply soon then I'd have to chance it on the door, which, given how exclusive the party was supposed to be – people had been bitching online all day that they couldn't get on the guest list – could very easily end in embarrassment. There were at least 1000 journalists in town covering CES so my 'I'm a journalist' card probably wouldn't work either. Seven thirty came, then 7.45 ... still no replies. It was hopeless.

'Hey!'

I looked up, expecting to see a waitress pestering me to buy another Egyptian-American-themed drink. But it wasn't a waitress.

'Sarah! I wasn't expecting to see you until tomorrow.' I looked guiltily at my glass of champagne. I was still almost sober, by my standards at least. Thank God.

'I'm just on my way to dinner. What are you up to?'

'I'm trying – and failing – to find a way to crash the Intel party.'

'Are you kidding? The one that Counting Crows are playing at? Why would anyone want to see Counting Crows?' And then her face turned to pity. 'Oh, yes, I forgot about your girly taste in music.'

'Well, quite.' Actually, I had no idea Counting Crows were playing, but a column's a column. 'I'm pretty sure I'm not getting in though.'

'You can have my wristband if you like.' She reached into her purse and pulled out the neatly folded strip of paper. 'I can't imagine anything worse.' I could have hugged her – but that would have wasted valuable seconds. It was almost eight o'clock and, assuming Counting Crows would be on stage around nine, I only had an hour left to work the room, getting the information I needed for my column and then escaping before I was punched in the ears by musical memories of my ex-girlfriend. There was no time to lose.

Fast forward half an hour and my work was done. Sarah's wristband had allowed me to go straight to the front of the queue and, with a single lap of the crowded club, I'd spoken to half a dozen of the attendees and had scribbled a list in my notebook under the heading 'everything you need to know about CES 09'.

Mobile computing company Palm were launching a new phone, apparently, and Microsoft were talking about a new version of Windows. Various companies were launching new flatscreen TVs. All very dull, but enough hard facts to wrap up in some colour about Vegas and the Luxor and my having to escape from the venue before Counting Crows began playing.

And so that was that: in just half an hour my entire week's research was done, leaving the whole of the next day free to write up the column before a catch-up dinner with Sarah and then a flight back to San Francisco the next morning. And, more importantly, I'd avoided having to see Counting Crows. I was just drunk enough to be emotional and the last thing I needed was to have to actually watch Adam Duritz singing my ex-girlfriend's favourite song. I headed for the door.

And I *almost* made it. But just as I was passing the stage, I felt a tap on my shoulder. It was Brian Solis, the PR guy who had organised the party I'd nearly ruined during my last trip to Vegas. The room had really started to fill up in anticipation of Counting Crows, so Brian was saving himself a spot right at the front of the stage; apparently he's a huge fan. Given my behaviour at his party, I figured the least I could do was to buy him a drink to say sorry. He gladly accepted, we shared an apology-forgiveness hug and I ran to the bar. I reckoned I could still make it out before the show; or at worst I'd have to suffer through one song.

By the time I'd made it back, forcing my way through the crowd with the drink held above my head, the club had filled to capacity. And that's when it happened – the exact moment I handed Brian his drink right at the very front of the room, the stage lit up and the whole crowd surged forward, pinning me to my spot. I was right at the front of the stage and I literally couldn't move in any direction.

'*Sha la lalalalala.*'

Of *course* they opened with 'Mr Jones'. But still, as Counting Crows worked their way through a set list consisting almost entirely of my ex's favourite songs, each of them sung straight into my face by the man she'd have left me for in a heartbeat, I managed to force a smile. This would certainly be colour for the column, and not only had I managed to get through an entire day in Vegas without being thrown out of anywhere but I'd caught up with Sarah – sober enough not to offend her again – and had even had a chance to apologise to Brian. See! I could do it if I tried: have fun, get work done, spend much of the day drinking and still not alienate any of my friends.

You know what happened the next day.

Of course you do.

1204

The day started fine. I woke up around noon – a slight hangover, but nothing ridiculous – and wrote up the column as planned. I had to start early as the time difference meant that my 6 p.m. London deadline was in effect a 10 a.m. Las Vegas deadline. Having finally filed around 3 p.m. local time – only five hours late – I spent the rest of the day soberly wandering around Vegas, hunting for porn stars, wasting money at the blackjack tables and generally enjoying the most ridiculous city on earth without getting drunk. I was due to meet Sarah for dinner at seven so fortunately I didn't have a huge amount of time to kill.

At about 6.30 my phone rang. The caller ID said 'Sarah Lacy'.

'Hey! Listen,' she said, without even waiting for me to say hello, 'I'm really sorry to do this but I've been invited to this journalists' dinner thing that I really should go to. The good news is it's in your hotel – is there any chance we could meet for a quick drink afterwards instead of dinner? Champagne is on me.'

'Of course, no problem – I'll just grab dinner somewhere and then find a bar to hang out until you're finished. Call me when you're done.'

'Perfect.'

And it was: the perfect plan. I went back to my room, had a shower, ordered another room-service burger and then fired up Twitter to see where the conference parties were. Mainly because I wanted to avoid them. Instead, I wanted to kill the few hours before meeting Sarah seeing some of the real Vegas; hanging out with some locals, maybe running into a porn star – that kind of thing. There was a bar downtown that I'd been meaning to try out – the Double Down Saloon – where they served a lethal cocktail called 'Ass Juice', and according to the chatter online was where some of the stars of the AVN conference were heading tonight. Porn stars drinking Ass Juice: that's the stuff amusing columns or blog posts are made of. I'd just head down there, have a couple of drinks and wait for Sarah to call.

1205

Noon.

It was checkout time at the Luxor, but my flight back to San Francisco left at 10 a.m. So why, then, was I just now waking up? What the hell had happened last night?

Ass Juice – that's what had happened.

I remembered arriving at the bar – sure enough, it was full of porn stars and creepy hanger-on guys with mullets. I'd ordered a beer and an Ass Juice. I remember it being about ten o'clock and me talking to a girl called – Misty, maybe? Amber? Something porny, for sure – and telling her I was a writer. There was some kind of party going on back at her hotel and I should come. I didn't go to Amber's hotel, but I definitely ordered more Ass Juice.

I think there had been a fight. A couple of the men with mullets had taken exception to a group of locals hitting on the porn stars. Chairs had been thrown – I definitely remember the chairs. At some point between the chairs being thrown and order being restored, Sarah had called. I don't remember the conversation; just looking at my phone and thinking 'about bloody time'. It was about midnight. And then – well – that's about it.

I reached for my phone to call Sarah. But it wasn't next to the bed, which is where I'd normally leave it. Nor was it in my pocket or anywhere else in the room. I must have left it at the bar, or wherever I'd gone to meet Sarah afterwards. I looked up her number on my laptop, picked up the hotel phone, and dialled. Straight to voicemail.

Shit. Had I actually met up with her last night? Had I acted like a drunken dick? I genuinely couldn't remember. Wait – was she staying at the Luxor too? That would make sense – lots of people from the conference were. I dialled reception.

'Hello, I wonder if you can tell me – do you have a guest called Sarah Lacy staying with you?'

A clicking of keys.

'We did have a Sarah Lacy here, yes, but Miss Lacy checked out this morning.'

Shit, shit, shit.

I threw everything into my bag and headed down to the lobby, and then hailed a cab to the airport where, hopefully, I'd at least be able to catch a later flight. I was still drunk – which was a slight blessing; I suspected everything was going to be much more difficult on an Ass Juice hangover. Arriving, sweating now and smelling of booze, at the American Airlines desk I was told that they didn't have another flight out of Vegas until late that evening. There was no way I could sit in departures for hours; not with this hangover, not without showering. I looked up at the departures board – there was a Virgin America flight leaving in an hour. I walked up to the booking desk.

'Yes, sir, we do have room on that flight – just one seat, actually – it'll be $350.'

'Jesus. Just for one way?'

'Yes, sir, would you like the ticket?'

'Yes, I suppose so.'

The booking agent printed out my ticket but, before handing it over, scribbled the letters 'SSS' in the corner.

'Oh, come *on*,' I said to no one in particular.

SSS stands for 'special security screening' and are three letters you really don't want to see on your plane ticket when you're hungover, tired and have less than an hour to get on your flight.

The fact that I had arrived at the airport looking and smelling like a hobo and was now booking a one-way flight using a foreign credit card, and with no checked bags meant that, in addition to the usual x-ray and metal detector fun, I'd also have to have a full body pat-down and have every single item in my suitcase swabbed for explosive residue. All of which, by the way, would take place in a special zone next to the main security area, in full view of the other passengers. For the hour and a half flight home, I'd be the terrorist suspect on the plane. And that was before I got back to San Francisco and found out from Sarah what behaviour I'd actually been guilty of.

1206

I made it all the way back to the Vertigo before Sarah finally answered her phone.

'Well, *hello* there,' she said in a way that telegraphed 'trouble'.

'Um . . . so I have no idea what happened last night.'

'No, I thought you might not. Do you remember meeting me in the Luxor bar?'

'Uh – no.'

'Jesus. Well, I'm just heading out to meet someone now, but if you want to meet me later for a *non-alcoholic* drink, I'll remind you of all the excruciating details.' She gave me the address of where she'd be.

'So you're still talking to me – that's a good sign, right?'

'I'll see you later.'

Click.

I walked into Homestead and Sarah was sitting at a table; in front of her was a beer and an orange juice. She slid the orange juice over to me.

'Good God, you were a mess yesterday,' she started before I'd even sat down. 'Do you really not remember anything? I'm amazed you're not dead.'

'Not really,' I mumbled, before taking a sip from my orange juice. I felt about two feet tall.

'Well, first of all, you stumbled into the hotel bar, tried to hug me hello, but missed and sort of fell into a sofa, nearly taking the whole table with you. Then you insisted on ordering champagne and trying to tell me about your night with porn stars or something. You were basically incoherent at this point.'

'Jesus.'

'Yeah, the barman was ready to call security and have you thrown out, but then you started arguing with him – telling him you were a journalist.'

'And then what?'

'And then I left and went to bed.'

'I'm sorry,' I said.

'You don't need to apologise to me,' she sighed and took a sip of her beer. 'Look, you're my friend and I care about you. But I still don't understand why you need to get so drunk all the time. Robert's worried too: he said you seem to think that people expect you to be drunk all the time, and that's when you turn into, what was it he says? Drunk Paul. I don't like Drunk Paul. Robert doesn't like Drunk Paul – none of your friends do.'

'But . . .' I started to protest. I wanted to point out all the adventures that alcohol had brought me – all of the fun and the girls and the column for the *Guardian* and everything else. But this wasn't the time. She was right; my drinking had got out of hand recently and my friends – including Robert – were clearly finding it less amusing than they once had.

'Yeah,' I said, 'I know – you're right. I really don't want to lose your friendship over this kind of crap.'

'You won't,' she said – 'but, well, it's like a woollen sweater with loose threads. Every time you behave like a drunken asshole, one of the threads of our friendship gets pulled away. It's fine at first, but pretty soon there's no sweater left.'

I knew that my friendship with Robert was made of sterner stuff, but it was true with him too, and with Anna and with all of my friends – my behaviour was starting to pull apart my friendships one thread at a time.

'I'm sorry,' I said again. And I meant it.

1207

20 January 2009

As I watched the hundreds of police officers lining President-elect Barack Obama's route down Pennsylvania Avenue I couldn't help but make a joke. 'The police escorting the motorcade are showing amazing discipline,' I said to the girl next to me at the bar.

'What do you mean?' she said.

'I mean I can only imagine the level of self-control it must have taken for American cops to see a black guy in such an expensive car and resist their natural urge to pull him over.'

'That's inappropriate,' said the girl.

The inauguration of any President is an event that brings America to a standstill, but the inauguration of the country's first black Commander in Chief was something truly special to witness, especially in San Francisco. Outside Chicago – Barack Obama's hometown – there wasn't a place in the country where the change was felt more keenly. The city is the heart of liberal America – a place that had been in a constant state of anger for the past eight years during which George W. Bush had been in office and the rights the people in this city held so dear – gay marriage, abortion, peace in our time – were slowly chipped away by a neoconservative oil monkey from Texas.

For the people of San Francisco this was not a day for jokes, which is a shame, because the inauguration was ripe for parody, starting with the motorcade but continuing through the President's inaugural speech – a homily so feel-good I half expected it to end, Oprah-style, with Obama giving each of the assembled crowd a puppy. 'You're getting a puppy, you're getting a puppy ...' And then there was poet Elizabeth Alexander who read an excruciating verse – 'Someone is trying to make music somewhere with a pair of wooden spoons on an oil drum ... A woman and her son wait for the bus ... A farmer considers the changing sky' – which sounded less like a piece of spoken art and more like someone reading out Twitter. And then . . .

But no. The more I watched, the more I couldn't really bring myself to make any more jokes. Not to the girl next to me, in her 'Hope' pin badge, not to the bartender who was serving all drinks on the house during the ceremony itself, and not even to myself.

My hotel was two blocks from Bush Street which, for one day only, had been renamed Obama Street: somebody had gone down the whole street the previous night, changing dozens of road signs. All day, in every café, grocery store, bar and private home, televisions were tuned to the non-stop coverage of the inauguration and the parade that followed. And later that evening, I had been invited to an inauguration party at Eris's new boyfriend's apartment, complete with 'Yes We Canapés'. The pun was my contribution to the festivities.

The mood was like in *Ghostbusters II* when the river of evil flowing beneath New York grips the city in collective paranormal madness, except in San Francisco that January day it was a river of change, putting the populace in the grip of hope.

You didn't have to be from San Francisco to feel it, of course, or even be an American. Most of the world was watching on television – welcoming an era of what Obama had called 'change we can believe in'.

The thought had been rattling around in my head for a while, but this was the moment – sitting in a bar, watching the inauguration – that everything coalesced into a fully-formed decision.

For all my globe-trotting, the place I kept ending up in was America, and specifically San Francisco. I'd fallen in love with the city at first sight, but with every trip I'd made new friends, discovered new places to visit and bought further and further into the American dream.

As I watched Obama being sworn in, I realised for the first time that I didn't want to leave when my visa waiver expired. I wanted to stay here to see what happened next, to witness the effects of an

Obama presidency on the most liberal and technology-savvy city in America. But of course I couldn't.

In a few days I was due to travel to Munich for yet another conference, before heading back to London for a week and then a flight to Verbier, where a bunch of successful young entrepreneurs had organised a skiing trip in the Alps. Thanks to the restrictions of the visa waiver scheme and the nomadic lifestyle I'd created for myself, I had to keep moving.

1208

I looked at my watch: time to go and get changed for the party. I'd bought socks with American flags on them – adding to my sock inventory was a big deal, but momentous times call for momentous decisions – and Robert's business partner, Scott, was picking me up at six. Except that Scott wasn't Robert's business partner any more – a few weeks earlier he'd been offered a job as chief technology officer for a company in San Francisco, starting immediately. The company was paying for his relocation and contributing towards the legal fees required for him to get an 'alien of extraordinary ability' visa on grounds of his scientific qualifications. As a – and, of course, I laughed at these words when he said them – respected journalist, Scott asked if I'd be prepared to write him a letter of recommendation to the US State Department.

In the car on the way to the party, I listened to Scott talk about his new job and for the first time in over a year I was actually envious of someone with an apartment and a job that forces them to stay in a single city and a single country.

It's not that I was ready to stop living in hotels, or to become rooted to one spot – but somehow my constant travelling didn't feel liberating any more. Rather it felt like I was trapped on a treadmill; unable to stay in the US – and in the city I'd fallen in love with – for longer than three months at a time; forced to keep moving. By the time we arrived at the party, and I saw the outside of the house decked in star-spangled banners, I'd made my decision.

I was going to get a visa. And I was going to make San Francisco the place I called home.

1209

My plane from Munich landed back in Gatwick at noon.

It was 27 January 2009, almost exactly a year since I'd given up my flat in London and decided that I never wanted to live in one place again. Now I was determined that by the end of the following month I'd have a US visa.

I'd done hours and hours of research online, and by this point I knew almost everything there was to know about the various classes of visa available for people who want to move to the US, without actually becoming citizens. I also knew from friends who already had visas that February was the perfect month to apply; far enough away from the tourist season, or any other peak travel times, that there wouldn't be backlog. I should only have to wait a couple of weeks for an appointment at the US embassy in Grosvenor Square, which was perfect as it would give me just enough time to fill in the lengthy application forms, get the specific sized passport photos they needed and generally prepare myself psychologically for the interview. At the embassy they'd grill me about my reasons for wanting to be allowed to stay in the US for an extended period, and then they'd carry out various background checks to ensure that I wasn't likely to overthrow the government or anything like that.

Settling into my hotel – the Grafton on Tottenham Court Road, where I'd checked in for a one-month stay at £70 a night – wiping out all of the budget savings from my twenty-day stay at the Vertigo – I picked up the phone and dialled the US embassy. Calls to the embassy cost £1.20 per minute. God bless America.

After holding for ten minutes – £12 – my call was answered by a man who sounded like he was in Leeds. 'American embassy,' he said, unconvincingly.

'Hello,' I said, 'I'd like to arrange an appointment for a US visa.'

He asked me various questions about the class of visa I was applying for, and also reminded me of the standard application fee of $131 which was non-refundable even if they refused my application. Once that was done, he tapped away at his keyboard to arrange a time for the interview.

'When would you like the appointment?' he asked.

'As soon as possible,' I replied, praying that it would be less than four weeks.

'How about Friday morning?' he asked.

'Uh – this Friday?' It was Monday.

'Yes,' he said, 'the computer says we have a spare appointment; maybe someone cancelled. Or I can put you in for three weeks' time.'

'Er . . . no . . . Friday will be fine,' I said.

And that was that. I had to report to the embassy at eight o'clock on Friday morning, carrying all my completed forms, my passport photos, my various references. I couldn't believe it – four days! That was brilliant!

Wait.

No.

It was fucking terrible. I hadn't even printed out the paperwork, let alone filled it in. I didn't have my reference letters, I didn't even have my passport photo. I immediately went into a flat spin of panic. First I fired off emails to my referees – subject line 'HELP!' – asking if there was any chance of them writing their letters right away. Fortunately they were all based in London but I'd still have to spend a few hours travelling around collecting them.

The passport photo was another challenge. Annoyingly, American passport photos are a different size from those in Europe. Just slightly bigger, as if America is trying to make a point. As a result, you can't get them from normal photo booths and instead have to go to a special studio off Oxford Street where you join a steady line of would-be visa holders paying £10 a time to get their photographs taken. The wall of the studio is amazing, lined with hundreds, no, thousands, of passport photos of their rich and famous clients. It's like the photos of celebrated patrons you see in Italian restaurants, except, these being passport photos, special care has been taken to capture each subject in his or her least flattering light. There was Sting, probably taken sometime in the seventies, looking like Carlos the Jackal. There was Channel 4 News anchor Jon Snow, also looking like Carlos the Jackal. One day it'll be my tiny, contorted, terrifying face up there, I thought, as I took my place on the stool and remembered that you're not allowed to smile.

I arrived back at my hotel, thoroughly pleased with myself. All my referees had managed to adjust to my ridiculous new timetable, I had my photos and now all I had to do was fill in a dozen or so forms. The hotel has a business centre with a printer so I took my laptop down to that and began printing, starting with the embassy's checklist of things to make sure I have with me for my interview.

As it came out of the printer, I started to glance down the list: referee letters, fine; photos, fine; four billion pages of application form; fine and then . . .

And then it felt as if every drop of blood had drained from my body. I stood staring at the last item on the list for a few seconds, and then literally collapsed into the business centre's swivel chair. Had the chair not been there, I would have hit the floor.

There, right at the bottom of the list, apparently less important than anything else, was the one thing I hadn't thought of. Except now it seemed obvious. Of *course* they'd need that. Three words.

ACPO police certificate.

That was it. Game over, not just for my visa – but potentially for any further visits to America. The ACPO police certificate is exactly what it sounds like. A piece of paper, produced by ACPO – the Association of Chief Police Officers – showing details of your entire criminal history. Or, rather, showing that you don't have a criminal history and so are therefore suitable for entry to the US.

The fact that I didn't have one of these certificates, and had no idea how to obtain one, wasn't what worried me. What worried me was what mine would certainly show when it arrived: two arrests, including one caution, for crimes that – technically at least – fell under the heading of fraud. There was no way on God's earth that they'd allow a self-confessed fraudster into the country.

My brain wasn't capable of processing the implications. If I took the certificate to the embassy and was refused a visa – which now seemed like an absolute certainty – then I'd also no longer be eligible to enter the country under the visa waiver scheme. One of the first boxes you tick on the visa waiver form is to say you've never been refused a visa.

But then it got even worse. As I started to Google for the immigration authorities' attitude towards admitting fraudsters, I discovered to my horror that the fact that I had been arrested for a crime involving fraud – a so-called crime of 'moral turpitude' – meant I almost certainly shouldn't have even been using the visa waiver at all. Had the Americans randomly stopped me at the airport and asked permission to check my UK police record* I would have been deported for a visa violation and possibly banned from travelling to the US for anything up to ten years.

Without realising it, I'd been taking a huge risk every time I arrived on American soil – a risk that I couldn't possibly continue to take. Whatever happened I had either to get a visa, or stay out of America for ever. The only glimmer of sunshine was that ACPO offered a forty-eight-hour delivery service for emergency certificates, at a cost of £90. I could still get it in time for my Friday appointment. At least I'd know my fate sooner rather than later.

1210

The two days between applying for my ACPO certificate and it arriving were the longest, most terrifying of my life. Much of that comparison, of course, is tied to the fact that I've never been kidnapped by insurgents in Iraq, or been in a plane crash in the

---

* Contrary to what many believe, unless you're a terrorist the police in Britain tend not to share criminal records with their American counterparts. All the Americans can do is ask for your permission to request the records before deciding whether or not to allow you into the country. Of course, if you refuse, they'll deport you anyway. Freedom is fun.

Andes. Only a simpering middle-class *Guardian* columnist would describe waiting for paperwork as 'terrifying'.

But it *was* terrifying, so, to calm my nerves, I scoured online immigration advice forums for any information that might give me a reason to be hopeful. What I was looking for was just one example of someone who had a criminal record subsequently being approved for my type of visa. Unbelievably, there didn't seem to be a single person who fit those criteria.

What I did find, though, was lots of advice for non-criminals as to how they should behave in a visa interview.

The most important factor is preparedness – if you didn't have all your paperwork in order, you ran the risk of being sent home and having to book a new appointment. As I would be able to confirm a few days later, the US visa system is shockingly efficient. They process thousands of people every day and still don't have much of a backlog. Much of this is down to their lack of tolerance of people who can't read simple instructions: there just isn't the demand in America for idiots who can't read checklists.

Being calm and confident is also critical; for many people a visa is the most important document they'll ever apply for – it can make or break careers, marriages and families. Tensions run high, but if you raise your voice at the interviewer, or give the impression that you're lying, you're done for.

The most important advice, though, was to be completely honest. Every single site repeated that advice: answer every question you're asked by the interviewer with the truth, the whole truth and nothing but the truth. There was no way of knowing how much background information the embassy could access on you – by applying for the visa you were agreeing to let them dig into your past as much as they liked – and, if you were caught in a lie, that would put paid to your chances of ever entering the US again, perhaps for life.

Until I'd read that, I was allowing myself one tiny hope: that somehow the same administrative cock-up that had meant the police outside Karen's flat had no record of me would mean that my ACPO certificate would come blank. But now I realised that, even if it did, I still had to admit to the arrests or risk the end of my American dream. Lying to blag my way into a nightclub is one thing; lying to blag my way into a country is just idiotic.

I'd asked for the certificate to be sent to my hotel and I was expecting delivery by the end of Wednesday. Wednesday came and went, as did Thursday morning. 'No, sir, as I've told you, we'll deliver any mail directly to your room.' I think I was starting to irritate the concierge. Finally, at just after five o'clock on Thursday evening – less than fifteen hours before my appointment – came a knock on the door and a man in a porter's uniform clutching an A4-sized white envelope with an ACPO franking stamp.

I couldn't bear to open it.

Since I'd left London – really since I'd decided to stop trying to be an entrepreneur and go back to writing – I'd been the author of my own destiny. Literally. I'd been able to travel where I liked, do what I liked, drink as much as I liked, and – barring the odd night behind bars – my behaviour had had zero consequences. So what if I woke up naked in a hotel corridor, or shattered the peace of an entire Spanish village, or turned up outside my ex's house and nearly got arrested for the second time in a week? I could just check out of my hotel, get on a plane and head somewhere else. It was the perfect life without consequences. And it went further than that – I was paid, by the *Guardian* and by my publisher, to write about those travels, which meant I could choose which ones would be remembered, and how I'd like to remember them. The night at Karen's house, or a week staying in a renovated halls of residence? Struck from the public record. Never happened. The hairdressers and the Icelandic rock star and the glamorous book launch party? All there in black and white, tweaked and packed and edited to present me in my best light.

The contents of the envelope were the precise opposite of all of that. Inside was a single piece of paper, written by a computer, and detailing only things I'd like to forget. I couldn't edit it, tweak it or spin it in a positive way. And, unlike an inconsequential newspaper column, the consequences of the information this one piece of paper held couldn't be more serious, for me at least. It had the power to ban me from the country and the city that I'd fallen in love with.

I sat on my hotel bed, holding the envelope, my hands shaking.

I knew what it was going to say, and I knew the next morning that I was going to have to hand it to a man in a uniform at the American embassy who would use it to decide my future.

I finally pulled myself together enough, and stopped my hands shaking enough, to tear open the envelope.

1211

Eight a.m., and the queue at the embassy already snaked along one side of Grosvenor Square. There were people of all nationalities: I heard French and German and Arabic and what I'm pretty sure was Russian. I heard British accents, too, and Australian and Canadian. All of us were there for the same reason, though: we all wanted to go to America.

The instructions from the embassy had been explicit and underlined, in bold. All I was allowed to bring with me was my paperwork, and a book or magazine for the inevitable five-hour wait inside. I'd heard stories of people being there for twelve hours or more. I was in the middle of reading Al Franken's *Lies and the Lying Liars Who Tell Them* – a satirical indictment of the Bush administration – but on my way to the embassy I'd decided to throw it away lest it prejudice my case. Which was ridiculous, really, but that's how paranoid I was about upsetting the Americans. Instead I'd stopped at Borders on Oxford Street and bought a copy of Bill Bryson's *Notes from a Big Country*. Everyone loves Bill Bryson, the man who does for modern-day Anglo-American relations what Roosevelt did in the 1940s. He's like a bearded Lend-Lease.

Apart from my book, I was allowed to bring no other entertainment devices, and certainly nothing electronic. No iPod, or phone, or laptop – the embassy even bans electronic car key fobs. The man in front of me in the queue apparently hadn't got the memo; not only was he listening to an iPod, with the earbud tucked into just one ear, but he was also managing to talk loudly on his mobile, which was pressed against his other ear. He must have felt like he was permanently on hold.

'Yeah, mate, I'm just at the embassy, innit?' he said – or maybe asked – at the top of his voice.

'Nah, should be done soon. Just got to get this fucking visa for Florida, innit?' The poor fellow was crippled by uncertainty.

I weighed up whether or not to say something. Part of me wanted to do the decent human thing and tell him about the no-electronic-devices rule. He was still far enough back in the queue that he could run to one of the nearby cafés that offers property lockers for embassy visitors and make it back without missing his appointment time. If he got all the way to the front and then was turned away, he'd have wasted his whole day. Another part of me, though, couldn't help but think 'this guy sounds like a total twat'. And, anyway, why should the rest of us have taken the time to read the instructions and spent a whole week panicking about our visas when he clearly couldn't give a toss?

No, I decided: him being a twat shouldn't stop me being a good Samaritan. Moral high ground and all that. Frankly, I needed all the karmic help I could get. 'Excuse me,' I said once he got off his phone. He turned around a little too quickly, as if I'd punched him in the back of the neck. He was obviously someone for whom the words 'excuse me' were usually followed by 'can you stop shouting into your phone, you twat'.

'What?'

'Sorry,' I said, because I'm British, 'just thought you should know that you're not supposed to bring electronic items into the . . .'

'Yeah, they don't mean phones, innit,' he said, with far more aggression than I'd anticipated. 'Mind your own business, mate.'

He turned around and put the other iPod earbud into his other ear.

I was about to tap him on the shoulder, and point out that, not only do they explicitly say that they do mean phones, but that the iPod he was now listening to wasn't a fucking phone. But he'd had his chance; and, anyway, he was a twat.

'Ignorant twat,' I said to his back.

He spun around again.

'What did you say?'

Now, I have to say, ordinarily I wouldn't have been so belligerent. He was a big guy, and could almost certainly have killed me, like those people you read about being stabbed on London buses because they asked a teenager to stop throwing chips. But on this occasion I was emboldened by my environment: the outside of the American embassy is one of the most highly policed areas in London. No more than two feet away from us was a policeman carrying a machine gun. A few feet away from him were five more policemen, all heavily armed. Sure, iPod man might get the first punch in, but at least I'd have the satisfaction of watching him being brought down in a hail of automatic gunfire. He looked at me, then he looked at the policeman, and at the gun. He knew it, I knew it.

'I said you're an ignorant twaaat.' Slowly and with relish this time.

One more glance at the policeman: he was looking back at us now. The twat turned back around. I felt a small jolt of victory – despite being the equivalent of the kid who pulls faces at the bully from behind teacher's back. Still, for the next half-hour, as the queue slowly shuffled towards the first of several security checkpoints, I was at least distracted from my visa panic by the impending joy of watching him be turned away. When the moment came it was even more satisfying than I'd expected.

'You what, mate?' he shouted at the security guard. 'That's fucking well out of order, innit.' A policeman edged closer. 'Fuck this,' said the man, eventually, and stormed off across the square.

I handed the security guard my paperwork, he glanced at it

casually and, satisfied that everything was in order, ushered me towards the metal detectors.

Here we go.

1212

The ACPO certificate had indeed contained the truth about my laughably unsordid criminal past – my recent caution was listed, along with the arrest date and police station – but not the whole truth; my first arrest was missing. According to the ACPO website, that was because the certificate only shows convictions and cautions, and the previous arrest had resulted in neither. The difference between convictions and cautions was my only possible saviour; by accepting the caution I'd been forced to admit guilt, but because I hadn't gone to court it wasn't a conviction. Most of the advice I'd found online suggested that the Americans only cared about convictions, not things you'd been cautioned over, but some self-styled legal experts still insisted that cautions were 'taken into account'. I wouldn't have to wait long to find out.

1213

After passing through the metal detector, I ended up in a large waiting area that looked much like every government waiting area you've ever been in. I was given a printed ticket with a number on it and asked to wait to be called. Having been told to expect long delays, I settled down with my book.

No more than ten minutes later, I heard my number being called. I was being fast-tracked!

No I wasn't. The first call simply took me to a glass window where I handed over my paperwork so the embassy staff could begin their background checks. Up until then I hadn't even been in the system. Now the real waiting could start. And so I waited.

And I waited.

And waited.

Two hours passed – it was approaching noon and I was making significant headway through Bill Bryson's folksy tales of regional post offices and the perils of taking children on long car journeys. But the numbers on the huge digital display seemed to be moving quickly enough: I was number 373 and I'd just seem numbers 350 and 351 be called. I estimated maybe another half-hour at most.

Half an hour passed.

Then four more half an hours. It was 2.30 p.m. Numbers 372 and 374 had been called over an hour ago, and now they were calling people in the high 400s. Had I missed my number? I was sure I hadn't: I'd been sure to look up every time a number was called.

I decided that all was probably lost. Obviously they'd looked at my police record and had spent the past four hours deciding the best way to break the news to me that I'd never be allowed to travel to the US again. They'd probably called up all my American ex-girlfriends and asked them to come down and help them do it, perhaps in the form of a song. This was the moment the entire American nation took its revenge.

And then.

Buzzzzzzz.

'Number 373.'

1214

I don't know what I was expecting – a special interview room, I think. One with a door and a table with an interviewer on one side and me on the other. Ironically, I think I was imagining something like the interview room at a police station.

That's not what visa interviews are like. Instead, I was directed to a row of windows made of what looked to be bulletproof – or at least incredibly thick – glass. In front of each window was a low plastic chair, and behind each sheet of bulletproof glass sat a man or woman in a US embassy uniform.

'Take a seat, Mr Carr,' said the first American voice I'd heard in my whole time at the embassy. Everyone up until that point – the security guards, the policemen, the people who took my forms and who directed me to take a seat – had been British.

'So . . .' began the interviewer. I glanced down at his name badge: Charles Dickens. I started to smile but stopped myself. This was surely a man who spent his entire day hearing people say, 'Oh, wow, your name is Charles Dickens'. Adding to their numbers would not help my case. It was an enormous challenge, but I returned my focus to the interview.

Charles Dickens – ha! – launched into his questions. Why did I want the visa? What would I be doing in the US? Did I have family there; friends – a girlfriend? I answered truthfully, except for a tiny white lie about how, sadly, I worked too hard to have time for girls. No sense in making him think I was on the hunt for a green card. He seemed happy with my answers, and we even shared a joke about my use of the visa waiver. I can't remember what it was, though. I was running entirely on panic and adrenaline.

And then came the moment. He'd worked through all the forms I'd filled in, and put them neatly to one side in a tray. Just one remained. The ACPO certificate.

'Now,' he said, with a definite sigh, 'tell me about this.'

I could sense the sick feeling making its way up my throat. 'Ah, yes,' I said, 'an embarrassing story, actually.'

And I told the whole story – every embarrassing detail, about my most recent arrest and caution. The fact that I'd had too much to drink, the fact that the police had kicked down the door and – yes – the fact that it was the second time it had happened. 'It's not on the certificate,' I said, 'but I want to be entirely honest with you.'

'I appreciate that,' he replied, not smiling.

Once I was done, Charles Dickens – hee! – was frowning. This was not good news.

'Right,' he said, 'that's all I need. You'll need to leave your passport at the courier table by the door and we'll have it back to you in a few days.' He reached for a large stamp and punched some red ink on to my form. I couldn't read what it said.

I sat there, waiting for him to continue.

He stared back through the bulletproof glass.

'You're all set,' he said.

I stayed sitting.

Finally he spoke again. 'Do you have any questions?'

'Um . . . when you say "I'm all set" . . .'

He laughed. 'I mean, that's all fine. Your passport and your visa will be returned to you in a few days. Enjoy the United States.'

'Uh – I – OK . . . thank you.' I couldn't believe it. I had so prepared myself for disappointment, so psyched myself up to be banned from America for ten years, or the rest of my life, that I simply couldn't process the idea of being approved for the visa. I'd told the truth and everything had turned out fine.

I had to get out of there before they changed their mind. Clearly this was some kind of hideous administrative error.

I walked slowly to the courier desk, got the receipt for my passport and walked, still slowly, to the door. I walked out of the building, back through security and across Grosvenor Square. I didn't look back – just kept walking. I felt like I'd just committed the perfect heist. I stood calmly on the escalator down into Bond Street tube station and on to the waiting train, heading towards my hotel. Only when the doors slid closed did I smile. And then I laughed and laughed and laughed. I looked like a lunatic, but I didn't give a shit. I was moving to America.

Chapter 1300

Trending Downwards

1 March 2009

The two weeks since my visa arrived had passed with significantly less chaos than would normally accompany a move to a new country. To move to a new country, one would ordinarily have to move *from* somewhere else. Not me. I wasn't packing up an old house and arranging for things to be shipped to a new one, I didn't have to say goodbye to friends or leave a job or any of that crap – I'd done that more than a year earlier. Really, my arrival at San Francisco International would be no different from the half-dozen other ones I'd made in the previous twelve months, except that, instead of filling out the green visa waiver card on the plane, I'd be carrying a five-year visa in my passport. I was even checking into my usual hotel.

When I told friends that I was moving to San Francisco, most of them assumed it meant the end of my living in hotels. They couldn't have been more wrong: if the rates offered by hotels when you stay for a month are impressive, then the discount for a three- or six-month stay is insane.

My first stop would be the Vertigo while I got my bearings – they were offering a rate of $65 a night if I stayed over a month – but I'd also sent emails to the reservations departments of all of the other decent independent hotels in San Francisco and my inbox was full of replies. The global economic downturn was my friend.

According to the San Francisco convention and visitors bureau, the average San Francisco hotel room rate in March 2009 – including everything from no-star hovels to five-star palaces – was $160.25 a night. The Steinhart Hotel next door to the Vertigo (averaging 4.5 stars out of 5 on Trip Advisor, with 91 percent of guests recommending it) offered me a suite for $55 a night – $1650 a month – while the brilliantly named 'Gaylord Suites' down the road (averaging 4 out of 5 stars, 83 per cent recommendation) was willing to go even lower. None of which would incur any additional tax, of course, because I'd be staying more than thirty days. Those rates would include wifi, maid service, heat, light, power and all other amenities in a city where the average downtown rent was a little over $2000 a month, before amenities. Given those numbers, I'd be an idiot not to keep living in hotels.

All the visa really meant was that I would be free to spend a few uninterrupted months in my favourite city, getting to know the place even better and, more importantly, making a start on writing my book about living in hotels. After the usual negotiations over advances and royalties and delivery dates, the contract with W&N was finally signed. My agent had pitched the book as a sort of blagger's guide – telling the stories of life in hotels, but also giving tips on scoring cheap rooms, getting into parties through – well, lying – and all the other things I'd learned in the previous year.

The manuscript was due in December – nine months' time – and, if I had any hope of making that deadline, I'd have to stop travelling for a while and actually focus on pulling together something resembling a narrative. I also still had to write my weekly column, promote the previous book and continue blogging adventures often enough to keep everyone interested in me. San Francisco seemed like the perfect place to achieve all of those things.

1301

There comes a point after making any irreversible life decision – usually a couple of weeks in – where one of two things hits you. Either a feeling of euphoric disbelief that you didn't make the decision sooner, or a gut-wrenching realisation that you've made such a gargantuan error that no number of mitigating factors will ever douse the flames of regret tearing through your brain. You're on a road to heaven or hell, but either way there's no turning back.

My own moment of realisation came halfway through my first month in my new home, at a little under 90mph, with Rob Dougan's 'Clubbed to Death' cranked up to eleven, just after Scott and I had pulled on to the Pacific Coast Highway in our (borrowed) convertible Porsche Boxster. We'd just had brunch at Buck's in Woodside and were heading down the coast for no reason other than to enjoy the clear skies and the view. That was how I spent my weekends now.

Glancing down at the date on my phone, it suddenly occurred to me that a year ago – very nearly to the day – I was on this exact same road, driving an equally convertible 1971 Dodge Challenger from LA to San Diego for ETech. And I couldn't believe it had taken me twelve whole months to decide to move here.

As the weeks passed and I became more settled in my new home, I kept expecting the novelty to wear off. But that didn't show any signs of happening. There was literally nothing about the move that I regretted; in fact, the only downside was that, just two weeks after being a California resident, I'd gone from being a hard-drinking cynical Brit to a hard-drinking sunny and optimistic expat. Even something as mundane as opening an American bank account filled me with joy – to the point where I was in danger of turning into one of those writers who moved to the US and spent the rest of his career churning out trite nonsense about the differences between 'them' and 'us'.

Indeed, every day brought at least one such trite observation, which I dutifully wrote down in my notebook, ready to be deployed in a forthcoming column. Or book . . .

Trite Observations about America, from the Point of View of a British Expat
- At some point in America's linguistic development they apparently decided that herbs should be pronounced as 'erbs' and fillet as 'fill-ay', like French people do. To compensate for this, they call

a cafetière a 'French press' and a croissant a 'crescent roll'.

- There is nothing funnier than hearing an American order a Cockburn's after dinner.
- Each hour of American television can be broken down as follows: 10 minutes of commercials for junk food, 10 minutes of commercials for prescription medication (which can be further broken down into one minute of benefits, nine of side effects), 10 minutes of commercials for lawyers who can help you claw back money to pay for more junk food and medication, 13 minutes of an announcer telling you what you are currently watching, 13 minutes of an announcer telling you what's 'up next', two minutes of cop show reruns, two minutes of a family-based cartoon series.
- Seeing advertising banners on the international version of the BBC website is like seeing your dad giving Satan a reach around.
- Opening a bank account in this country – even if you're not a citizen – is a joy. Ten minutes, two forms of ID, in and out. And when you walk through the door, a nice lady says hello to you. This is very unsettling.
- They also set up Internet banking and your ATM pin while you wait. To a former Barclays customer, this is like witnessing magic.
- If anyone's looking for all the chrome, it's on the fire engines.
- Apparently there is a newspaper in the world called *The London Times*.
- And tea can be served with cream.
- Tea served with cream tastes like a baby has been sick in it.
- Perhaps in response to the fact that I keep giving cab drivers $50 bills instead of $5s, the US Treasury has slowly started to add tiny flashes of colour to distinguish between different denominations of bill. At the current rate, money will be full-colour by 2096, like the world's longest remake of *Pleasantville*.
- For some reason, when San Francisco shopkeepers or bartenders hear a British accent, they feel the need to use the word 'cheers' instead of 'thanks'. This sounds as odd as a Brit using 'bucks' as slang for dollars or an Australian speaking French.
- Cab drivers in San Francisco have no idea where anything is. If

you asked one to drive you to one end of the road and back again, you'd still have to tell him the cross-street.

- But even if you made that journey back and forth till the end of time, it would still cost you less than taking a black cab halfway down the length of Oxford Street.

- Even using a British debit card, and with the pound in the toilet, you can still fill up a Porsche Boxster and have change from thirty quid.

- Except over here the pound isn't 'in the toilet'; it's 'using the restroom'.

- American service is astonishing. You could give a Labrador puppy a hand job with a Prozac glove and it still wouldn't be as pleased to see you as the staff of the Leland tea shop on Bush Street.

- There are more than 80,000 kinds of American toast, seven hundred ways to cook an American egg but only one way to make American bacon. And it isn't pretty.

- In restaurants, it is impossible to finish a glass of water before it's refilled. The state of California is permanently in the grip of a water shortage. No one seems to have connected these facts.

- Free universal healthcare is tantamount to Communism. Free soft drink refills are a basic human right.

- Newcastle Brown Ale is a delicacy.

- Adoption of new technology here is highly selective. Minicab drivers have Priuses, hookers accept PayPal but the idea of a three-pin plug is only just beginning to catch on.

- The *Onion* newspaper's headlines are brilliantly satirical, but the body of its editorial often stretches the joke into unfunniness. The Fox News Channel does the exact opposite. Both are still wonderful.

- Almost no one here has heard of *Father Ted*, *Jonathan Creek*, *Yes Minister* or *Blackadder*. And yet they can all hum the *Benny Hill* theme tune.

- Thanks to Frost/Nixon, when you mention David Frost to an American, they picture Tony Blair doing an impression of Austin Powers.

- 'Double the tax' sounds simple in theory but only natural-born Americans will ever understand the rules of tipping.
- See also: American football.

Another huge difference between Britain and America is their attitude to drinking. Of course, this was hardly news to me but there was something about actually moving to the place that really drove it home.

During the time I was applying for the visa, I'd started to pay attention to Robert and Sarah's concern about my drinking, and had made a concerted effort to cut down. But now that I'd actually made it to San Francisco, my intake had started to ramp up again. Part of this was cockiness – getting the visa despite my record made me feel invincible – but there was also a practical reason: to get enough material to a write the column each week without leaving San Francisco I'd had to throw myself wholeheartedly into the party scene.

Every night was the same: I'd grab my notebook and head to whichever of the town's maybe five big venues was hosting the best party to promote some dot com company or other. Then I'd avail myself of the free bar while talking to partygoers and taking notes of anything amusing they might say. The parties would generally wind down about eleven, and it was at this point that the difference between Brits and Americans would make itself most apparent. In London, 11 p.m. is the time when my friends and I would head on to a late bar or a club to continue drinking, basically until one or more of us fell over. We'd do this six or seven nights a week: I tended to hang out with journalists and entrepreneurs; groups of people who can set their own hours and so are unafraid of hangovers on a school night.

In San Francisco I was partying with entrepreneurs and journalists too, but, for reasons I couldn't understand, come 11p.m. they'd go home. Some of them were still so sober that they'd actually drive; in fact many would drive even if they weren't sober – Californians obsess over pilates and frown at the notion of eating carbs but their attitude to drink driving is straight out of an episode of *The Sweeney*. Occasionally I'd be able to convince someone to stay out for a late drink – but, even then, California's licensing laws meant that even the late bars were closed by two.

My solution to this problem was twofold. First of all, I would start drinking early. This was the easiest fix, but it also meant that by the time the parties got started, I was already drunk. I was quickly getting a reputation as the drunk British writer at every party, a reputation I did absolutely nothing to counter as it only drew more attention to me, and by extension the columns that I was writing. Wherever I went in the world, people still gave me a pass for my appalling behaviour on the basis that I was a journalist – in America they gave me a second pass because they assumed that being a drunken idiot was just how British people behaved.

My second trick was to hang out more with Brits, which in San Francisco isn't particularly difficult to arrange. Every week at least one entrepreneur from London would make the pilgrimage across the Atlantic either to meet their Silicon Valley counterparts or to beg for money from one of the valley's super-rich venture capitalists. And, of course, for those who read my *Guardian* column, I was the first person they'd email or call. Could they take me for a drink to tell me about their company? Of course they could; and what started as one drink always ended as an all-day binge.

Life was good, work was good and the drinks were free.

1302

April

If my liver had fists, it would have been pounding them on the mat and begging for mercy. I was covered in strange bruises, I had no idea what day it was – and in about half an hour I was heading out again to yet another party.

I hurt.

Webmission week had rolled around again, and the Brits had invaded San Francisco in their dozens. My last vivid memory from the previous evening was watching a British entrepreneur – who should probably remain nameless – standing on a bar, pouring tequila into the gaping mouth of a journalist from the Daily Telegraph. Meanwhile, across the bar, another entrepreneur – who should definitely remain nameless – was making plans to take one of the barmaids home, as his friend failed to gain support for a belching competition. An hour or so later, with the Brits having drunk the bar dry, we decided to move things on to the Beauty Bar on Mission Street, but not before someone handed me a black bag containing something heavy.

'What's in there?' I asked.

'A wooden duck.'

'Why have you put a wooden duck in a black bag?'

'Because otherwise they'll realise we're stealing it.'

I blacked out shortly afterwards.

I woke up the next morning at Kelly's house. Kelly was one of the few American girls who drank almost – at least half – as much as I did, and so was less put off by my drunken behaviour than most. But still I could tell that even she was starting to tire of the constant hangovers and drinking with Brits until the sun came up. It was only a matter of time before she came to her senses.

I'd become increasingly aware that my American friends had started to give me a wide berth since I'd move to San Francisco. I'd seen Eris and her boyfriend maybe once or twice since arriving – both times it was at a party and I was drunk. We would make vague plans to catch up, but she was always busy, usually with work. Scott was busy with his new company and so had dropped off the social scene, at least as far as I was concerned.

The person, though, who had made her wide berth the most obvious was Sarah. Before I moved, we'd virtually become best friends – emailing most days about book woes, speaking on the phone as often as international calling rates would allow. It was nice for us both to have a friend who could critique our writing and to whom we could vent about editors and publishers. It was Sarah who said that if I ever decided to move to San Francisco she'd be happy to introduce me to people in 'the Valley', and generally help me make a start in building a network of professional contacts to rival the one I had in London. At the start of the year she'd accepted a job at TechCrunch – organisers of the TechCrunch 50 conference – as Editor at Large, further increasing her professional profile.

We'd had lunch a few times during my first weeks in town, but she too had since become increasingly 'busy' and the few times we'd run into each other at parties – usually while I was drunk – she'd made it pretty clear that she didn't have time to talk. Frankly, I felt patronised: like I was some errant child who had let her down. I mean, yes, she had a point – in a few months I was going to turn thirty and I should probably be giving more serious thought to my health and my career – but I was also being paid handsomely for writing about being a drunk expat curiosity in San Francisco; the party invitations were showing no signs of drying up, and in a few months I'd finish writing my book about living in hotels and – well – being a drunk curiosity. Be as disapproving as you like, I thought, but, as jobs go, mine isn't a bad one.

1303

May

Seven months until my book deadline, and I was a little behind schedule. It wasn't my fault, of course; I'd spent the previous two and a bit months getting used to my new town; slipping into the social scene, making new friends, arguing with Kelly, that kind of thing. She'd started off gently trying to persuade me that waking up every morning with no memory of the previous night was not the optimum way to live – she was worried about me. But soon she too had become frustrated by my complete unwillingness to cut down on booze.

All of that stuff – getting drunk, being dumped – takes up a lot of time, and I had to write 900 words a week for the *Guardian*, so I could hardly be blamed for slipping a bit when it came to writing my next book. And anyway, I reasoned, all of the parties and the drinking and the girls were technically research, so it wasn't like I hadn't done *any* work. I just hadn't written as many actual words as possibly I should have done. Which is to say, I hadn't written a single one.

Of course the story I told Alan, my publisher at W&N, was slightly different. Every so often he'd email to check on progress and I'd happily report that all was 'going fine' or that I was 'ploughing ahead'. My editor at the *Guardian* would email me every so often too – enquiring why the column was sometimes as much as twenty-four hours late. 'I'm sorry,' I'd explain, 'I'm just racing towards my book deadline – so much going on right now.'

And then I'd close my laptop and head out to meet whichever Brit was in town, and spend the rest of the day getting trashed.

Life was good, as far as I could remember.

1304

June

'Wait, you're going to Butt Lands?' Kelly seemed surprised.

'Butlins. I'm going to But*lins*. It's a holiday camp in England where poor people who are scared of flying go on holiday.'

'Butt Lands sounds like more fun.'

She had a point.

It was now five months until my book deadline and I'd finally decided to start taking it seriously. I had loads of good material about staying in hotels, and I was pretty sure I had enough amusing stories to fill a book – but I wanted some extra colour. Having stayed in a villa and a student halls of residence, I decided I needed to try at least one other alternative to hotels. And when my friend Paul Walsh called me from London, I knew I'd found it.

'Hey, buddy – how do you fancy flying back from San Francisco for a weekend in Butlins?'

Apparently Butlins had hired a new PR person who had decided, inexplicably, that it would do their brand a world of good if they invited a group of 'influential Internet users'* to travel down to Bognor Regis† for a weekend-long 'social media party'.‡

I hesitated for all of ten seconds: did I really want to fly 5000 miles to spend three days in Bognor Regis with a group of bloggers, even if it would be a funny addition to the book? Yeah, of course I did – not only was there probably a chapter in it, but there was also at least one column and a half-dozen blog posts.

The deal was sealed, though, when I realised what date it took place on. The trip came a week before the arrival in London of the Traveling Geeks – the American version of Webmission, where a group of entrepreneurs and journalists from Silicon Valley travel to London to, well, I suppose to give themselves the smug satisfaction that things really are better back home. A few of my friends from Silicon Valley would be on the trip, including Sarah.

I missed Sarah. Since we'd stopped talking regularly, I would often find myself stuck with a line in a column, or trying to understand some element of entrepreneurship in the Valley, wishing I could pick up the phone and ask her. I'm sure she'd have answered had I called, but there was something about the change in her manner towards me that made it obvious that she wouldn't exactly be thrilled to hear my voice.

And yet I couldn't think of anything specific I'd done to offend her. Maybe if we could catch up in London I could find out what had gone wrong, and how I could fix it. Robert would be in town too, of course, and I knew I could always rely on him to have a good word for me when all those around me had lost theirs.

Come to think of it, I hadn't heard from Robert for a few weeks

---

* I shit you not.
† Really, I shit you not.
‡ I can't emphasise how much I'm not shitting you.

either, but according to the published invitation list he was going to be at Butlins too. That was the final deciding factor. I booked my ticket.

Chapter 1400

Butt Lands

In his book *How to Lose Friends and Alienate People*, Toby Young writes about his first trip back to London after spending a few months in New York. He talks about seeing England through the eyes of an American: 'The people, with their sallow complexions and cheap, non-designer clothes, looked so drab . . . Britain was so dowdy . . . as if everything was covered in a thick layer of dust.'

As Robert and I sat on the train from Victoria to Bognor Regis – my transatlantic flight having landed only a few hours earlier – I knew exactly what he meant. Even the name Bognor Regis sounds dowdy and British – for years I'd assumed it only existed as a punchline in comics.

We'd decided the best plan, if we were going to survive the weekend – me with my jetlag and both of us with the fact that we were heading to Butlins – would be to start drinking early. Specifically, we decided that the best plan would be to sit in the vestibule between the train carriages, drinking Marks & Spencer champagne from paper cups, as if to underline how ironically we were treating the whole trip.

The decision proved to be a sound one as we'd dramatically misjudged how far away Bognor Regis is from London. 'I think it's about half an hour,' said Robert as the train pulled out of Victoria station. The champagne ran out after about an hour, around about the time the train divided into two halves, somewhere past Gatwick. 'We should have bought a second bottle,' said Robert. 'We should have bought a whole case,' I replied.

If the point of the trip was to confound our snobbish expectations of Butlins then things got off to a shaky start as we were checking in.

Walking towards the reception desk, our way was unintentionally blocked by half a dozen fat men in black t-shirts bearing the slogan 'Ken COCKS stag'. As if the comedy value of Mr Cock's name was too subtle, even with the capitals and the missing apostrophe, each shirt also sported a huge cartoon penis, ejaculating over the text. 'Oyoy!' hinted one of the men, at the top of his lungs. 'Ave it!' suggested a second. The receptionist looked ashamed of herself, as well she might.

Our visit coincided with one of Butlins' 'Big Weekends' (adults only – no children allowed) and, despite the company's terms and conditions emphasising that stag weekends were not welcome, it would be fair to assume from the COCK chaps that a few had snuck in. Furthermore, each group of men had determined that their coordinated fancy-dress costumes – which they wore for the whole weekend – would be the most brilliantly hilarious in the camp, through a combination of blunt irony and shock value. Accordingly, the whole place was full of drunk 118–118 runners and gangs of overweight Essex boys in drag. The hen-weekend girls, meanwhile, had all taken their cue from American college chicks at Halloween and were resplendent in a variety of 'slutty' variations of traditional costumes – slutty cats, slutty soldier girls, slutty ballerinas and slutty nuns, each with her name and alliterative description written on her back ('Naughty Niccie', 'Cute Chantelle' just two real examples). By far my favourite, though, was slutty Tinkerbell – who, on the second night, we watched having an absolutely screaming row with a man dressed as a fat Peter Pan. 'You need to fucking grow up, mate,' she yelled, brilliantly.

The people, it soon became clear, were more entertaining than the actual organised entertainment. On the night we arrived, we were treated to a performance in the resort's nightclub by the three remaining members of S Club 7, as well as 911 (pronounced 'nine one one' and not, as Milo Yiannopoulos, a stereotypically posh *Telegraph* journalist who was also on the trip, suggested, 'nine-eleven') and Lee Ryan, formerly of the boy band Blue. Ryan was the headliner, presumably after winning a game of rock-paper-scissors against the other acts. A man dressed as a fat, masked Captain America tried gamely to talk his way into the VIP area (a roped-off section of the main nightclub, guarded by an off-duty Redcoat) using the line 'do you know who I am?', which was almost as brilliant as Tinkerbell vs Peter Pan.

On the second day, we all went go-karting, an experience that ended with Robert nearly flipping his kart over thanks to some clumsy oversteering and me trying to undertake him on a hairpin bend. As we were leaving the track – heading towards an archery lesson that would see Robert being stabbed in the leg by Milo – we overheard a woman complaining that she had suffered whiplash. Clearly the daytime TV message was getting through to these people: where there's blame there's a claim. After that it was time to head for the high ropes course and the climbing wall, where a man dressed in a pink tutu and tights complained about having to wear a helmet because 'it makes me look stupid'.

If all of these encounters had reinforced my prejudice about holiday camps, there was one area where my expectations were completely confounded.

Brought up on old episodes of *Hi-de-Hi!*, I knew exactly what to expect from Butlins: dated self-catering chalets with peeling wallpaper and TVs that you had to put 10p coins into every half-hour to keep them switched on. Having already written, in my head, a hilarious chapter about trying to sleep in the equivalent of a garden shed, I was actually disappointed when I realised that we'd be staying in a proper hotel within the camp. Worse still, my room was really, unironically, nice: far better than a lot of the rooms I'd had in four- and five-star hotels in London.

The PR person, hearing I was from the *Guardian*, had decided to pull some strings and I'd been upgraded to the best room in the resort. Leather sofas, a king-sized bed, a minibar and wine chiller – but better than all of that, a huge roof terrace with a telescope pointing out across the sea. This isn't *Hi-de-Hi!* anymore, Toto.

Sure, some of the attempts to make Butlins 'posh' were laughably brilliant – the copies of the *Daily Mail* and the *Sun* in reception were on wooden sticks, like in upmarket members' clubs ('Oh, look, the *Sun* on a stick,' said Milo from the *Telegraph*) and on arrival each member of our group received a pot of strawberry and champagne jam in a little bag. But all in all, every aspect of the accommodation surpassed my expectations by a considerable chalk.

'In fact,' I said to Robert, as we sat in the camp's Burger King, on the last night, 'if only the people who stayed here weren't so predictably hideous, I could just about live here permanently.'

I gestured at the scene outside Burger King, which was situated in the main Big Top – a sort of poor-man's Millennium Dome filled with fast food outlets and arcade games and shops selling scrunchies and pregnancy test kits (but not, as far as I could see, condoms. Know your audience). It reminded me of that scene in the film version of *Fear and Loathing in Las Vegas* where Dr Gonzo and Raoul Duke are off their tits on ether, making everyone look grotesque and twisted and loud and terrifying. Except I wasn't on ether – the people were just grotesque and twisted and loud and terrifying. One man was surfing on the roof of a ride-on Bob the Builder dumper truck, another was scaling the outside of the children's climbing area – it was a bit like watching *Street Crime UK* parkour.

'I mean, look at them,' I continued. 'They can hardly walk – how can they live like this?'

Robert just looked at me. He didn't smile.

'You realise that's how you look some nights?' he said.

I laughed. He didn't, just carried on talking.

'I'm worried about you, mate – and coming from me that's saying something. Everything I hear about you from San Francisco is about you being drunk. I don't just mean from friends, but total strangers – how they saw you at a lunch event and you were already well on your way, or how you were still drunk at breakfast meetings. It used to be that you would turn into Drunk Paul when you drank too much, but that the rest of the time you'd be this nice guy who everyone liked. Like a Jekyll and Hyde thing. But I'm worried the analogy is getting a bit too accurate. I care about you, mate, and I don't want you to end up poisoning yourself to death.'

The man on the Bob the Builder truck lost his footing and fell to the floor laughing.

'Oh, come on,' I said, 'I'm not that bad. And at least I get paid to be an arsehole.'

'Yeah, but that's my point,' said Robert, 'that guy on the floor has a real job. He works all year and then come to Butlins for a weekend of acting like a twat. That's just a normal Tuesday night for you. I know people love reading about it – I love reading about it, too – and you keep getting paid for it, but most of the people who are your biggest fans don't know the real you; they don't give a shit if you kill yourself.'

It was quite a speech, and one that hit its mark. My drinking was seriously out of control again, probably worse than it had ever been. But I was trapped again. I'd built a career – or at least the beginnings of one – as a drunken scapegoat. The guy who failed at business, and at relationships and at just about everything else, and then wrote about it so everyone could laugh and thank their lucky stars they weren't me. If I stopped being that guy, then what? The first instalment of my new book advance had just hit my bank account. I might be killing myself, but I was being paid well to do it. What was I suppose to do? Call up my editor and say 'sorry, I've decided to quit drinking – no more drunken adventures from me. Here's your cheque back, I'm going to get a job in Starbucks.'? No. For better or worse, this was the career I'd decided on and I had to see it through. I was too far down the road.

1401

One thing I did decide, though, was that I wasn't going to drink while Sarah was in town. I'd be spending a week with her and Robert and this was my chance to show them both that I wasn't totally out of control.

I arrived back in London from Butlins on Monday evening. The Traveling Geeks were due to arrive on Tuesday afternoon. I'd have one quick drink on Monday night and then that would be it for a week.

Tuesday morning came, and I woke up in my hotel next to Amy – a producer for the BBC who I'd met on my flight back from San Francisco and, if my hungover memory served me correctly, I'd drunk-dialled at about eleven o'clock the previous night, insisting that she come down to Adam Street where I was enjoying a quick post-Butlins drink with Milo from the *Telegraph*.

I looked at the time. Still four hours until Sarah's plane landed – plenty of time. I gently moved Amy's arm off my shoulder and tried to figure out how to crawl over her and get to the shower. It was then that I realised something heavy was on the end of the bed, trapping my feet.

I craned my neck up to see what the hell we'd left on the bed. Judging by my headache it was probably a keg of beer.

'What the fuck?'

My whispered shout woke Amy up. 'What's going on?' she asked.

'Look at the end of the bed,' I said. She craned her neck too.

'What the fuck?' she said. There, curled up on the end of the bed, like a little fully clothed dormouse, was Milo from the *Telegraph*.

'What the hell is he doing on the end of the bed?' I asked. I didn't even remember Amy coming back to the hotel with me, let alone Milo. At least he was still dressed, I suppose, which was more than could be said for Amy and me.

Amy shrugged. Just another morning in London.

1402

After half an hour in the shower, removing the smell of alcohol from my body, I headed out to meet Sarah. I'd suggested a lunch to welcome her to London and her response was less than enthusiastic. But she could hardly fly all the way to London and not at least meet me for lunch.

'Hey!' I said, as I walked into her hotel lobby and found her already waiting, checking her email.

'Hi,' she said, forcing a smile, but clearly not sure that this was a good idea at all. I swear she was looking me up and down, trying to tell if I was drunk already.

'Don't worry,' I said, 'I'm not drunk yet.'

'Yet,' she said.

Lunch itself, though, was far better than I'd expected. After a few more minutes of awkwardness, we both realised how much we'd missed our bitching sessions about the publishing industry, journalism, Silicon Valley and our mutual friends. Sipping a glass of water, I told her about Butlins – minus most of the drinking – and she asked how my book was going. I told her the truth – that it was going really, really badly, and she sympathised, raising me the fact that she was still slaving away on the chapter plan for her next book, an investigation into global entrepreneurship in emerging markets. We talked for an hour without either of us really taking a breath; it was just like old times – two best friends catching up.

'This is great,' I said.

She nodded. 'It really is. I have to say, I was really not looking forward to seeing you. I just didn't want to have to *deal* with you, you know?'

But I didn't know. Or at least I didn't think I knew. She must have seen the hurt in my eyes and the confused look written across my whole face.

'You really don't see it, do you?'

'I know I've been drinking a lot,' I said, starting to apologise. First Robert, now Sarah. I knew where this was going.

'It's got nothing to do with the drinking,' she said. 'Or at least, that's just a symptom. I drink, everybody drinks. Yes, I'd prefer it if you didn't act like a drunken asshole towards me, but that's not what my problem with you is.'

'Then what is it?'

'It's the fact that you've stopped caring about what you do.'

1403

For the next hour, Sarah explained.

'When you said you were moving to San Francisco, I was really happy for you. I was going to introduce you to people and help you make connections there. But what happened? You got off the plane and you immediately decided you wanted to go to every party with a free bar and make this big splash as the new drunk British guy in town. You could have decided to arrange meetings and focus on the one big advantage you had – being one of the few people who writes about technology for a British newspaper but who actually lives in Silicon Valley. You could have got some real stories about them and then you could have written it in your slightly drunken Brit style that everyone loves reading; that I loved reading; and you'd have had the best of both worlds – the fan base who loves the fact that you're a loser, and the people in Silicon Valley who would be interested in reading some proper analysis on the industry written by an outsider.'

'Loved reading?' I interrupted, caught up on the past tense.

'Yes, loved reading – past tense – once you decided to focus on the drinking, and to spend your whole life either drunk or hungover, it became really obvious from your writing. Look back at the early columns you wrote and compare them with the stuff now. You barely write about technology any more; it's just a string of stories starting with 'I woke up . . .' They're funny for the first few times, but now they're the rule not the exception. Also, you make no effort to hide your contempt for the people and things you write about – like your ignorance is a badge of honour. You write about drinking with Brits, or Americans who want to be around Brits, and about the hangers-on who go to every party there's a free bar. And you do that like it's where you want to be: that you want to be a drunken hanger-on too, and that anyone who actually takes the time to get to know serious people in the Valley or start serious companies or – I don't know – write serious journalism, is somehow not worth getting to know. I lost count of how many times I had to tell people that you weren't really like that, that you were a really nice guy and that when you were sober you wrote really well. I told them about your book, that you were just going through some kind of phase. And then . . .'

'And then what?'

'And then it stopped being true. The drinking took over, and the ego, and the don't-give-a-shit persona you adopted in your writing stopped being a persona. It just became you.'

I didn't have any response. Sarah was saying the same thing as Robert had said a few days earlier about my drinking, but to her the drinking was just a part of it. I'd become a hideous caricature of myself – a belligerent, egotistical drunk who forgot that it was supposed to be an act.

The evidence was pretty damning: I was less than six months away from submitting a book that I hadn't even started to write and I was basically just phoning in my *Guardian* columns, assuming that as long as I packed them with enough drunken stories, they wouldn't realise that I had stopped trying.

Looking back, it was an absolute miracle they hadn't fired me.

1404

The next day the *Guardian* fired me.

1405

From: Charles Arthur
To: Paul Carr

Hi Paul . . .

Oh, I don't like to have to write this email. The past not-quite-a-year of your column has been enormously entertaining, and what's more you haven't managed to attract a single libel lawsuit. I'm not sure whether to be amazed, delighted, surprised or disappointed. But I've liked them all.

However, the economic situation has increasingly begun to chew off first our feet and more recently our legs. Our latest budget for the Media and Technology 'pod' has been cut by 10% on last year, and then had an additional 15% lopped off that, because the Guardian is spending enormously more money than it's getting in. Even with people leaving the paper through a redundancy scheme, the ends are far from meeting.

Which is why I'm really sorry to say that in recasting the budget I can't, at present, find a way to keep paying for your weekly column. Obviously you're free to take your ideas elsewhere.

I'm really sorry that it's come to this; if it's any comfort, you're far from alone. We're simply having to take an axe to all sorts of contributions because there isn't the money to pay for them.

If you've any questions, then do get in touch.

Best,
Charles

And that was that. Economics, pure and simple. With times being so hard for newspapers – ironically because the web is killing their advertising-based business model – the *Guardian* simply couldn't justify continuing to pay me to write a weekly column about getting drunk. As Charles said in his email, they were having to give lots of freelancers the boot, not just me, but, looking at the ones they kept, it was easy to see the trend. The writers left behind were the ones who added actual value: hard news, or proper industry analysis. The stuff that brings in serious readers. For all my ego, that's really what mattered.

1406

'Are you OK?'

For everything she'd said at lunch the previous day, Sarah seemed genuinely upset when I told her the news. 'I know it meant a lot to you,' she said. 'Still, at least you can concentrate on the book now.'

That was true – and yet losing the column symbolised a lot more than a few hours a week saved; it meant I no longer had an excuse for living the way I was. The excuse that someone paid me to act like an ass had been my only real justification, to Robert, to Sarah, to all my other friends and to everyone else I met. I could go back to just writing the blog, but it would be obvious to everyone that it was a step backwards – that people had fallen out of love with my shtick.

And then there was an even bigger problem: losing a regular pay cheque was a pretty dramatic change in circumstances – I had no idea how it would affect my eligibility to live in the US. I had less than a week until I was due to fly back to San Francisco.

'So, what are you going to do?' asked Sarah 'Have you had any other offers?' A few hours earlier, I'd updated Twitter with the news of my firing – more out of frustration than anything else, but also partly in the hope that someone might offer me another job.

'Actually, yes,' I said, 'the *Telegraph* want me to blog for them.'

'Well, that's good, right?'

And it was, except for the fact that to most of my liberal friends moving to the *Telegraph* was like going from the ACLU to the KKK. Accepting their offer would be the very definition of whoring. More importantly, though, the blogs editor had made it clear that I would be bound by the paper's strict 'no swearing' rule.

'Maybe,' I said, 'but it's certainly no replacement for the *Guardian*.'

Sarah sat silently for a moment, clearly weighing something up in her head.

'Have you heard from Mike?'

Chapter 1500

A Second Chance

Michael Arrington began his career as a corporate lawyer. Then, after years of advising Silicon Valley entrepreneurs on their businesses, he decided to launch a blog about the people and deals behind the second dot com wave. So-called 'Web 2.0'. As Web 2.0 had grown, so had his site and his personal influence. By 2008 Arrington was listed by *Time* magazine as one of the one hundred most influential people in the world.

The name of his site was TechCrunch, regarded by almost everyone – including me – as the most influential technology news site in the world, with millions of weekly readers including everyone who is anyone in Silicon Valley. And since Sarah had begun writing for TechCrunch, Arrington had gone from being her friend to her boss.

As it happens, I had heard from Mike. We'd met a few times at events in San Francisco and we'd got on reasonably well. Despite the fact that I'd taken occasional jabs at him in my column, he claimed to read it every week – mainly, I assumed, to reassure himself that TechCrunch had nothing to fear from the *Guardian*. A few hours after I'd broadcast news of my firing, he emailed me with simply the words 'you're hired'. I'd replied back: 'make me an offer' but hadn't got a reply. I assumed he was joking.

There were, after all, a number of reasons why me writing for TechCrunch would be ridiculous. For one, I only wrote one column a week at the *Guardian* – TechCrunch, like most new sites, is published twenty-four hours a day, seven days a week. Its writers are well paid but they're expected to write more than one article a day, let alone a week.

Also, I tend to write long; my column at the *Guardian* should have been 900 words, but it often ran to over twice that. TechCrunch was all about short, newsy posts, tuned to the ADHD attention span of the average Silicon Valley entrepreneur or investor.

And, finally, something told me the drunken, sweary ramblings of a clueless Brit whose behaviour since he moved to Silicon Valley had alienated everyone remotely serious wouldn't fit well on the pages of the web industry's paper of record.

Mike's email was a nice gesture – and also a slight victory lap on his part, I suspected – but we both knew it wouldn't come to anything. I explained all this to Sarah.

'I could talk to him if you like.'

I literally didn't know what to say.

'I . . . You'd really do that?' I asked.

I'd considered trying to act cool – 'I don't need your charity' and all that crap, but, given our recent conversation, it didn't seem like the time for acting. 'I mean, you told me a few days ago that you were embarrassed by my writing.'

'I am,' she said, 'but this could be your chance to fix that. You'd have to stop with all the grandstanding crap and actually start doing proper work. Keep the voice, lose the attitude, you know? Can you even remember how to start a paragraph without the words 'I woke up . . . '?'

'I think so,' I said, feeling thoroughly ashamed of myself, but also genuinely amazed at what I was hearing. 'Do you really think Mike would hire me?'

'Let me speak to him,' she said.

My flight back to San Francisco was due to leave in three days.

1501

While I waited to hear back from Sarah, I had time to think and to make some serious decisions. The first decision, unsurprisingly, was to stop drinking. Not to cut down, not to stop writing about drinking but still have the occasional beer with friends, but to actually stop drinking – for a few months at least. Until I'd got myself back on track, and actually started to make some progress on the hotel book. Robert and Sarah were right – I was spending more time as 'Drunk Paul' than I was sober.

I still knew that, even with Sarah's help, there was almost no chance of my being hired by TechCrunch but she was showing a huge amount of faith in me even to try. It was one thing me writing stuff for the *Guardian* that embarrassed her, but quite another to write it for a publication for which she was an editor. For that faith alone, stopping drinking was the least I could do.

And, anyway, the more I thought about it the more convinced I was that drinking was really just a stage prop for me. I was perfectly capable of having ridiculous adventures sober: I'd been sober at the toga party, I'd been sober driving the Challenger, I'd been . . . no, actually, that was about it – but the point stood: there had been times that I'd been sober and had fun. There was no reason I couldn't survive without drink.

Whatever the news from TechCrunch, I was going to quit. For Robert, for Sarah, for all my other friends, and also for Karen and everyone else my drunken behaviour had hurt. Most importantly, though, I was going to quit to prove to myself that I could.

1502

'Hey!' Sarah's call came the day before my flight. 'Mike's going to email you.'

'What's the verdict?' I said.

'Well, amusingly, at first he thought he wouldn't be able to afford you. I assured him he could.'

'Thanks. I'm not sure how to take that.'

'Nor me. I'm not sure Internet editors realise how badly paid newspaper columnists are. The point is, he thinks your column – assuming you make the changes we talked about – could work really well as a weekend thing, published on a Saturday or Sunday morning. You could write long, and he'll probably be fine with you swearing, too.'

'Holy shit, really?'

'Just check your mail. He's going to send you an offer today.'

'I really don't know what to say,' I said.

'Just don't fuck it up.'

'I won't,' I said, 'and in fact I've decided to stop drinking. I'm going to focus on writing for the next few months and spend less time acting like a drunken idiot at parties.'

I don't know how I expected her to react, but in hindsight she said exactly the right thing.

'I don't believe you, but it would be nice if I were wrong.'

1503

And she was wrong. At first at least. I arrived back in San Francisco on 20 July and checked into the Gaylord Suites for two months, at $50 a night.

I spent the whole of the first week working on my TechCrunch column. The first one is always the easiest, just introducing myself and setting out my stall for the column, and yet I still worked harder on it than I had on my previous dozen or so *Guardian* columns. The opening paragraph read ...

> I don't know about you, but I give this ridiculously misguided experiment three weeks. Three weeks until – at best – Arrington comes to his senses and realises that there's a reason why I've been fired from every job I've had, most recently as a columnist for the *Guardian*. Three weeks until – at worst – I say something so insanely actionable about a deep-pocketed venture capitalist that Tech-Crunch finds itself sued out of existence ...

I was joking, of course, but there was truth in that introduction. I was pretty sure that it would be just a matter of time before I did something stupid, and ended up fired again. But in the meantime, news of TechCrunch's latest 'hard-drinking' hire got around quickly and almost immediately the party invitations started back up again – as well as emails from PRs who decided that the way to my heart would probably be through my liver. In the week after the first column, no fewer than four separate PRs invited me to drinks, each of them mentioning rum. I had to at least give them credit for doing their homework.

Still, I resisted the invitations. I had lunch with Sarah, with Scott and with Eris and with a few other friends I hadn't seen for far too long, but generally stayed locked away in my hotel room. I decided that the best way to avoid drinking was to avoid temptation – so instead I bought a new notepad and began sketching out a plan for the new book. There was no reason why my calming down for a while should stop me writing a book telling others how to do the opposite. I saw the book as a kind of lifestyle manual – part (in deference to my publisher) blagger's guide but also part manifesto; encouraging others to follow in my footsteps, at least as far as living in hotels goes. Having lived that way for seventeen months, I couldn't imagine ever going back to renting an apartment; at least not until I got married to a girl who demanded her own cushions.

The Kings of the Road Club name had stuck; both as a working title for the book, but also among those people I know who had either joined it or were seriously considering doing so. Eris was the latest recruit; over lunch she told me that she'd decided to quit her ridiculously high-paying job and, inspired by my travels, was going to hit the road in search of adventure. I happily gave her the benefit of my advice: which was basically not to plan anything in advance, as she'd probably wake up naked in a hotel corridor and fuck everything up.

1504

There were some problems with advocating the life I'd led since leaving London.

As a freelance writer, I was able to work from anywhere and to focus my writing on whichever place I happened to find myself.

Rob is an entrepreneur without any permanent employees, and so enjoyed similar freedom. Eris would be able to do freelance design work as she travelled, but even so she only intended to live nomadically for a few months before returning to San Francisco. The truth is, for most people living as a permanent nomad was at best impractical and at worst impossible; their jobs and other personal circumstances just don't allow it. It seemed disingenuous at best – plain dishonest at worst – to write a book advocating a lifestyle that most people simply couldn't replicate.

But then I started reading other so-called 'lifestyle manuals' and was amazed how often the lifestyle being described in them could only be achieved by someone who started with almost the exact same circumstances as the writer. And even then there was a marked contrast between what was written, and reality.

On my flight back to San Francisco from London, I'd reread Tim Ferriss' *The 4-Hour Workweek*, which had gone on to become a *New York Times* Best Seller. Since first reading the book in San Diego, I'd seen Tim at various conferences and had heard him talk about how one of the best ways to cut down on your work load is to say 'no' to things. In fact, I'd run into him at ETech, at South by Southwest, at TechCrunch 50, at LeWeb and at about half a dozen other events. Coupled with his daily blog, TV and radio appearances and guest articles in the press, I'd say, at a conservative estimate, Tim Ferriss spends about a hundred hours a week promoting his four-hour-a-week work life.

The point, I suppose, is not that you're supposed to live exactly as Tim describes in his book – but rather that you draw inspiration from his overall message, picking the elements that you can apply to your own life.

Once I understood the secret behind lifestyle manuals: that they're basically bullshit, it was like I'd unlocked the gate to a magical garden. It wasn't just the 4-Hour Workweek: every aspirational media brand in the world worked the same way. No one, apart from Hugh Hefner, can possibly live the way that *Playboy* describes, but the magazine was successful because it was just convincing enough that every reader believed buying a copy was the first step to living an unobtainable dream. No one who reads *Vogue* can afford to buy all the clothes in its pages, but they can buy the magazine and maybe one pair of shoes and feel like they're on their way. No one who reads Tim Ferriss' book can work just four hours a week, but they can buy the dream. My book would work the same way: no one who read it would be able to abandon their flat, live in hotels around the world, blag their way into ridiculous situations and still remain alive and employed – but they could do some of it. The living in hotels aspect, for example, is perfectly viable in most cities, even if you have an office job and no intention of travelling.

This realisation also helped with my second problem: my lifestyle hadn't even been sustainable for me. In fact, it had nearly killed me, along with driving away friends and getting me arrested. But those were minor details that could be safely ignored in the book – I'd just big-up the good times and the one-night stands while ignoring the hangovers and the screaming outside ex-girlfriends' flats. It wasn't like anyone was going to be dumb enough to mimic me. Satisfied with my plan, I started sketching out some chapter headings. As long as I kept away from booze, I'd easily have the thing finished by December.

Chapter 1600

Once You're Lucky

The cravings were the worst thing. Three weeks without a drink and alcohol was all I could think about. I'd started going to parties again – I was trying to focus on serious issues in my column, but there's some information that you can only get from drunk people – and amazingly I'd managed to stick to water and Diet Coke throughout. As much as my sobriety was about keeping productive, it was just as much about not letting Robert and Sarah down.

Robert's pep talk at Butlins had not come easily to him: he'd always been hugely supportive of my drinking, and I could see he thought he'd helped create a monster. Sarah had put herself out on a limb to get me the job at TechCrunch and I'd made her a promise that I'd quit drinking and work hard. San Francisco is a small town – precisely seven miles by seven miles – and I knew that if I started drinking again, she'd hear about it – and so by extension would Robert. Knowing that kept me honest; frankly, I wasn't sure I had the willpower on my own. Every time a beer commercial came on TV, I'd salivate. I was Pavlov's drunk.

1601

My first 'fuck-up' was a combination of factors. Factor one: a group of Brit entrepreneurs arrived in town from London and invited me for a drink to pitch their new company for a mention on TechCrunch. Factor two: they suggested a bar that I'd never been to before, not somewhere frequented by any of my San Francisco friends. Factor three: Sarah had starting researching her new book, and so was spending most of her time in other countries, away from the San Francisco gossip circle. I almost certainly could have got away with drinking occasionally and neither she nor Robert would ever find out.

In hindsight, I should have realised that this was a combination of factors too risky for someone who was starting to appreciate that maybe doing without alcohol wasn't as easy as he'd thought.

But I'd managed to stay sober this long – three whole weeks – and, hell, going to a place where I could get away with drinking – if I wanted to – would be the perfect test of my willpower. There was no reason I couldn't stick to Diet Coke all night. And so I would.

The evening of the meeting came around and I sat in the bar, drinking black fizzy water by the gallon, as the three entrepreneurs told me all about their business. Their idea didn't quite warrant a whole column, but I promised to keep an eye on them, and would write about them if they secured funding and started to expand. The business portion of the meeting over, the conversation soon turned social – gossip from London, that kind of thing. The entrepreneurs ordered shots, but I stuck to Diet Coke. It was 11p.m. and I was totally sober. And then it happened – such a stupid thing: someone messed up a bar order and came back to the table with four pints of Stella and a Diet Coke instead of three pints and a Diet Coke.

The pint just sat there, looking at me.

I looked back.

Just the one. I could wash it down with the Diet Coke; no one would ever know.

'Help yourself,' said one of the entrepreneurs. 'It'll just go to waste otherwise.'

'No,' I said, 'thank you.'

1602

'I woke up . . .'

Ah, fuck.

1603

The guilt I felt the next morning was worse than any guilt I'd ever felt after any previous night of drinking. Worse than the morning after showing up at Karen's house, and worse even than either of the two mornings I'd woken up in a cell. Or at least it was a different kind of guilt: not for my behaviour – I hadn't actually done anything bad – but for the first time in my life, the guilt was for the act of drinking itself.

For one thing, I'd let down Sarah and Robert, and everyone else who had for the past few weeks patted me on the back and congratulated me for cutting out the booze. But also, trite as it is to say, I'd let myself down – badly. Up until that night I'd always assumed that I didn't need to drink; that it was an active choice I was making in order to make my night more relaxing or fun. But I'd made it to eleven o'clock last night without drinking; I could have gone home and the night would still have been a success. And yet I still had the drink.

Worse than that, after a couple more beers the entrepreneurs had gone back to their hotel. But I'd stayed in the bar; just me and a roomful of strangers, drinking until closing time. As I'd ordered my second beer I remember thinking 'well, I've had one now; I've fallen off the wagon, I might as well make the most of it.' But the truth is, I couldn't stop. Physically could not stop. I had to keep drinking until I was drunk.

1604

And, of course, it happened again. I'd got away with it the first time and I'd sworn to myself that it was just a blip. I'd tested myself, and I'd failed, so next time I'd avoid the situation.

But then my friend Richard came to visit, and suggested we catch up over a Sierra Nevada. He specifically mentioned the brand; it was one of the things he liked best about coming to San Francisco. It was rude not to join him for one. Just one.

But then it was Oktoberfest in San Francisco, and my friend Andy was in town. I couldn't not see him and, well, you can't not have a beer at Oktoberfest. Just one.

And on and on and on, until I was actively watching Twitter and Facebook and anywhere else on the Internet where my Brit friends detailed their travel plans. Coming to San Francisco? Let's go for a beer – I know an out-of-the-way place.

My 'lapses' – and I still thought of them as that – only happened about once a week and they weren't affecting my work. Nor was anyone important in San Francisco seeing them. I convinced myself that was the main thing: that I wasn't embarrassing myself, or anyone. I was just having a drink, like everyone else does. Except when everyone else went home, I couldn't stop. I'd just sit at the bar, drinking on my own, making the most of it because I didn't know when my next excuse would roll into town.

I think I was the last person to realise that I was the dictionary definition of an alcoholic, and the only person to be surprised when it turned out that I couldn't quit. And yet it baffled me. Like any addict, I'd assumed that I could just stop whenever I wanted to. That it was just a social prop. I never got drunk on my own. Or at least I didn't get drunk on my own until that was the only way I could get away with it. Then I did.

It was only a matter of time before I got caught.

Chapter 1700

Twice You're Screwed

I'd been out for dinner with Kelly. We hadn't seen each other for a while, and she was one of the few people I knew I could trust to drink with me in San Francisco without telling anyone. In American psychology-speak she was 'an enabler' – in London she'd be called 'a drinking buddy'. We started out easy, with just a few glasses of wine with dinner but by 1 a.m. we'd worked our way through several rounds of rum (me) and vodka (her). I was doing the lion's share of the drinking and at some point she'd decided to leave me to it.

I made it back to my hotel not long after 2 a.m. I'd got away with it for another night; aside from Kelly, no one else in San Francisco knew I was drinking. Robert was safely in London and Sarah was on another research trip: this time to Beijing. I staggered into my room and had just crawled into bed when my phone rang. It was an unknown number. I knew it wouldn't be Sarah at 2 a.m., especially not calling from China, and Robert never called me on my mobile because he knew I'd get hit with the roaming charges.

In my drunken haze, then, I reasoned that this made it safe for me to answer. It might have been a girl; or, even better, it might have been another drink.

'Hello,' I slurred.

'Hey!'

Shit.

1701

It was Sarah, calling from China. She'd calculated the time difference wrong and thought she was calling me in the early evening.

I should have hung up. And, had I not been drunk, I would have
done. But like a teenager arriving home from a party and trying to
hide the fact that he'd been drinking, I thought I could get away
with it. 'Oh, hi, it's you, hello' I slurred – or at least I imagine I tried
to.

'Have you been drinking?'

'Yes,' I should have said. 'I'm sorry.'

'No,' I said, 'what makes you shay that?

Ten minutes later, Sarah hung up. I know this because that's
what my phone told me the next morning. I also know that because
Sarah had thoughtfully emailed me a summary of the conversation,
assuming that I'd have forgotten most of it.

It wasn't that I'd been drinking that annoyed her. She'd always
said she didn't think I'd be able to quit without getting help. It was
the fact that I'd lied about it and then – apparently – blamed her
for falsely accusing me, even though I could barely form the words
to do so.

As she put it in her email, she wasn't angry, she just doesn't
really like being yelled at by Drunk Paul when all she was doing
was calling to see how I was getting on with my book.

1702

Every recovering alcoholic I've spoken to since that moment has
told me about the moment they hit 'rock bottom'. The moment
they knew they had to get help to quit, because they just weren't
capable of doing it themselves. Speaking to Sarah that night was
my moment. I knew that she would almost certainly mention the
incident to Robert next time they spoke, and that even if she wasn't
mad, I'd get a lecture from him. About how Sarah had risked

her own professional reputation to vouch for me, and that I was throwing it back at her, while fucking up my health at the same time. He'd dress it up as being worried about me, of course, and he'd probably make a joke, but I knew I'd let them both down, badly.

It was also the moment that I understood – really understood – that I couldn't quit on my own.

It was time to get help, and I knew where to get it.

1703

I first met Ruth Fowler in 2006 when she was working as a stripper, and I was pretending to be a publisher. Specifically, she was a Cambridge graduate who had grown up in Wales but had decided to smuggle her way into America to work illegally as a stripper in one of the most prestigious strip clubs in Manhattan and blog about the experience. I had been sent to New York to convince Ruth that ours should be the company to publish her book based on that blog.

I didn't succeed in securing the book rights, but Ruth and I became good friends; a friendship that had grown over the years as she'd stopped stripping, become a published author, moved back to London, moved legally to Los Angeles to work as a screenwriter, decided to quit drinking, joined Alcoholics Anonymous and recently celebrated her seventh month sober. As people in AA are wont to do, she'd emailed every so often to encourage me to attend a meeting. She could recognise the signs, she said. As people who don't realise they're alcoholics are wont to do, I brushed her off, pointing out that I wasn't an alcoholic, I just enjoyed drinking.

But now that I was finally ready to admit that I had a serious problem, I knew it was time to find out more about AA. I couldn't bear to call Ruth and admit that she was right and I was wrong. So I emailed her. Just one line.

'*Hey – if I come to LA – will you come with me to an AA meeting?*'

She emailed back in less than five minutes.

'*Yes. Come now.*'

1704

There were A A meetings in San Francisco, of course – dozens of them, according to the Internet – but I had two very good reasons for wanting to travel to Los Angeles instead. For a start, going to a meeting in LA meant that Ruth could come with me. I knew that if I tried to go on my own then I'd put it off, first for a day or two while I picked the meeting that sounded best for me, then for a few more days while I wrote that week's column, then for a week or so because, hell, there was no rush. Soon I'd be back drinking again.

The second reason was that, by going to LA, there was little to no chance anyone in San Francisco would find out.

The idea of going to Alcoholics Anonymous embarrassed me. This was an organisation that was the exact opposite of everything I'd stood for. For one thing, I'd made no secret of my drinking. In fact, I'd so been proud of it that I'd made it one of my defining professional characteristics. Even when I'd started writing for Tech-Crunch and had ostensibly given up, I had still continued to cultivate a fictitious drunken persona. The last thing I wanted was for readers to find out that not only was my drinking so out of control that I'd had to quit, but that I'd actually joined A A to help me do it. My ego just couldn't stand it.

I booked a plane ticket from San Francisco to Los Angeles. It cost me $90 return, which seemed quite reasonable for a trip that might save my life. Then I fired up Google and decided to do some research about what lay in store for me when I got there.

What I discovered annoyed the hell out of me. For a start, Alcoholics Anonymous is incredibly – and pompously – religious. They'd clearly tried to tone down the explicitly-Christian aspect in modern times with lots of talk of 'God as you understand him to be' rather than just 'God', but there was still no getting away from the idea that the only way one could quit the sauce was by asking for divine assistance. In fact, not only did members have to ask God to help them stop drinking, but according to the organisation's 'twelve steps' they had to 'turn [their] entire lives over to His care, get closer to Him through prayer or meditation in the hope that [they] could have Him remove [their] shortcomings'.

In short, Alcoholics Anonymous is a place where alcoholics can hide from their friends and plead with a deity that may or may not exist to magically cure them of their addiction. It's the antithesis of personal responsibility and accountability. Put another way, going to Alcoholics Anonymous would be little more than a formalised, religious extension of what I was already doing – except that instead of promising close friends like Robert and Sarah that I was going to get my shit together and quit drinking, I'd be promising a roomful of strangers.

And then I had to ask for help from a deity who – it should be noted – hands the stuff out every Sunday. Hell, if the New Testament is to be believed, this is a God – as I understand him – who taught his son how to turn water into wine. You might as well pray to Oliver Reed for help.

If the thought of Robert and Sarah being disappointed in me hadn't been enough, then would my new self-righteous AA buddies have any more success? Of course they wouldn't.

1705

I was trying to talk myself out of seeking professional help. I knew that. But I also knew that I was serious about giving up. One of the reasons I've always been so good at getting away with things is that I've always obeyed the golden rule of the blagger: know when it's time to stop. Recognise when you really have reached your last chance; and don't push it an inch further.

AA wasn't going to work for me, I knew that. I'd end up going to the meetings and then going for a beer afterwards, knowing that I'd get away with it. If I was going to quit then I had to acknowledge the two things that were keeping me drinking. The first was ego:

I was still acting like a gonzo wannabe and I still hadn't shaken the idea that 'my readers' expected me to drink. The second was opportunity: by only telling a very small number of people that I was quitting, I could still get away with drinking as long as they didn't find out.

Somewhere deep inside my brain, a synapse fired. Tzzziz.

I opened up my email programme and began to write an email. In the subject line, I wrote three words: 'I'm quitting drinking'. I clicked BCC and added everyone from my address book: friends, professional contacts; everyone I might possibly run into in the coming weeks and months.

My plan was to write an email telling everyone I knew about my decision to quit, and the reasons behind it. I'd ask for their help: if you see me drinking, I'd say, please stop me.

But then I stopped. Who was I kidding? All I was doing was expanding the list of people I couldn't drink around. Even if I sent the email, and even if I recruited all of my friends to watch over me, there was still a whole world of strangers out there; a planetful of bars where I'd never get caught. Thanks to my years of creating a persona of drunkenness, there was always the chance that I'd run into someone – particularly in a town as small as San Francisco where it seems like everyone reads TechCrunch – who would offer to buy me a drink. In my own little world at least, I was famous for my inability to say no.

And *that's* when it hit me.

A ridiculous idea.

That settled it.

Chapter 1800

Going Public

The half-finished email was still glaring out from my laptop screen. I read it back and laughed. Even though it was only a few minutes old, it now seemed ridiculously naïve; full of jokes and half-excuses. My ego simply wouldn't let me look pathetic in the eyes of even my friends, let alone people I only knew tangentially.

Being honest about my inability to stop drinking went against the whole character I had spent years building; the hard-drinking, doesn't give a fuck, never apologises, never explains asshole. The asshole who wrote my column for the *Guardian*, and the asshole who in two months was supposed to file a book on how to be just like him. Robert called him Drunk Paul, Sarah thought his problems went far deeper than drinking and I . . . well, I don't know what I thought. Apart from this . . .

That asshole had to die. It was him or me.

I got up from my chair and walked laps of the room, thinking through the consequences of what I was about to do. Then I lay on my bed and stared at the ceiling. An hour passed; maybe longer. Finally, I managed to summon up the kind of courage that would normally take me a couple of beers and a shot of rum. I closed the email window and opened a fresh browser window. I typed in the address of my blog and clicked the button to write a new entry. It started with a title . . .

'The trouble with drink, the trouble with me'

And then a quote that seemed apt . . .

'The chief reason for drinking is the desire to behave in a certain way, and to be able to blame it on alcohol' – Mignon McLaughlin

Then I wrote . . .

I mulled for a ridiculous amount of time over whether I should post this. Not because it's hopelessly self-indulgent – that's never stopped me before – or because it's too personal – ditto – but rather because there's so much weirdness and angst and back-story that I would really need a whole self-indulgent book to tell it all. Lucky I'm writing one, I guess.

Getting straight to the point: a few days ago I decided to stop drinking. Or, rather, I decided to stop properly. Completely.

It was actually back in July – during my month-long London visit – that I realised I needed to take a break from the ridiculously Bukowskian cycle I'd got myself (back) into. And – with a few dramatic exceptions – I was doing ok. But then, as someone pointed out after my last binge, in recent weeks those dramatic exceptions had started to move closer together – to the point where they were inevitably going to collide. Almost-quitting is just not something I'm capable of. It's all, or it's nothing.

One complicating factor (in my head at least) is that I've forged a career – and a respectable income – from drinking too much, doing idiotic things and writing about them. My last book floated on a sea of booze, and if you were to ask anyone who knows me to give you three keywords about me, drink would certainly be one of them. Barely a week goes past without a PR person trying to bribe me with a bottle of good rum (really, it's got weird now – and each thinks they're the first to think of it); and the look of disappointment on people's faces when I say I'm not drinking is heart-breaking. Last week I was at a party where someone said – and I swear this is true – 'of course you'll have a drink . . . you're Paul Carr'.

Jesus.

But the thing is, there's a line between doing entertainingly idiotic things under the influence and doing irreversibly damaging things. And what sells the most books and makes people read blog posts – losing loves, getting arrested, being fired, inching towards cirrhosis of the liver – is not actually that much fun when it's you doing it. The truth is there are people in my life who I would rather trade every single funny anecdote I have just to avoid hurting them again. Or in certain cases, just to speak to them again. When you get to that point the decision isn't the difficult part. The difficult part is the execution.

To be honest, drinking for me became a habit – a prop – rather than a necessity; I'm perfectly capable of doing dumb things stone cold sober, and it's not like I need a fucking confidence boost. I also never – ever – write while drunk. But having a drink in my hand – and another, and another – is also one of those habits that has proved incredibly hard to break. Hence the decision to write this post.

I figure by making the statement – I'm not drinking – I don't really have anywhere to hide. Maybe people who have read this and who see me drinking will look as disappointed as those who previously were disappointed that I wasn't.

I've been lucky enough to get advice on quitting from some really good friends in the past week or so, including one friend who has been sober for seven months despite previously writing a drink-fuelled memoir of her own. No doubt some of the advice will work, and some of it won't. But I'm going to try it all. I might write a follow-up post on the subject, or there might be more in the book, or I might just get on with it. It's too early to tell. All I know is that it's my 30th birthday in a couple of months, and I really hope I'll be spending it sober. And alive. And with friends. Those are decent enough goals for now.

And to those worried that a non-drinking me means fewer hilarious fuck-ups, don't be. The only difference is I'll be able to remember them in the morning.

God help me.

. . .

I clicked the 'Publish' button and the post immediately appeared on the front page of my site. From there it was automatically sent out to the 20,000 or so people who had registered to be notified whenever I posted something new. Just to make sure, I posted a link on Twitter and sent it out to the thousands of people who follow me there. As often happens on Twitter, people started reposting – 'retweeting' – the link to their own followers. The first was Michael Arrington, who appended his own message to the retweet . . .

'We're here for you, dude.'

By the end of the day, more than 100,000 people had read the post. By the end of the week, it was closer to a quarter of a million. I had nowhere left to hide.

Epilogue

I don't notice the man in the grey suit taking my bag.

I mean, I do notice him – but in his smart grey Savile Row suit and his patent leather shoes, he looks just like any other hotel guest. I'm dimly aware of him gliding past me as I'm signing the guest register but, by the time I turn around, he's gone. And, with him, my bag.

A professional.

I smile.

December 2009. It's the day before my thirtieth birthday and I've flown into London on my way to speak at the LeWeb conference in Paris. The receptionist at the Lanesborough hands me back my back-up debit card, having just pre-authorised it for £1000 in incidentals; just in case I feel the urge to have a green-painted Dalmatian puppy delivered to my room.

The room itself, though, is free: a birthday present from the head of the PR agency I consulted for last year. The Lanesborough is one of her clients and they're charging her their top-secret media rate. Every hotel has one.

Walking into room 237, I smile again. Marcus, the butler, has unpacked my bags and almost everything is exactly where I'd normally put it, right down to the razor on the little towel by the sink. The only difference is that, instead of turning on the shower to remove the creases from my shirts, he's sent them to be pressed. That works too.

I head into the living room. On the table, next to a chocolate birthday cake and a card from the hotel's head of PR, sits an ice bucket and two half-bottles of champagne, with the compliments of the manager. Perfect. It's been two months since I last had a drink and I'm not planning on starting again*. Instead, I take out my phone and snap a picture with the built-in camera. Later I'll post it on my blog with a note about how the Lanesborough was determined to tempt me to drink, but I'd resisted. Another small victory for my ego.

Ah, yes, my ego: the cause of and – as it turned out – solution to my drinking problem. Since my blog post about quitting went live, it has been read by well over a quarter of a million people. Some of those people – just over a hundred at last count – have emailed me to wish me luck, or to share their own struggles with booze. But most readers remain anonymous, which suits me just fine. Whenever I walk into a bar, anywhere in the world, I have no way of knowing if one of them is watching. But if they are, and they catch me drinking, they'll know I've failed – something my ego can't possibly allow. Where once my obsessive need to maintain an image made me think I had to keep drinking, now that same obsession demands that I keep quitting.

More importantly, it turns out that American girls are big on the whole 'reformed drunk' thing. A few minutes after I posted my blog link, a girl called Amelia from Los Angeles sent me a message – 'That's the sexiest thing I've ever read' – and suggested I look her up next time I'm in town. In the days and weeks that followed, several similar messages followed – including one from Jenny, the girl who is flying into town for my birthday party tonight. I still don't quite understand why being a recovering alcoholic attracts women but, as rewards for sobriety go, it's hard to fault.

As I'm putting my phone away, I notice that Sarah posted a message on Twitter: '*Massive happy birthday to my best friend Paul. Wish I could have been in London with you tonight.*' Given that Sarah is one of the two people responsible for saving my life, I wish she could be here too, but I'll forgive her absence just this once: she's in Chile, researching another chapter of her next book. And,

---

* www.ispauldrinkingagain.com

anyway, after Paris, I'm heading to her hometown of Memphis where she and Geoff have planned a couple of days of gorging on local food and seeing the sights. Sights including the city's famous Peabody Hotel, with its family of trained ducks which swim around a fountain in the lobby all day, before being led back along a special red carpet to their very own mini hotel on the roof. Even ducks are starting to realise the benefits of living permanently in hotels.

I'm looking forward to seeing Sarah and Geoff, just like I'm looking forward to seeing all of my friends – Hannah, Michael, Michelle, Zoe and a few dozen others – who will be at Adam Street tonight for my birthday party. I've finally become a bona fide member, and it didn't cost me a penny: the club's way of saying thank you for the flurry of prospective members who joined their waiting list after reading about Adam Street in my last book.

For a long time, I really believed that alcohol was the common factor in every fun adventure I'd had. Since quitting, though, I've realised that the real common factor was my friends – Michael and Michelle in Vegas, Scott in Spain, Zoe in Austin, Eris in San Francisco and, of course . . .

'Open the fucking door, you twat.'

I let Robert in and show him around my room with its crystal decanter minibar, hydraulic television and free pornography. There's no mistaking the look in his eyes: envy. 'Your life is officially ridiculous,' he says. But his jealousy only goes so far – after all, he's enjoying an equally ridiculous existence.

His next stop after London is a luxury villa in the mountains overlooking the Côte d'Azur. It has all the facilities he's come to demand from his temporary homes – swimming pool, bar, amazing view – but as an added treat this place is set in the middle of a private twenty-acre forest. 'I've always fancied my own forest,' he said. The villa is far too big for just him, but that's not a problem. He's just launched his latest business: the YesAndClub – an organisation for people who don't let practicalities get in the way of a good idea. The business has a mission statement that's amusingly close to that of the Kings of the Road Club, and its first event just happens to be a two-week retreat in the mountains overlooking the Côte d'Azur. The attendance fees from members will cover the villa's rental costs twice over, and, of course, attendees are expected to keep the fridge stocked with food and drink.

Whether I'll be able to join Robert in France will depend on how quickly I can finish writing this book. My deadline is now less than a month away, but I've been making good progress since I threw away my first draft and decided instead to tell the whole story of the past two years, not just the part that suited my image. I have no idea what my publisher will think when he reads the resulting manuscript – between the arrest and near-arrest, the slumming it in Easy Hotels, the near-death experiences and the painful hangovers, it's not exactly the feel-good blagger's guide he had in mind.

And yet, and yet . . . somehow it still satisfies all the criteria of a successful lifestyle guide. The past two years sound great on paper – a story of luxury hotels, pretty girls, fast cars and drunken adventures. It was all perfectly affordable too; at the end of my first year of travel I added up all my hotel bills and found that I had actually come in under budget. In fact, I'd saved about £800. But, like all good lifestyle guides, it wasn't sustainable. Not even for me.

Through trial and error, though, I've managed to figure out which aspects of life as a high-class nomad *are* sustainable. And the surprising answer is that, without a crippling drink problem, almost all of them are. My income may have taken a sharp upward turn now that I'm actually taking my work seriously, but my monthly outgoings are still about the same as they were two years ago – possibly less, adjusted for inflation. This despite the fact that, through a combination of rate-blagging and a ridiculous spiral of long-stay upgrades, I now keep a permanent suite at an amazing hotel a few blocks from San Francisco's Union Square. A suite that's costing me just a shade over $75 a night.

And whenever I get bored with San Francisco, I know I can just hop on a plane. Thanks to the secrets I've learned these past twenty-four months, I know I have my pick of fully staffed accommodation in every major city on earth, a fleet of luxury cars at my disposal night and day and year-round access to villas in the Spanish mountains, and across most of Europe.

For me, none of this is a break from the pressures of my normal, everyday life – a nice birthday treat before returning to the rat race. This is my normal, everyday life.

And all I had to do to start living it was to make one simple, life-changing decision.

The golden rule of the blagger.

I had to decide when to stop.

Acknowledgements

There are so many people to thank and so few pages left in which to thank them, but first an important disclaimer:

Everything you've read in this book is true, to the best of my recollection. It is impossible to overstate, though, how much alcohol I consumed in the past few years and so it's inevitable that my recollection is more than a little fuzzy in places. Wherever possible, I've checked the stories with the people involved or with the official police record. I've also relied on the half-dozen notebooks that I filled during my travels, plus emails, blog posts, Twitter updates and all that stuff. Inevitably, though, there will still be mistakes. *Mea culpa*. Email me at paul@kingsoftheroadclub.com and I'll be sure to fix them in any future printings.

In almost all cases I've used real names for people featured in the book. A couple of names have been changed where I've wanted to avoid embarrassing people, particularly girls who have been misguided enough to become involved with me. There are no composite characters though: everyone in the book is a real person . . .

And so, to the thank-yous . . .

Thanks firstly to every single person who agreed to allow me to write about them. In particular, Michael Smith, Michelle, Zoe Margolis, Scott Rutherford and Ruth Fowler. A special additional thank you is due to Eris, Hannah and Kelly. I still have no idea what you saw in me, but I'm glad you saw it, however briefly. I'm ridiculously grateful that we're still friends.

Thanks also to those who were fortunate not to have been included in the book, but without whom much of it wouldn't have been possible: Oli Barrett, Richard Moross, Sarah Bee, Stuart

O'Connor – and in particular Olivia Hine for always having a better idea.

Thank you to Charles Arthur and Michael Arrington for being the two best editors in the world. Your patience, support and encouragement are appreciated more than I can say.

Speaking of patience, thanks once again to my parents for continuing to hide their disappointment at the path their eldest son has chosen for his life. I owe them everything.

Thanks to my agent, Robert Kirby at United Agents, and my editor at W&N, Alan Samson, for believing that I had a second book in me. I have no idea if you were right, but here it is. Thank you to Rebecca Gray for continuing to humour me even though you're still not convinced I had even a first book in me, let alone a second. And thank you to Bea Hemming for once again doing all of the things required to turn a pile of electronic pages into this real live book.

More than any of the above, though, thank you to my best friends, Robert Loch and Sarah Lacy. There simply aren't the words to thank you for staying with me for the ride, even when I threatened to swerve off the road. Without you I'd be dead, emotionally and probably literally. This book is dedicated to you both.

www.kingsoftheroadclub.com